RESEARCH IN GOVERNMENTAL AND NONPROFIT ACCOUNTING

Volume 10 • 1999

Research in Governmental and Nonprofit Accounting

Paul A. Copley, Editor
George D. Sanders, Associate Editor

EDITORIAL BOARD

Leslie Aronovitz	U.S. General Accounting Office
William Baber	George Washington University
Rajiv Banker	University of Texas, Dallas
Dennis Beresford	University of Georgia
Vivian Carpenter	Florida A&M University
James Chan	University of Illinois at Chicago
Edward Douthett	Texas Christian University
Ehsan Feroz	University of Minnesota, Duluth
Dana Forgione	University of Baltimore
Ken Gaver	University of Georgia
H. Perrin Garsombke	University of Nebraska, Omaha
Gary Giroux	Texas A&M University
Michael Granof	University of Texas, Austin
Robert Ingram	University of Alabama
Saleha Khumawala	University of Houston
Barry Marks	University of Houston, Clear Lake
Penny Marquette	University of Akron
James Patton	University of Pittsburgh
Kris Raman	University of North Texas
Robin Roberts	Iowa State University
Mark Rubin	Miami University
George Sanders	University of Western Washington
Mary Stone	University of Alabama
Wanda Wallace	College of William and Mary
Penny Wardlow	Governmental Accounting Standards Board
Earl Wilson	University of Missouri

RESEARCH IN GOVERNMENTAL AND NONPROFIT ACCOUNTING

Editor: **PAUL A. COPLEY**
J.M. Tull School of Accounting
The University of Georgia

Associate Editor: **GEORGE D. SANDERS**
University of Western Washington

VOLUME 10 • 1999

JAI PRESS INC.
Stamford, Connecticut

Copyright © 1999 JAI PRESS INC.
100 Prospect Street
Stamford, Connecticut 06901-1640

JAll rights reserved. No part of this publication may be reproduced, stored on a retrieval system, or transmitted in any form or by any means, electronic, mechanical, photocopying, filming, recording, or otherwise, without prior permission in writing from the publisher.

ISBN: 0-7623-0169-4
ISSN: 0884-0741

Transferred to digital printing 2007

CONTENTS

LIST OF CONTRIBUTORS	vii
EDITOR'S COMMENTS *Paul A. Copley*	ix
INFORMATION INTERMEDIATION AND SEASONED MUNICIPAL BOND YIELDS *Robert W. Ingram and Earl R. Wilson*	1
THE DIFFERENTIAL EFFECT OF STATE GOVERNMENT PENSION FUNDING PRACTICES ON BOND YIELDS ACROSS VARYING MATURITIES *Cynthia Sneed and John Sneed*	33
THE INFLUENCE OF AUDITOR CHANGE AND TYPE ON AUDIT FEES FOR MUNICIPALITIES *Bruce W. Chase*	49
AUDIT FEES AND NONAUDIT FEES IN THE GOVERNMENTAL SECTOR: A SELF-SELECTION ANALYSIS *Randal J. Elder, Susan C. Kattelus, and* *Edward B. Douthett, Jr.*	65
A COMPARISON OF ALTERNATIVE MODELS OF BUDGETARY BEHAVIOR: EVIDENCE FROM CALIFORNIA CITY DEPARTMENTS *Alberto M. Bento and Lourdes F. White*	87
AN ANALYSIS OF CROSS-SECTIONAL VARIATION IN THE RATE OF FINANCIAL RATIO ADJUSTMENT BY CITY GOVERNMENTS *Paul A. Copley and Sharon S. Seay*	111

FACTORS AFFECTING THE RELATION BETWEEN
DONATIONS TO NOT-FOR-PROFIT ORGANIZATIONS
AND AN EFFICIENCY RATIO
  Daniel Tinkelman 135

HEALTHCARE ACCOUNTING RESEARCH:
A REVIEW OF THE PROFESSIONAL LITERATURE,
MODELS, DATA, AND RESEARCH OPPORTUNITIES
  Dana A. Forgione 163

A COMPARATIVE ANALYSIS OF THE EVOLUTION
OF LOCAL GOVERNMENTAL ACCOUNTING IN
ALGERIA AND MOROCCO
  Alan D. Godfrey, Cherif Merrouche and Patrick J. Devlin 201

LIST OF CONTRIBUTORS

Alberto Bento	University of Baltimore
Bruce Chase	Radford University
Paul Copley	University of Georgia
Patrick Devlin	Glasgow Caledonian University, UK
Edward Douthett	Texas Christian University
Randal Elder	Syracuse University
Dana Forgione	University of Baltimore
Alan Godfrey	Glasgow Caledonian University, UK
Robert Ingram	University of Alabama
Susan Kattelus	Eastern Michigan University
Cherif Merrouche	Glasgow Caledonian University, UK
Sharon Seay	Mississippi College
Cynthia Sneed	University of Nebraska at Kearney
John Sneed	University of Nebraska at Kearney
Daniel Tinkelman	Pace University
Lourdes White	University of Baltimore
Earl Wilson	University of Missouri-Columbia

EDITOR'S COMMENTS

I am pleased to present Volume 10 of *Research in Governmental and Nonprofit Accounting*, the only series annual exclusively dedicated to governmental and nonprofit accounting and reporting issues. With Volume 10, the series returns to an unsolicited manuscript format with anonymous referees. The purpose of *Research in Governmental and Nonprofit Accounting* is to stimulate and report high-quality research on a wide range of governmental and nonprofit accounting issues. A quick review of the titles suggests that we were successful in attracting a wide range of topics, and I am confident that a thorough reading of the papers will reveal that the research quality is excellent.

A number of papers appearing in Volume 10 differ from much of our existing empirical work. The *Bento and White* and *Copley and Seay* studies use time-series data over relatively long intervals. In the case of the *Sneed and Sneed* and *Elder, Kattelus, and Douthett* studies, the authors use methodologies which have not been employed in previous studies in either the public or private sector. To the extent that these methodologies permit investigation of previously unexplored issues, the papers will be of interest to researchers outside of the governmental and nonprofit area.

Governmental and nonprofit accounting represents an undeveloped research area which would benefit from rigorous examination. I believe that the government and not-for-profit sectors are also becoming increasingly attractive research areas. There are new standards of reporting for not-for-profit entities and a proposal for a dramatic change in state and local government financial statements. Change is always an opportunity for new research. As evidenced by the *Forgione* chapter, data exists and is becoming increasingly available.

INFORMATION INTERMEDIATION AND SEASONED MUNICIPAL BOND YIELDS

Robert W. Ingram and Earl R. Wilson

ABSTRACT

This study examines whether seasoned municipal bond yields impound accounting information on a timely basis and, if so, the mechanism by which accounting information is impounded in these yields. As in prior studies, we find that accounting information is linked with seasoned municipal bond yields. Unlike prior studies, however, we provide evidence that this linkage relies on information intermediation by underwriters of new bond issues and bond rating agencies. Thus, our evidence suggests that seasoned bond yields, rather than responding directly to accounting information, appear to respond *indirectly* to accounting information provided in association with new bond issues and accompanying ratings. At other times, when new issues are not being marketed, seasoned bond yields are driven largely by the level and term structure of interest rates and by broad estimates of default risk as proxied by bond ratings. This research suggests that additional mandated disclosure of accounting information may have only limited effectiveness in reducing the potential mispricing of seasoned debt.

I. INTRODUCTION

This study examines the extent to which seasoned municipal bond yields impound accounting information on a continuous basis and the mechanism by which accounting information is impounded in these yields. In particular, we consider whether seasoned bond yields are associated with accounting numbers at the time new bond issues are sold and in periods preceding the sale of new issues. If seasoned bond yields impound accounting information on an ongoing basis, we expect an association between the yields and accounting information at times other than when new issues are sold. If, instead, seasoned yields impound accounting information primarily at the time new issues are sold, we expect the association between yields and accounting information to be stronger at the time new issues are sold than at other times. Further, because accounting information is used in pricing new issues, we expect that much of the accounting information will be impounded in seasoned yields through an adjustment of these yields to the interest costs of the new issues. Accordingly, the new issues market is expected to be a major information intermediary for the seasoned bond market.

This research is useful for assessing whether additional mandated disclosure of accounting information is likely to reduce potential mispricing of seasoned debt. If accounting information is impounded in seasoned yields only in conjunction with ratings and new issues, additional disclosure requirements are not likely to reduce mispricing of seasoned debt on a timely basis.

A. The Problem

We provide evidence of a linkage between accounting information and seasoned municipal bond yields that relies on intermediation by underwriters of new bond issues and bond rating agencies. This evidence suggests that seasoned bond yields are not directly responsive to accounting information except at the time new issues are sold. Rather, they appear to respond to accounting information when it is provided in association with new bond issues and accompanying bond rating reviews or revisions. At other times, when new issues are not being marketed, seasoned bond yields are driven largely by the level and term structure of interest rates and by default risk as proxied by bond ratings.

Default risk normally is reevaluated by rating agencies only when new issues are marketed. Bond ratings are reviewed and are potentially revised in conjunction with new issues. In addition, investment bankers and brokers provide an information intermediation function in conjunction with marketing new issues. They evaluate information, including accounting information, provided by bond rating agencies and by issuers in setting yield and price parameters on new issues. Accordingly, accounting information potentially is impounded in bond yields when new issues are sold.[1]

We present evidence that, at the time a new issue is sold, seasoned bond yields of the same issuer adjust to a level consistent with the new issue yield, controlling for maturity differences.[2] Thus, accounting information is impounded in seasoned bond yields primarily as a result of the intermediation provided by the new issues market. During the interim between new issues, seasoned bond yields are free to drift away from values established at the time new issues are sold and are likely to differ from the economic values of the bonds that are established when information is impounded in association with new issues. Consequently, seasoned bond yields are likely to differ (substantially in some cases) from the yields that would be established if the market continuously impounded accounting and economic information like that impounded when new issues are sold.

B. Reasons for the Problem

Accounting and economic information about individual bond issuers is not followed closely by financial analysts on a continuous basis.[3] The fact that this information is not continuously impounded stems from both unavailability of reliable information on a timely basis (a concern of accounting regulators) and a lack of incentives to evaluate the information (not an apparent concern of accounting regulators).

Accounting and other information is disclosed by issuers infrequently. Annual reports are the primary source of accounting information (other than information provided with new issues), and these reports generally are released six to nine months after fiscal year end. Major economic events affecting a government are reported by the media, but implications of these events for the financial condition of a government generally receive little explicit analysis. A government usually does not disclose revenue or expenditure implications of these events.

Even when accounting information is available, there is no evidence that debt markets contemporaneously impound this information. Ingram, Raman, and Wilson (1987), for example, were unable to find evidence of a contemporaneous response of bond prices to the release of municipal annual reports. Individual issues seldom are traded actively (Public Securities Association 1990, 29). Accordingly, an incentive does not exist for analysts to monitor individual issuers because an active market does not exist for taking advantage of superior information.[4] We demonstrate that yields of seasoned issues are driven largely by the level and term structure of interest rates in comparison with the coupon rate and maturity attributes of a specific bond.[5]

Underwriters and traders have greater incentives to search for information at the time of a new issue than at other times because accurate bond valuation is essential to facilitate the purchase and sale of the new bonds in the primary market. Secondary market investors essentially are able to piggy-back or free ride on the information generated in the primary market. Further, any mispricing is evident by comparison of seasoned and new bond issues. Thus, traders and investment services that provide seasoned bond yield information have incentives to correct any obvious mispricing at this time.

C. The Accounting Issue

Factors affecting the pricing (and potential mispricing) of seasoned bonds have implications for accounting policy, in particular for current efforts to increase the amount of timely accounting information provided to bond markets. The SEC's Rule 15c2-12 requires underwriters to provide official offering statements to national information repositories (see Petersen 1989). These repositories are proprietary information services responsible for making information available to market participants. A 1994 amendment to Rule 15c2-12 (SEC 1994) prohibits underwriting of bonds unless the issuer agrees to notify the national repositories of material events and to provide annual financial reports. Causes of the SEC concerns are the large percentage of municipal bonds held by individuals, 76 percent in 1993 (SEC 1994), and recent defaults of the Washington Public Power Supply System (see Lamb and Rappaport 1987, 12), the bankruptcy of Orange County, California (see numerous articles in the *Wall Street Journal* 1994 and 1995), and possible financial misrepresentation by the District of Columbia in issuing $250 million of debt in 1994 (Taylor and Connor 1995).

Efforts to increase the availability of accounting information to municipal debt markets presumes that this information will be impounded in bond yields. The extent to which information is, in fact, impounded and the mechanism by which it is impounded are unknown, especially for seasoned debt. Unless seasoned bond yields respond to current information on a timely basis, the availability of additional information (as a result of regulatory intervention) will have little effect on the municipal bond market. Accordingly, additional disclosure and monitoring costs may be imposed on municipalities and the investment community that do little to reduce the potential mispricing of seasoned bonds.

A presumed objective of requiring more frequent disclosure of accounting information is to enable the secondary bond market to do a better job of establishing the economic values of these securities. This point is emphasized in a recent *Wall Street Journal* article (Taylor and Jeffrey 1994) that quotes Christopher Taylor, executive director of the Municipal Securities Rulemaking Board (an agency of the SEC) as commenting as follows about the intended effect of the 1994 amendment to Rule 15c2-12 (p. c1): "For one thing, new disclosure will have the effect of making bond dealers responsible for incorporating the latest and best information in the prices they quote to investors in the 'secondary market.'" He further is quoted as saying, "The real value of this to the investor is that the dealer is on the hook to incorporate the information into the price."

More frequent disclosure would appear to be of little value to the new issues market because most municipalities issue debt infrequently and generally disclose considerable information, accounting and otherwise, in conjunction with these issues.[6] We cannot rule out, however, that additional timely disclosure could reduce search costs for market agents and might be considered in pricing decisions. We find little evidence of this effect for the accounting measures examined in this study.

II. ACCOUNTING INFORMATION AND BOND YIELDS

Bond prices can be viewed as the present value of expected future cash flows:

$$P_{it} = \sum_{t=1}^{T} [C_{it}/(1 + Y_{it})^t], \qquad (1)$$

where P_{it} is the price of bond i at time t, C_{it} is expected cash flow (interest for each period $t = 1$ to T and maturity value at T), and Y_{it} is the discount rate or yield associated with bond i at time t. In this equation, expected future cash flows are the contracted amounts established by the coupon rate and maturity value of a fixed rate bond. Once established, the parameters are constant and are unaffected by new information. The probability of receiving the expected cash flows is measured by the discount rate which can change in response to new information. Thus, in this formulation, change in price depends only on a change in yield. For all practical purposes, both theoretically and empirically, bond prices and yields are two sides of the same coin. We examine yields in this study because they are more directly linked to accounting information, as discussed below. Substituting prices for yields in the empirical analysis discussed later produces essentially the same results, with signs reversed, as that discussed in this paper.

Yield can be expressed as the sum of two components:

$$Y_{it} = R_{ft} + R_{pt}, \qquad (2)$$

where R_{ft} is the rate of return associated with a default-free security of the same maturity as bond i at time t and R_{pt} is a risk premium associated with the default risk of bond i at time t. R_{ft} is a function of bond maturity and the general level of interest rates. Thus, it incorporates interest rate risk but not default risk. Jointly, maturity for bond i at time t and the general level of interest rates at time t capture the effect of the term structure of interest rates for bond i at time t. R_{pt} is a function of the expected ability of the issuer to make future principal and interest payments. A role of accounting is in providing information for assessing this expected ability, though accounting information is only part of the information set available for assessing default risk (see Public Securities Association 1990; Lamb and Rappaport 1987; Sherwood 1976).

Bond rating agencies are information intermediaries that assess default risk and provide this information to the bond markets. The process by which information about a bond issuer, including accounting information, is impounded in bond ratings is not completely known because the process is proprietary and includes heuristics, subjectivity, and negotiation between the rating agency and issuer.[7] Nevertheless, rating agencies examine accounting information, and empirical evidence indicates an association between accounting information and bond ratings and between accounting information and bond rating changes (a review of this literature is provided by Ingram, Raman, and Wilson 1987). Accordingly, evidence exists that accounting information affects bond yields (and therefore prices) through bond ratings. A bond rating for a particular issuer applies to all general obligation bonds of that issuer. Default risk is the same for all general obligation issues because these issues are all backed by the full faith and credit of the issuer.

Also, financial analysts examine accounting information, in addition to bond ratings, in marketing new bond issues (see Public Securities Association 1990, 123-131). Consequently, accounting information may have a direct effect on bond prices of new issues. During the marketing of these issues, analysts and investment bankers have incentives to assess the credit worthiness of issuers to ensure a reasonable spread and to protect the interests of buyers and sellers. New issues of municipal bonds often are for large amounts, so transaction fees are sufficient to compensate investment bankers for information search and analysis costs. Empirical evidence (though mixed) indicates that accounting information, in addition to bond ratings, is associated with the prices of new bond issues (for example, see Feroz and Wilson 1992). This evidence suggests that bond analysts also are information intermediaries with respect to the impounding of accounting information in municipal bond prices.

Both bond rating reviews and new issue sales are periodic events. For many issuers, these events occur only every few years. For some issuers, the events are rare, and for others, the events occur fairly regularly. For the sample of issuers examined in this study, the average period between new bond issues was approximately two years. The shortest average period for any issuer was approximately six months.

Thus, at best, these events provide limited opportunity for accounting information (or other issuer-specific information) to affect seasoned bond yields.

Once issued, municipal bond yields are tracked primarily by investment services. These services are proprietary and sell information to banks, institutional investors, governments, and brokerage firms for pricing bonds and portfolios. They price bonds daily from a matrix pricing system.[8] This system classifies bonds according to yield curves (coupon rates and maturities) and default ratings. As new information becomes available (for example, from trades or new bond issues), matrix prices are adjusted and issues are reassigned classifications in the matrix.

The matrix system is important because it provides a quasi-market for seasoned municipal bond prices. It complements the thin trading market for these securities by providing low-cost information intermediation for a segment of the market that otherwise has limited access to information on a continuous basis. How this system captures accounting information and the mechanism by which that information is captured is the subject of this study.

If the system captures accounting information on a continuous basis, seasoned bond yields should reflect contemporaneous accounting (and other) information, so that there is no evidence of mispricing of seasoned bonds relative to new bond issues when new bonds are sold. If the system does not impound information on a continuous basis (or if no information is available on a continuous or frequent basis), systematic adjustment of seasoned yields should be apparent around the date new issues are sold as seasoned yields adjust to the yields of the new bonds (controlling for maturity differences).

This study tests two related issues:

1. whether seasoned bonds are systematically mispriced relative to accounting (and other) information available when new bond issues are sold, and
2. whether new bond issues and associated bond ratings are important information intermediaries for providing accounting information to the seasoned bond market.

The first issue considers *when* the municipal bond market (investment services) captures accounting (and other issuer-specific) information. If the market captures information continuously, then additional timely disclosure of accounting information may benefit investors to the extent they are better informed of relevant economic events. If the market captures information only periodically, then additional disclosure is likely to be of less benefit to investors because it will not be impounded in seasoned bond yields on a timely basis.

The second issue considers the mechanism by which accounting information is impounded in seasoned bond yields. If seasoned yields rely exclusively on information intermediation through bond ratings and new issues, then additional disclosure regulation is not likely to be of major benefit to investors unless efforts are made to improve the intermediation process so that other mechanisms are created for impounding this information.[9]

To test these issues we examine three empirical issues:

1. whether yields of new bond issues are associated with accounting variables, either directly or through bond ratings that are associated with accounting variables,
2. whether seasoned bond yields are associated with accounting variables, after controlling for information provided by new bond yields, and
3. whether seasoned bond yields respond systematically to information contained in new bond yields at the time new bonds are sold.

Tests of the first issue support the conclusion that accounting information is relevant for pricing municipal bonds, particularly for evaluating default risk. Tests of the second issue support the conclusion that secondary bond markets do not continuously impound accounting information. Tests of the third issue support the conclusion that accounting information is impounded in seasoned bond yields at the time new issues are sold.

III. EMPIRICAL ANALYSIS OF ACCOUNTING INFORMATION AND BOND YIELDS

This section describes the sample, models, and variables used in the empirical analysis.

A. Sample and Data

The sample was based on new issues of general obligation bonds issued between August 1978 and August 1989. Data were obtained from the Bond Buyer MUNIFICHE database on 1,105 issues of 391 cities. The MUNIFICHE database represents nearly all advertised new general obligation issues of cities with populations in excess of 25,000. The accounting data were those for the fiscal year of the financial statements included in the offering statements for the new issues. This sample was matched with seasoned bond yields for the same period from Interactive Data Services (IDS), bond ratings from Moody's Investors Services, and accounting information from the Bond Buyer Database and annual reports. IDS is an investment service that supplies seasoned bond prices from a matrix system to banks and other institutional investors. Data were purchased from the service for particular issues with at least 10 years to maturity in 1978. The sample is representative of cities with populations in excess of 25,000 population throughout the United States. Smaller cities were omitted because accounting and other data often are difficult to obtain, often do not conform with GAAP (see Ingram and Robbins 1987), and data from sources such as the U.S. Bureau of the Census generally are not available for these cities.[10] After eliminating issues with missing data for one or more variables used in analysis, the final sample consisted of 592 new issues from 196 cities. The sample was geographically dispersed (including issuers from 31 states) but was restricted to larger issuers (over 25,000 population) that are more likely to be followed by national markets and that typically provide more information than that provided by smaller issuers. Observations were well distributed across years and months. No more than 13 percent of the new issues were sold in any year, and no more than 14.4 percent were sold in any month. Thus, event clustering was not a problem.

B. Empirical Models

Regression models were used to test whether accounting information is impounded in bond ratings and in the net interest cost of new bonds. Regression models also were used to test whether accounting information is impounded indirectly (through ratings and net interest costs) and directly in seasoned bond yields.

Bond Rating Model

The first model examined bond ratings using cross-sectional, logistic regression, in the form:

$$\text{Rating} = \alpha_0 + \alpha_1 \text{ Insurance} + \alpha_2 \text{ Population} + \alpha_3 \text{ Frequency} +$$
$$\alpha_4 \text{ Dept} + \alpha_5 \text{ Fund Balance} + \alpha_6 \text{ Surplus} + \dot{\varepsilon}. \quad (3)$$

Rating is the bond rating on a five point scale (AAA, AA, A1, A, and BAA). BAA and BAA1 ratings were combined into one class because of the small number of bonds of each rating. The sample contained 126 AAA, 253 AA, 107 A1, 81 A, and 25 BAA1 or BAA bonds. No bonds below BAA were contained in the sample. The (s are coefficients; α_0 is the intercept. In logistic regression with multiple classifications of the dependent variable, separate intercepts are computed for $n-1$ classes, where n is the number of classes (five in the bond rating model). α is random error. Insurance is a dummy variable set to one if bonds are insured and zero otherwise. A municipality purchases insurance to protect investors from default and to increase its bond rating. Approximately 10 percent of the sample bonds (58 of 592) were insured.[11] Population is the log of population and proxies for economic attributes of the issuer. Larger municipalities tend to be more diverse and less risky than smaller municipalities. Frequency is the number of new bond issues sold by the issuer between January 1978 and December 1989. More frequent issuers are monitored more continuously than less frequent issuers. They have established their abilities to market and repay debt, and thus generally exhibit lower default risk than less frequent issuers. Debt, Fund Balance, and Surplus proxy for accounting information. Debt is the ratio of total general obligation debt to total general fund revenues. A larger amount of debt relative to revenues indicates greater default risk, ceteris paribus. Fund Balance is the ratio of the general fund balance to total general fund revenues. This balance cushions a government against unexpected revenue shortfalls and reduces default risk.[12] Surplus is general fund revenues minus general fund expenditures, scaled by general fund revenues. It is a measure of the ability of a government to meet its current expenditure demands, including interest and debt payments. A surplus reduces default risk. All accounting numbers are measured at the date of the most recently audited financial statements contained in the new issue offering statements.

Debt, fund balance, and surplus were used in this study because they have been observed to be associated with bond measures (e.g., Wallace 1981; Wilson and Howard 1984; Feroz and Wilson 1992). A strong theory does not exist to guide selection of accounting variables, and we cannot rule out that other measures might exist that could produce different results from those reported. We believe the variables we use are representative of major accounting measures that should be of interest to investors.

The purpose of the bond rating model test was to determine whether accounting variables were associated with bond ratings for the sample used in this study. Earlier research has indicated an association (at least a weak one) between ratings and accounting variables (for example, Wallace 1981; Ingram and Copeland 1982; Wilson and Howard 1984). It is important for this study to determine if accounting information affects bond yields through intermediaries such as bond ratings. Accordingly, we must first establish that accounting information is associated with ratings.

The sample included data for each of the 592 new bond issues. Thus, it is a test of whether bond ratings were associated with accounting information at the time new issues were sold. This is an appropriate period for testing because ratings are reviewed (and revised if necessary) when new bonds are issued.

New Issue, Net Interest Cost Model

Net interest cost (NIC) proxies for the yield on new bond issues. It is the basis used by syndicates to bid on new issues and is measured as the ratio of total interest payments for the entire bond issue to the amount of bonds issued times the years to maturity of the bonds. The resulting calculation approximates the average yield to maturity of a bond issue (see Public Securities Association 1990, 181-183 for details).[13] An OLS regression model was used to test factors associated with NIC in the form:

$$\text{NIC} = \beta_0 + \beta_1 \text{ Bond Index} + \beta_2 \text{ Avg. Maturity} + \beta_3 \text{ AA} + \beta_4 \text{ A1} + \beta_5 \text{ A} + \beta_6 \text{ BAA} + \beta_7 \text{ Bids} + \beta_8 \text{ Callable} + \beta_9 \text{ Frequency} + \beta_{10} \text{ Debt} + \beta_{11} \text{ Fund Balance} + \beta_{12} \text{ Surplus} + \beta_{13} \text{ Insurance} + \varepsilon. \quad (4)$$

βs are coefficients. Bond Index is the Bond Buyer Index of 30-year municipal bonds for the same week as the new issues were sold and proxies for the general level of interest rates. Controlling for interest rate differences is important in a cross-sectional model without event clustering. The sample consisted of the 592 new bond issues described earlier. These issues were sold at various dates from 1978 to 1989. Avg. Maturity is the average maturity (in years) of the new bond issue.[14] Nearly all municipal issues are serial bonds. Therefore, the average maturity for the entire issue is used as a proxy for maturity. Together, the Bond Index and Avg. Maturity proxy for the effect of the term structure of interest rates at the time of a new issue. A higher value of the Bond Index and a higher Avg. Maturity are associated with higher NIC, ceteris paribus. AA, A1, A, and BAA are dummy variables representing bond rating classes and are set to one if a bond is rated in that class. If all dummy variables are zero, the bonds are rated AAA. The lower the rating class, the higher the NIC, ceteris paribus. Bids is the number of bids received from underwriters for an issue. A larger number of bids indicates greater competition for the bonds and lower NIC. Callable is a dummy variable set to one if the issue is callable. Governments pay a premium for the call privilege, thus increasing NIC. Approximately 70 percent of the bonds in the sample were callable. Frequency, Debt, Fund Balance, and Surplus are measured as in model one.

Insurance (a dummy variable) was included in the model to control for the effect of insurance on interest cost. Deleting the insurance variable from the model or omitting observations that were insured from the sample had minimal effect on the results.

The purpose of the NIC model was to determine whether accounting information was associated with new bond issue yields for the sample used in this study. Significant associations between accounting variables and NIC have been found in earlier studies (Wallace 1981; Wilson and Howard 1984; Feroz and Wilson 1992). Evidence of this association is important for assessing whether new issue data provide a potential information intermediary for seasoned bond yields. If accounting information is associated with new issue yields, in addition to the information provided by bond ratings, then these yields are a potential source of information for secondary markets in addition to that provided by bond ratings.

Seasoned Bond Yield Model

The third model examined the association between accounting information and seasoned bond yields using OLS regression in the form:

$$\text{Yield} = \gamma_0 + \gamma_1 \text{ NIC} + \gamma_2 \text{ Bond Index} + \gamma_3 \text{ Maturity} + \gamma_4 \text{ Debt} + \gamma_5 \text{ Fund Balance} + \gamma_6 \text{ Surplus} + \varepsilon. \qquad (5)$$

Yield is the bond yield on a seasoned issue from the IDS data. The γs are coefficients. NIC is net interest cost on a new bond issue from the same issuer as the seasoned bond. Data were for the 592 observations described earlier. Maturity is the remaining maturity (in years) for each of seasoned bonds. Other variables are measured as described above for the first two models. Bond Index and Maturity are included in the model to control for the term structure of interest rates. NIC is included to control for information provided by new issue data.

The model was tested both with and without this variable to assess whether accounting information is associated with seasoned bond yields separately from information provided by NIC. Also, the model was tested in the month the new bond issue was sold ($t = 0$) and three months prior to the sale ($t = -3$). These tests were used to assess whether accounting information was associated with seasoned bond yields in conjunction with new issues or in periods when new issue data were not available, or both. An association between accounting information and seasoned bond yields in periods other than when new issues are sold would suggest a continuous monitoring of accounting information.[15] If an association does not exist or exists only when new issues are sold, we can conclude that the secondary market is not continuously monitoring this information.

In addition to test results for the entire sample, we examined results for two subgroups of observations. The subgroups were for bonds issued by small and large cities, where small and large were defined relative to the median population of cities in the sample. The separation was prompted by the notion that large cities may disclose more information and may do so more frequently than small cities. Therefore, the market may be more alert to or find it more beneficial to monitor information for large cities.[16]

Seasoned Bond Yield Change Model

The fourth model examined the response of seasoned bond yields to new bond issues. It considers whether seasoned bond yields adjust systematically to the NIC of new bond issues. Each new issue in the sample was matched with a seasoned bond of the same issuer for the period surrounding the sale of the new issue. Changes in yields on the seasoned bond were examined during this period to determine whether the yields responded systematically to new issue data. The OLS regression model takes the form:

$$\text{Yield Change} = \delta_0 + \delta_1 \text{ NIC-Yield} + \delta_2 \text{ Bond Index} + \delta_3 \text{ Maturity Difference} + \delta_4 \text{ Debt} + \delta_5 \text{ Fund Balance} + \delta_6 \text{ Surplus} + \varepsilon. \quad (6)$$

Yield Change is the sum of the percentage change in yield to maturity of a seasoned bond during the month prior to and the month subsequent to a new bond issue:

$$(Y_0 - Y_{-1})/Y_{-1} + (Y_1 - Y_0)/Y_0 \quad (7)$$

where Y is yield to maturity of the seasoned bond for month -1, 0, or 1 relative to the sale of a new issue. Yield Change measures the shift in yield at the time of a new bond issue. δs are coefficients. NIC-Yield is the difference between the net interest cost of the new bond issue and the yield to maturity of the seasoned bond in the third month prior to the sale (Y_{-3}). This variable measures the disparity between NIC and the seasoned bond issue yield. If seasoned bond yields respond to new issue data, a large positive difference between NIC and the seasoned bond yield should be associated with a large positive Yield Change as the yield on the seasoned bond shifts upward to adjust to the higher NIC on the new issue. The seasoned bond yield in the third month prior to the new bond issue was used because there is little likelihood that information associated with the new issue would be available at that time. However, we also wanted to maintain close proximity between the measurement of the yield and NIC to avoid major shifts in general economic conditions between these dates. Maturity Difference is the difference between the average maturity of the new bond issue and the maturity of the seasoned bond at the date of the new issue (in years). Bond Index, Debt, Fund Balance, and Surplus are measured as in the earlier models.

The accounting variables are included in this model to determine whether they provide additional information beyond the information provided by new issue data at the time of the new issue. Thus, we can determine whether any shift in yield is associated with accounting information that might be considered by the secondary market at the time of a new issue, after controlling for the new issue yield. The fourth model is important for this study because it can help us understand the mechanism by which accounting information is impounded in secondary market yields. If seasoned bond yields adjust systematically to information provided by new issues, we can conclude that the new issue market is an important source of information for the seasoned bond market. It is then likely that new issues and bond ratings associated with these issues are important information intermediaries for the seasoned market. We examined results for bonds issued by small and large cities, in addition to results for the entire sample, as discussed in the previous section.

Description of Variables

Table 1 provides descriptive statistics for variables included in the empirical models, except for dummy variables and bond ratings described earlier. The table reports means, medians, standard deviations, minimum and maximum values for each variable. Distributions are symmetric and approximately normal.

The bond yield for seasoned bonds and the NIC for new issues are similar measures expressed as percentages. Both variables are measured in the month a new issue is sold. NIC is smaller on average than bond yield because of measurement differences described earlier. Another reason for the difference is the difference in maturities of new and seasoned issues. Seasoned issues in the sample have longer maturities, on average, than the average maturities of the new issues, as discussed below. Because the yield curve normally is upward sloping, longer maturities have higher yields. The difference between NIC and yield (Net Interest - Yield) is approximately a half a percentage point, on average (mean of −0.459). Minimum (−4.846) and maximum (2.388) indicate large differences for some observations. Yield change is the cumulative percentage change in yield for seasoned bonds for the two months surrounding a new issue. On average the change is approximately zero (mean of −1.8%). Relatively large positive (37.3%

Table 1. Descriptive Statistics for a Sample of 592 New Issues of General Obligation Bonds Issued between 1978 and 1989 by U.S. Cities with Populations in Excess of 25,000

Variable	Mean	Median	Std. Dev.	Min.	Max.
Yield (Seasoned)	8.338	8.000	1.921	4.531	14.469
Net Interest Cost	8.002	7.709	1.630	4.378	13.856
Yield Change	−0.182	−0.901	8.388	−39.038	37.336
Net Interest- Yield	−0.458	−0.320	1.124	−4.846	2.388
Bond Index	8.857	8.720	1.766	6.020	13.360
Avg. Maturity	9.773	9.900	3.305	1.100	23.600
Maturity (Seasoned)	12.228	11.750	5.171	1.250	33.833
Maturity Difference	−2.455	−2.317	5.758	−26.533	15.600
Bids	5.230	5.000	2.458	1.000	18.000
Frequency	5.669	5.000	4.398	1.000	22.000
Debt	1.141	0.906	1.017	0.020	8.640
Fund Balance	0.134	0.110	0.117	−0.152	0.643
Surplus	0.013	0.011	0.041	−0.162	0.200

Notes: Yield is the percentage yield to maturity on seasoned bonds. Yield change is the percentage change in yield for the period from the month before the issue of a new bond to the month subsequent to the issue. Net interest cost is the percentage cost for new bonds. Bond index is the Bond Buyer Index of 30-year municipal bonds for the same week as new issues were sold. Average maturity is the average maturity in years of new issues. Maturity difference is the difference between the average maturity of new issues and the maturity of the seasoned bond for the same issuer at the time the new bonds are sold. Bids are the number of bids received from underwriters for an issue. Frequency is the number of new bond issues sold by an issuer between January 1978 and December 1989. Debt is the ratio of total general obligation debt to total general fund revenues. Fund balance is the ratio of general fund balance to total general fund revenues. Surplus is general fund revenues minus general fund expenditures, scaled by general fund revenues.

maximum) and negative (−39.0% minimum) changes occurred for some observations, however. Accordingly, seasoned yields appear to have changed at the time of new bond issues for some observations. The Bond Index measures the average yield of long-term municipal bonds in the month of the sale of new issues. The values are similar to those for NIC and Yield, though higher, on average, than either NIC or Yield. The Index is for 30-year maturities, longer than the average maturities of new issues or the maturities of the seasoned bonds in the sample.

Average Maturity is the average maturity in years for the new bond issues. For example, a 20-year, serial bond issue with an equal amount of repayment each year would have an average maturity of 10 years. Maturity of seasoned bonds is the remaining life of the bonds in years. Maturity Difference is the Average Maturity of a new issue minus the maturity of a seasoned bond with which it is compared. Maturity differ-

Table 2. Correlation Coefficients for Primary Variables for 592 New Issues of General Obligation Bonds Issued Between 1978 and 1989 by U.S. Cities with Populations in Excess of 25,000

	Yield	NIC	Yield Change	NIC-Yield	Bond Index	Avg. Mat	Maturity	Mat Dif	Bids	Frequency	Debt	Fund Balance	Surplus
Yield	1.000	0.895	0.110	−0.400	0.904	0.025	0.363	−0.318	−0.222	0.012	0.030	−0.045	−0.018
NIC		1.000	0.014	−0.102	0.924	0.192	0.163	−0.045	−0.261	−0.006	0.039	−0.030	−0.023
Yld Chn			1.000	0.522	−0.017	0.019	0.052	−0.026	−0.053	0.049	0.024	−0.011	−0.017
NIC-Yield				1.000	−0.267	0.280	−0.409	0.532	−0.023	0.013	0.027	0.031	−0.015
B Index					1.000	−0.032	0.106	−0.120	−0.176	0.023	0.024	0.032	0.011
Avg Mat						1.000	0.129	0.449	0.000	0.048	0.132	0.047	0.007
Mat							1.000	−0.828	−0.092	0.080	0.023	−0.179	−0.073
Mat Dif								1.000	0.081	−0.038	0.059	0.189	0.071
Bids									1.000	0.082	−0.066	0.101	−0.024
Freq										1.000	0.224	0.024	−0.054
Debt											1.000	0.154	0.078
F Bal												1.000	0.419
Surplus													1.000

Notes: Coefficients with absolute values > 0.08 are significant at the 0.05 level.
Yield is the percentage yield to maturity on seasoned bonds. Yld Chn is the percentage change in yield for the period from the month before the issue of a new bond to the month subsequent to the issue. Net interest cost (NIC) is the percentage cost for new bonds. B index is the Bond Buyer Index of 30-year municipal bonds for the same week as new issues were sold. Avg Mat is the average maturity in years of new issues. Mat is the maturity of seasoned issues. Mat Dif is the difference between the average maturity of new issues and the maturity of the seasoned bond for the same issuer at the time the new bonds are sold. Bids are the number of bids received from underwriters for an issue. Freq is the number of new bond issues sold by an issuer between January 1978 and December 1989. Debt is the ratio of total general obligation debt to total general fund revenues. F Bal is the ratio of general fund balance to total general fund revenues. Surplus is general fund revenues minus general fund expenditures, scaled by general fund revenues.

ences are apparent and are large (positive or negative) in some cases. On average, the maturities of the seasoned bonds are approximately two and half years longer than the average maturities of the new issues. Consequently, it is important to control for maturity effects in the empirical analysis.

Bids is the number of bids from underwriting syndicates for the new bond issues. The sample included only competitively bid issues. The range of number of bids (one to 18) is large. Therefore, this variable also is controlled in the empirical analysis. Frequency is the number of new bond issues sold by a municipality during the test period, approximately 10 years. The range of this variable (one to 22) also is large and is controlled in the empirical analysis.

Debt is the ratio of general long-term debt to general fund revenue prior to the new bond issues. Fund balance is the ratio of general fund balance to general fund revenue, and Surplus is the excess of general fund revenue over general fund expense, scaled by general fund revenue. The ranges of these variables indicate large variations in the sample.

Correlation coefficients are in Table 2. The only intercorrelation involving accounting variables of statistical significance is that between Fund Balance and Surplus. The R^2 for the association is 0.160. None of the other independent variables was significantly associated with the accounting variables. Multicollinearity was examined using variance inflation factors and multiple regressions of accounting variables on other independent variables. No evidence of a problem was identified.

IV. EMPIRICAL TEST RESULTS

This section presents regression model results and analysis of these results.

A. Bond Rating Model Results

Table 3 reports coefficients, standard errors, and p values for the bond rating model. The signs of all coefficients are in the expected direction and, except for Surplus, are significant at the .05 level. Insurance, population, and frequency are associated with higher bond ratings. Higher debt to revenue is associated with a lower rating, and higher fund balance is associated with a higher rating. The model is highly significant (Chi-Square of 349.6 with 18 degrees of freedom).

Table 3. Bond Rating Model
Summary logistic regression statistics for bond rating =
$\alpha_0 + \alpha_1$ insurance $+ \alpha_2$ population $+ \alpha_3$ frequency $+ \alpha_4$ debt $+ \alpha_5$ fund balance $+ \alpha_6$ surplus $+ \varepsilon$.

Variable	Coefficient	Std. Err.	P Value
Intercept1	−4.096	0.492	0.0001
Intercept2	−1.804	0.462	0.0001
Intercept3	−0.737	0.460	0.1087
Intercept4	0.927	0.488	0.0575
Insurance	4.293	0.609	0.0001
Population	0.405	0.093	0.0001
Frequency	0.087	0.021	0.0001
Debt	−0.270	0.081	0.0008
Fund Balance	1.464	0.671	0.0291
Surplus	1.092	1.515	0.4710

Notes: Chi-Square (18 DF) = 840.93, P value = 0.0001, N = 592. Data are for U.S. municipal bond issues for cities with populations in excess of 25,000 from January 1978 to December 1989. Dependent variable is bond rating on a five-point scale. Insurance is a dummy variable set to one if an issue is insured and issued after 1983. Population is log of municipal population. Frequency is number of new issues sold during test period. Debt is the ratio of general obligation debt to general fund revenue. Fund Balance is the ratio of general fund balance to general fund revenue. Surplus is the difference between general fund revenue and general fund expenditures, scaled by general fund revenues.

The results of the bond rating model are consistent with the conclusion that accounting information is associated with bond ratings. These results are consistent with prior research (Wallace 1981; Wilson and Howard 1986) and with the bond rating literature (Sherwood 1976). Therefore, bond ratings appear to be an important information intermediary for conveying accounting information to the bond market, both new and seasoned issues.

B. Net Interest Cost Model Results

Table 4 reports summary regression statistics for the NIC model. This model examines the relationship between NIC for new issues and explanatory factors, including accounting information. The model is highly significant (R^2 of 0.933 and F value of 639.87). The Bond Index and Average Maturity variables are highly significant and coefficients are positive as expected. Also, a higher NIC is associated with lower ratings. Callable bonds pay higher interest, and more bids are associated with lower interest. Of the control variables, only Frequency is not significant.

Table 4. New Issue, Net Interest Cost Model
Summary OLS regression statistics for NIC = $\beta_0 + \beta_1$ bond index + β_2 avg. maturity + β_3 AA + β_4 A1 + β_5 A + β_6 BAA + β_7 bids + β_8 callable + β_9 frequency + β_{10} debt + β_{11} fund balance + β_{12} surplus + β_{13} insurance + ε

Variable	Coefficient	Std. Err.	P Value
Intercept	−0.502	0.129	0.0001
Bond Index	0.847	0.010	0.0001
Avg. Maturity	0.104	0.006	0.0001
AA	0.111	0.054	0.0388
A1	0.312	0.063	0.0001
A	0.356	0.065	0.0001
BAA	0.931	0.098	0.0001
Bids	−0.043	0.008	0.0001
Callable	0.123	0.045	0.0065
Frequency	0.003	0.005	0.5109
Debt	−0.030	0.019	0.1172
Fund Balance	−0.504	0.153	0.0011
Surplus	−0.412	0.348	0.2372
Insurance	0.211	0.067	0.0019

Notes: $R^2 = 0.934$, F Value = 604.09, P Value = 0.0001, N = 592. Data are for U.S. municipal bond issues for cities with populations in excess of 25,000 from January 1978 to December 1989. NIC is net interest cost on new bond issues. Bond Index is the Bond Buyer average yield on 30-year municipal bonds. Avg. Maturity is the average maturity of the bond issue. AA through BAA are dummy variables for rating classes. Callable is a dummy variable (1 = callable bond issue). Frequency is number of new issues sold during test period. Debt is the ratio of general obligation debt to general fund revenue. Fund Balance is the ratio of general fund balance to general fund revenue. Surplus is the difference between general fund revenue and general fund expenditures, scaled by general fund revenues. Insurance is a dummy variable set to one if an issue is insured.

Of the accounting variables, Fund Balance and Surplus have the correct sign. Fund Balance is highly significant. These results are consistent with earlier research (Wilson and Howard 1984; Feroz and Wilson 1992) and provide evidence that accounting information is associated with NIC in addition to information provided by bond ratings. Consequently, we can assume that new bond issues also are an important potential source of accounting information for the seasoned bond market.

C. Seasoned Yield Model Results

Table 5 provides summary results for the seasoned yield models. The table presents data for two periods. One period (panel A) uses the Yield for the third month prior to new issues as the dependent variable. The other period (panels B and C) uses the Yield for the month of new

Table 5. Seasoned Bond Yield Model
Summary OLS regression statistics for yield = $\gamma_0 + \gamma_1$ NIC + γ_2 bond index + γ_3 maturity + γ_4 debt + γ_5 fund balance + γ_6 surplus + ε

	Small Cities			Large Cities		
Variable	Coefficient	Std. Err	P Value	Coefficient	Std. Err	P Value
Panel A: Dependent Variable is Yield in Month - 3 Relative to New Issue in Month 0						
Intercept	−1.561	0.303	0.0001	−1.366	0.211	0.0001
Bond Index	0.987	0.031	0.0001	0.989	0.022	0.0001
Maturity	0.110	0.012	0.0001	0.096	0.007	0.0001
Debt	−0.017	0.044	0.6946	−0.027	0.038	0.4802
Fund Balance	−0.156	0.425	0.7137	−0.589	0.367	0.1092
Surplus	1.022	1.305	0.4343	1.103	1.029	0.2834
$R^2 = 0.810$, F Value = 249.46, P Value = 0.0001; $R^2 = 0.807$, F Value = 491.51, P Value = 0.0001						
Panel B: Dependent Variable is Yield in Month of New Issue in Month 0						
Intercept	−1.546	0.196	0.0001	−1.051	0.228	0.0001
Bond Index	0.973	0.020	0.0001	0.947	0.023	0.0001
Maturity	0.104	0.008	0.0001	0.093	0.007	0.0001
Debt	0.018	0.028	0.5198	−0.020	0.059	0.7281
Fund Balance	−0.228	0.274	0.4068	−0.797	0.435	0.0682
Surplus	0.386	0.841	0.6468	−0.213	1.011	0.8332
$R^2 = 0.909$, F Value = 580.10, P Value = 0.0001; $R^2 = 0.869$, F Value = 396.74, P Value = 0.0001						
Panel C: Dependent Variable is Yield in Month of New Issue in Month 0						
Intercept	−1.646	0.184	0.0001	−1.166	0.219	0.0001
Net Interest	0.337	0.052	0.0001	0.356	0.067	0.0001
Bond Index	0.692	0.047	0.0001	0.637	0.062	0.0001
Maturity	0.096	0.008	0.0001	0.089	0.007	0.0001
Debt	0.009	0.027	0.7241	−0.046	0.056	0.4202
Fund Balance	−0.187	0.256	0.4652	−0.171	0.433	0.6931
Surplus	0.465	0.786	0.5546	−0.049	0.968	0.9596
$R^2 = 0.920$, F Value = 560.54, P Value = 0.0001; $R^2 = 0.880$, F Value = 366.06, P Value = 0.0001						

Notes: Data for 592 U.S. municipal bond issues for cities with populations in excess of 25,000 from January 1978 to December 1989. Small (large) cities are those below (above) the median population of the sample. Yield is yield to maturity of seasoned bond issues. Net Interest is net interest cost of new issue. Bond Index is the Bond Buyer average yield on 30-year municipal bonds. Avg. Maturity is the average maturity of the bond issue. Debt is the ratio of general obligation debt to general fund revenue. Fund Balance is the ratio of general fund balance to general fund revenue. Surplus is the difference between general fund revenue and general fund expenditures, scaled by general fund revenues.

issues as the dependent variable. Results for two regressions are provided in each panel. One is for small (below median population) cities, and the other is for large (above median population) cities. The regression models in panel C differ from A and B in containing the net interest cost (NIC) variable. All models are highly significant with R^2s ranging from 0.807 to 0.920. Control variables, NIC, Bond Index, and

Maturity, are all highly significant and coefficient signs are in the expected direction.

None of the accounting variables are significant for the small cities in any of the models. Any accounting information impounded in the seasoned yields is provided by the net interest cost variable. That is, it is provided indirectly through information used in pricing new issues. NIC and Bond Index both capture effects of general economic conditions and are intercorrelated. Removing NIC from the models has little effect on explanatory power. The primary effect of removing NIC is to increase the coefficient of Bond Index. Removing NIC has little effect on the magnitude or significance of the accounting variable coefficients. Adding bond ratings to the models (not reported) further reduces the association of the accounting variables.

For the large cities sample, Fund Balance is marginally significant in the third month prior to the sale of a new issue (panel A) and significant at the 10 percent level in the month of a new issue when NIC is omitted from the model (panel B). These results indicate that some accounting information is associated with bond yields for larger cities, though the association is stronger at the time new issues are sold. The association is insignificant when NIC is included in the model (panel C). Consequently, we again conclude that accounting information is impounded in seasoned yields primarily through information made available at the time new issues are sold. Results are consistent with incentives being larger for market agents to monitor accounting information of larger cities to a greater extent than that for smaller cities. The results are inconsistent with market agents monitoring accounting information for smaller cities except at the time new issues are sold. NIC and bond ratings associated with the sale of new issues appear to be important intermediaries for conveying accounting information to the seasoned bond market.

D. Seasoned Yield Change Model Results

This section presents evidence that seasoned bond yields respond systematically to new issue data. Figure 1 illustrates the response. The figure provides mean seasoned bond yields for the sample for months −4 to +4 relative to new issues in month 0. All observations in the sample were ranked by the difference between NIC and seasoned yield in month 0 (Net Interest - Yield). The ranked observations were then

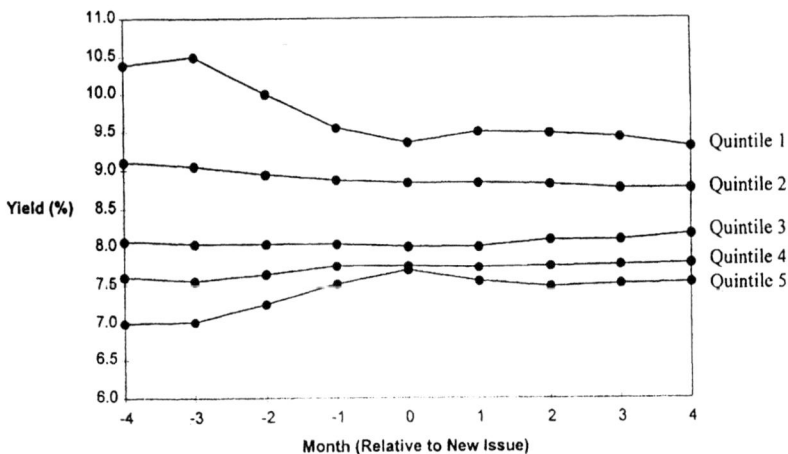

Notes: Data are mean monthly yields for a sample of 592 observations of seasoned bonds issued by U.S. cities with populations in excess of 25,000 between 1978 and 1989. Quintiles were formed by ranking observations from lowest (quintile 1) to highest (quintile 5) by the difference between the net interest cost on a new issue sold in month 0 and the yield on a seasoned bond of the same issuer in month −3.

Figure 1. Changes in Seasoned Bond Yields Surrounding the Issue of New Bonds in Month 0

divided into quintiles (approximately 120 observations in each quintile). The mean yield for each quintile was computed for each month, as plotted in Figure 1.

The quintile with the highest NIC - Yield difference is at the bottom of the graph, and the quintile with the lowest difference is at the top. Table 6 reports descriptive statistics for the quintiles. Data are reported for NIC - Yield, for NIC, and for Yield in months −3 and 0. The mean NIC - Yield difference ranges from -2.154 for quintile 1 to 0.967 for quintile 5.

As Figure 1 illustrates, seasoned yields adjust systematically at the time of new issues. When yields are high relative to the NIC of new issues (quintile 1), the yields adjust downward from month -3 to month 0. When yields are low relative to NIC (quintile 5), the yields adjust upward from month -3 to month 0. Lesser adjustments occur in quintiles 2 and 4, though some adjustment is apparent by comparing yields in months -3 and 0 for these quintiles in Table 6.

Table 6. Descriptive Statistics for Yield Difference (NIC - Yield) Quintiles

Quintile	Mean	Std. Dev.	Min.	Max.
NIC - Yield				
1	−2.154	0.704	−4.846	−1.219
2	−0.886	0.178	−1.215	−0.592
3	−0.316	0.146	−0.591	−0.092
4	0.182	0.162	−0.092	0.484
5	0.967	0.429	0.496	2.388
Net Interest				
1	8.349	1.816	4.905	12.678
2	8.173	1.897	4.378	12.694
3	7.732	1.622	5.419	13.856
4	7.737	1.318	5.542	12.344
5	7.985	1.378	5.619	12.231
Yield (−3)				
1	10.503	2.000	6.336	15.500
2	9.059	1.932	5.094	13.672
3	8.048	1.628	5.656	14.188
4	7.556	1.329	5.375	12.125
5	7.018	1.437	4.578	11.375
Yield (0)				
1	9.358	1.807	5.773	13.297
2	8.834	2.111	4.531	14.469
3	7.996	1.739	4.906	13.531
4	7.755	1.597	4.719	13.484
5	7.689	1.778	4.859	13.438

Notes: Data are for 592 U.S. municipal bond issues for cities with populations in excess of 25,000 from January 1978 to December 1989. Quintiles were formed by ranking observations from lowest (quintile 1) to highest (quintile 5) by the difference between the net interest cost (NIC) on a new issue in month 0 and the yield on a seasoned bond of the same issuer in month −3 (NIC - Yield). Net Interest is net interest cost on new issues. Yield (−3) is seasoned bond yield in month −3 relative to new issue in month 0. Yield (0) is seasoned bond yield in month 0.

The data in Figure 1 and Table 6 do not control for other differences among observations. For example, quintile 1 bonds have higher yields, on average, than those in the other quintiles. Maturities and other factors also differ (statistics are not reported). Table 7 reports summary statistics for an OLS regression model that controls for these factors.

The dependent variable in the model in Table 7 is the cumulative change in seasoned bond yield for months −1 to +1 relative to a new issue in month 0. Results are reported separately for small and large cities. The coefficient of the difference between NIC in month 0 and seasoned yield in month −3 (NIC - Yield) is highly significant and positive for both groups. This result is consistent with the data in Figure 1. When

Table 7. Seasoned Bond Yield Change Model
Summary OLS regression statistics for yield change = δ_0 + δ_1 NIC-yield + δ_2 bond index + δ_3 maturity difference + δ_4 debt + δ_5 fund balance + δ_6 surplus + ε

Variable	Small Cities			Large Cities		
	Coefficient	Std. Err.	P Value	Coefficient	Std. Err.	P Value
Intercept	−0.1243	0.0240	0.0001	−0.0905	0.0205	0.0001
NIC-Yield	0.0657	0.0047	0.0001	0.0609	0.0040	0.0001
Bond Index	0.0090	0.0024	0.0002	0.0052	0.0021	0.0140
Maturity Difference	−0.0005	0.0001	0.0001	−0.0004	0.0001	0.0001
Debt	−0.0007	0.0033	0.8398	−0.0035	0.0051	0.4997
Fund Balance	−0.0178	0.0278	0.5500	0.0905	0.0380	0.0180
Surplus	0.0005	0.0007	0.4939	0.0005	0.0009	0.5891

$R^2 = 0.395$, F Value = 32.43, P Value = 0.0001; $R^2 = 0.445$, F Value = 39.66, P Value = 0.0001

Notes: Data for 592 U.S. municipal bond issues for cities with populations in excess of 25,000 from January 1978 to December 1989. Small (large) cities are those below (above) the median population of the sample. Yield change is the cumulative monthly percentage yield change on seasoned bonds from month −1 to month 1 relative to a new issue in month 0. NIC - Yield is the difference between the net interest cost on a new issue in month 0 and the yield on a seasoned bond of the same issuer in month −3. Bond Index is the Bond Buyer average yield on 30-year municipal bonds. Maturity Difference is the difference between the average maturity of the new bond issue and the maturity of the seasoned bond issue for the same issuer. Debt is the ratio of general obligation debt to general fund revenue. Fund Balance is the ratio of general fund balance to general fund revenue. Surplus is the difference between general fund revenue and general fund expenditures, scaled by general fund revenues.

NIC is higher than the seasoned yield (in months prior to the sale of a new issue), the yield adjusts upward toward NIC. When NIC is lower, the yield adjusts downward. Bond Index and Maturity Difference are included in the model to control for differences in general economic conditions across time and for differences in maturities between the new and seasoned bonds. Both variables are highly significant for both groups.

None of the accounting variables is significant for the small cities, but Fund Balance is significant for the large cities. These results, along with those in Table 6, indicate that accounting information is impounded directly in seasoned yields at the time new issues are sold. Thus, there appears to be some monitoring of accounting information in addition to that associated with the pricing of new issues. Nevertheless, the sale of new issues appears to be a major event that stimulates the monitoring and impounding of accounting information.

Results of the yield change model are important because they support the conclusion that seasoned bond yields adjust systematically to new issue data. Seasoned yields often are systematically mispriced relative to new issues. Again, it is apparent that new issue data are an important information intermediary for seasoned bonds and that these data are important for correcting the mispricing of seasoned issues.

CONCLUSIONS AND IMPLICATIONS

Our results provide evidence that accounting information is associated with bond ratings and new bond issue data and that seasoned bond issues impound accounting information primarily at the time new issues are sold. Seasoned bond yields impound accounting information primarily through information intermediaries associated with new issues, including bond ratings. Accordingly, increased regulation of issuers to mandate additional and more frequent disclosure of accounting information is likely to have minimal effect on seasoned bond markets. Under current institutional arrangements, additional and more frequent disclosure has little opportunity to affect seasoned bond yields because the secondary market relies primarily on information intermediation by the primary bond market. It is unlikely that additional regulation would increase the amount of information available at the time new issues are marketed. Therefore, this additional information would have little opportunity to affect seasoned bond yields.

For additional disclosure to affect the secondary market, new mechanisms will be needed to provide incentives for analysts and traders to access this information. Regulators, especially the SEC, appear to have given little consideration to the process by which information is impounded in the bond market. Consequently, regulations mandating additional disclosure are likely to impose costs on issuers and traders without substantially improving the ability of the markets to avoid mispricing seasoned bonds.

Accounting research has focused primarily on the quantity and quality of governmental accounting information. Policy setters and regulators have attempted to improve both quantity and quality by imposing reporting standards and disclosure requirements. Additional attention should be given to the institutional processes by which this information is made available to decision makers and the incentives of decision makers to act on this information. Lacking mechanisms and incentives to access the information, decision makers are not likely to benefit greatly from additional disclosure requirements. In particular, it is not clear how additional disclosure alone can prevent or reduce the impact of occasional municipal defaults and bankruptcies on holders of local government bonds.

This study examined a broad spectrum of municipal issuers and conclusions are based on results for this cross-section. Another approach would be to isolate important economic events that might be conveyed through accounting information, if additional disclosures were provided, to evaluate whether seasoned bond yields respond to these events at the time the events occur. Restricting the sample to specific events could improve the power of the tests to identify significant associations between yields and particular disclosures rather than general accounting information, as examined in this study.

ACKNOWLEDGMENT

We appreciate the comments of Paul Copley, Jere Francis, Tom Howard, Inder Khurana, and the anonymous reviewers on earlier drafts of this paper. Remaining errors are the sole responsibility of the authors.

NOTES

1. Discussion of the institutional arrangements involving new municipal issues is available in Public Securities Association (1990, chap. 4).

2. Wilson, Gotlob, and Lawrence (1996) provide evidence that accounting measures are associated with seasoned municipal bond returns during new issue periods, but only for infrequent issuers.

3. About 1.5 million bond issues are sold by 50,000 municipal entities in the United States (Spiro et al. 1993), which effectively precludes close following by analysts.

4. Institutional arrangements for the sale of seasoned municipal bonds are described in Public Securities Association (1990, 85-88). Sales generally are made from dealer inventories. Short sales are not common because of the difficulty of borrowing bonds in a thin market.

5. Other studies (e.g., Marks, Raman, and Wilson 1994; Raman and Wilson 1990, 1994) provide evidence that seasoned bond prices provide useful information to investors.

6. The Securities and Exchange Act of 1934 was amended in 1975 to require considerable amounts of disclosure by issuers and underwriters. Rating agencies also require large amounts of disclosure from issuers (see Sherwood 1976, 115-135).

7. The municipal bond rating process is described by Lamb and Rappaport (1987) and Sherwood (1976).

8. Exact information about these prices is proprietary. General information is available from the investment services. Additional discussion and analysis of these data are provided by Ingram (1985).

9. We presume municipal bond market efficiency (see Ingram, Brooks, and Copeland 1983; Ingram, Raman, and Wilson 1989). The failure of the market to impound information may be the rational result of the cost of information processing exceeding the benefit when large numbers of issues exist, securities are thinly traded, and profits do not accrue from monitoring existing information. Markets are efficient if they impound information at the time the information is available in conjunction with the marketing of new issues, at which time there are incentives to impound the information.

10. The U.S. Bureau of the Census annually publishes financial and economic data for cities with populations in excess of 25,000 population in *Survey of City Government Finances*.

11. Moody's did not adjust bond ratings for the effects of insurance prior to 1984. Therefore, we set the dummy variable for insurance to zero in periods prior to 1984. Also, we ran the tests without insured bonds. Results were almost identical to those reported.

12. Municipal bond analysts and municipal finance professionals (see, e.g., International City Management Association 1980, 55-57) view a prudent fund balance as being at least 5 percent of a year's revenue requirement. In practice, a fund balance to revenue level of less than 5 percent is now regarded as a "red flag," indicating possible financial stress. Municipal annual reports often contain a discussion of the city's policy on fund balance level, with goals of 10-20 percent being typical.

13. Though NIC has been criticized in the literature for its failure to incorporate the time value of interest payments (Public Securities Association 1990, 181), it remains a primary measure of the cost of new bonds. In addition to NIC, we examined reoffering yields, the yields associated with the prices underwriters attempt to charge for their bonds. Reoffering yield data also are subject to criticism because underwriters are known to discount bonds to brokers and dealers relative to the official yield. We examined reoffering yields in addition to NIC. Results were substantially the same and are not described in this paper.

14. A case can be made for using log of maturity because of the exponent term in the present value equation (equation (1)). Log and non-log forms were tested. The results were essentially the same.

15. Limited information is available about the relationship between seasoned yields and accounting information. Ingram and Copeland (1982) provide some evidence of association between yields and state regulation of accounting practices. Ingram (1983) examined state accounting practices and yields and found evidence of a statistical association for one variable, the ratio of expenditures to revenues. Ingram, Raman, and Wilson (1989) found no significant relationship between bond returns and the release of annual reports by municipalities.

16. Additionally, we examined results for subgroups based on the number of bond issues sold during our test period. Frequent (infrequent) issuers were those above (below) the median for the sample. Results were similar to those reported in this paper for the entire sample and are not included.

REFERENCES

Feroz, E. H., and E. R. Wilson. 1992. Market segmentation and the association between municipal financial disclosure and net interest costs. *The Accounting Review* 67 (July): 480-495.

Ingram, R. W. 1983. The importance of state accounting practices for creditor decisions. *Journal of Accounting and Public Policy* 2 (Spring): 5-17.

———. 1985. A descriptive analysis of municipal bond price data for use in accounting research. *Journal of Accounting Research* 23 (Autumn): 595-618.

Ingram, R. W., L. Brooks, and R. Copeland. 1983. The information content of municipal bond rating changes. *Journal of Finance* 38 (June): 997-1010.

Ingram, R. W., and R. Copeland. 1982. State mandated accounting, auditing, and finance practices and municipal bond ratings. *Public Budgeting and Finance* 2 (Spring): 19-29.

Ingram, R. W., K. K. Raman, and E. R. Wilson. 1987. Governmental capital markets research in accounting: A review. *Research in Governmental and Nonprofit Accounting* 3, Part B: 111-126.

———. 1989. The information in governmental annual reports: A contemporaneous price reaction approach. *The Accounting Review* 64 (April): 250-268.

Ingram, R. W., and W. A. Robbins. 1987. *Financial Reporting Practices of Local Governments*. Stamford, CT: Governmental Accounting Standards Board.

Lamb, R., and S. P. Rappaport. 1987. *Municipal Bonds*. New York: McGraw-Hill.

Marks, B. R., K. K. Raman, and E. R. Wilson. 1994. The effect of municipal bond rating change announcements on seasoned bond prices. *Municipal Finance Journal* 15 (Fall): 17-35.

Petersen, J. E. 1989. The new SEC rule on municipal disclosure: Implications for issuers of municipal securities. *Government Finance Review* (October): 17-20.

Public Securities Association. 1990. *Fundamentals of Municipal Bonds*. New York: PSA.

Raman, K., and E. Wilson. 1990. The debt equivalence of unfunded governmental pension obligations. *Journal of Accounting and Public Policy* 9 (Spring): 37-56.

———. 1994. Governmental audit procurement practices and seasoned bond prices. *The Accounting Review* 69 (October): 517-538.

Securities and Exchange Commission. 1994. Municipal securities disclosure: Final rule. *Federal Register* (November 17): 59590-59610.

Sherwood, H. C. 1976. *How Corporate and Municipal Debt is Rated*. New York: John Wiley & Sons.

Spiro, L., K. Holland, L. Light, D. Griesing, and M. Schroeder. 1993. The trouble with munis. *Business Week* (September 6): 44-51.

Taylor, J., and J. Connor. 1995. SEC probes District of Columbia's data on financial woes at time of note sale. *The Wall Street Journal* (February 8): A3, A11.

Taylor, J., and N. Jeffrey. 1994. New SEC rules aim to help muni buyers step out of the dark and into the know. *Wall Street Journal* (November 15): c1, c17.

Wallace, W. 1981. The association between municipal market measures and selected financial reporting practices. *Journal of Accounting Research* 19 (Autumn): 505-521.

Wilson, E. R., D. Gotlob, and C. Lawrence. 1996. The effects of new issue accounting information on seasoned municipal bond prices. Working paper, University of Missouri.

Wilson, E. R., and T. Howard. 1984. The association between municipal market measures and selected financial reporting practices: Additional evidence. *Journal of Accounting Research* 22 (Spring): 207-224.

THE DIFFERENTIAL EFFECT OF STATE GOVERNMENT PENSION FUNDING PRACTICES ON BOND YIELDS ACROSS VARYING MATURITIES

Cynthia Sneed and John Sneed

ABSTRACT

We examine the relationship between states' unfunded pension obligations and borrowing costs for general obligation debt. The study adds to the literature by examining this relationship across different maturities. We present a statistical technique to deal with cross-sectional dependence, a problem inherent in the use of multiple observations from a single bond issue. The results suggest it is important to control for the term to maturity when examining the relationship between states' unfunded pension obligations and their borrowing costs. States with larger unfunded pension plans are found to pay higher borrowing costs for bond issues with long-term maturities but not for bond issues with short-term maturities.

We examine the effect of state pension funding practices on the yield of general obligation bonds issued by state governments between 1990 and 1992. Our study is an extension of Raman and Wilson (1990) using data gathered from pension disclosures reported in state government annual reports. Our analysis differs from previous studies in that we treat individual maturities under a serial bond issue as separate observations. This allows us to test for differential effects of unfunded pension liabilities across different serial maturities. In so doing, we demonstrate a technique (Froot 1989) that addresses the problem of correlated residuals which is inherent in the use of multiple observations from the same bond issue.[1]

We find a significant positive relation between unfunded pension liabilities and borrowing costs for state governments for long-term bond maturities, or maturities greater than 10 years. However, we find an insignificant relation for short-term bond maturities, or maturities less than 10 years. Thus, states that currently underfund their pension plans do not pay higher borrowing costs in the short term, but the borrowing costs are higher for long-term issues when they will have to provide additional funding.

I. INTRODUCTION

The purpose of this study is to provide additional insight into the relationship between states' unfunded pension obligations and borrowing costs. Raman and Wilson (1990) argue that, while there is no well-developed theory linking unfunded pension obligations with the default risk on general obligation bonds, such a linkage is intuitively appealing.

Several studies (General Accounting Office 1979; Munnell and Keefe 1982; Woodruff 1983; Zorn 1992) indicate that state and local pension plans are substantially underfunded. From the bondholders' perspective, unfunded pension obligations represent a claim on the future resources of the government and thus represent a significant competing claim with general obligation debt for future cash flows. If this is so, a higher unfunded pension obligation increases the default risk and borrowing cost.

Underfunded pension obligations are of sufficient magnitude to be a significant competing claim with bondholders for the cash flows of state governments.[2] However, the timing of the pension funding is uncertain. An unfunded pension obligation represents a liability that will not have to be paid immediately, but several years in the future when current employees retire. Most states issue serial bonds for their general obligation debt, where some principal is repaid each year over the life of the bond issue. Therefore, it is conceivable that different maturities will be affected differently by unfunded pension obligations.

The difficulty in analyzing the effect of unfunded pension obligations on bond yields for state governments is that there is no set maturity date where the states will be required to fund the plans. Presently states must only fund amounts sufficient to meet the retirement claims of current retirees.

As the population ages and the baby boom generation reaches retirement age, states will be required to increase their pension contributions to meet the increased cost of the pension benefits. Some states currently have large unfunded pension obligations, indicating that they have chosen not to prefund their plans, postponing the required contributions until future years.

Since it is projected that the baby boom generation will start retiring in large numbers in approximately 10 years,[3] unfunded pension obligations may become a competitor with general obligation debt for a state's cash flows at that time. Thus, we expect the unfunded pension obligation to be positively associated with borrowing costs for bond issues with long-term maturities.

Because states with large unfunded pension obligations choose not to fund their plans until close to the time that the additional funds will be needed to pay retirees, the unfunded pension obligation will not compete with general obligation debt for a state's cash flows in the near future. Thus, we do not expect unfunded pension debt to be associated with borrowing costs for bond issues with short maturities.

II. REVIEW OF PRIOR LITERATURE

The Governmental Accounting Standards Board (GASB) identifies "investors and creditors" as a primary user of governmental financial reports (GASB 1987, p. 12) and attempts to make governmental information more useful to this user group (GASB 1986, 1988; Ives 1988).

However, little is known about the information content of governmental pension data or whether governmental bond markets impound this information in bond prices (Raman and Wilson 1990).

Initial studies (Copeland and Ingram 1983; Marks and Raman 1985) examining the relationship between unfunded pension obligations and borrowing costs for governmental units use pension ratios to proxy for underfunded pension debt, because measures of the unfunded obligation were not available.[4] Copeland and Ingram (1983) find that pension ratios are not related to bond yields for cities. Marks and Raman (1985) find that the relationship is not significant for cities, but is significant for states.

Later studies (Marks and Raman 1987, 1988; Raman and Wilson 1990) use pension underfunding estimates by Kotlikoff and Smith (1983) to examine the relationship between unfunded pension obligations and the cost of government debt. Marks and Raman (1987) find that unfunded pension obligations affect municipal rating decisions. Marks and Raman (1988) find the unfunded accumulated benefit obligation is associated with the yield on new state bond issues, while the incremental increase to the projected benefit obligation is insignificant. Raman and Wilson (1990) find that unfunded pension obligations are partially impounded in the yield of seasoned bond issues, but had a smaller incremental effect on bond yields than general obligation debt.

We use the unfunded pension obligations reported by the states in the footnotes to their comprehensive annual financial reports. The unfunded pension obligation measure used in the analysis is the unfunded pension benefit obligation per the requirements of GASB Statement No. 5, "Disclosure of Pension Information by Public Employee Retirement Systems and State and Local Government Employers." This study extends prior research by examining the relationship for bond issues with short-term maturities versus bond issues with long-term maturities.

Prior studies treated each serial bond issue as one observation, using the average yield and the average maturity for each serial bond issue. In this study, each serial maturity is treated as a separate observation. Thus, a 20-year serial bond issue is treated as 20 observations.

III. DATA AND METHODOLOGY

The dependent variable, yield to maturity, for all new state bond issues from 1990 to 1992 was collected from Bloomberg's Financial Markets database. This database is used extensively by investors on Wall Street to track security prices.

Twenty-six states combined for a total of 78 new bond issues during this period. However, many states had several bond issues within one year. We limited the sample to only one bond issue per state per year. We selected the issue closest to the end of the year, since the financial variables are measured at year end. After deleting the multiple bond issues by one state within a year, the final sample consisted of 42 bond issues from 26 states (see the Appendix for a listing of the state/year combinations of new bond issues).

The majority of state bond issues are serial bonds, where a portion of the principal is repaid each year over the life of the bond. Bloomberg's reports a separate yield to maturity for each of the principal repayment maturities. We treat each maturity under a serial bond issue as a separate observation, resulting in 720 observations. This sampling procedure allows us to examine the relationship between unfunded pension obligations and bond yields across varying maturities.

The following regression model is estimated to examine the relationship between unfunded pension obligations and bond yields for new state bond issues:

$$YTM_{i,t} = b_{0i,t} + b_1 LMAT_{i,t} + b_2 COUPON_{i,t} + b_3 IRATE_{i,t} + b_4 LPOP_{i,t} + b_5 PCINC_{i,t} + b_6 STDR_{i,t} + b_7 GODEBT_{i,t} + b_8 OWNREV_{i,t} + b_9 UPO_{i,t} + E_{i,t}$$

where: YTM = yield to maturity; LMAT = term to maturity, natural log; COUPON = coupon rate associated with each observation; IRATE = market interest rate for the week the bonds were issued; LPOP = the states' population, natural log; PCINC = per capita income; STDR = short-term debt/general revenues; GODEBT = general obligation debt per $1,000 of personal income; OWNREV = ratio of general revenues from own sources to total general revenues; UPO = unfunded pension debt per $1,000 of personal income for all residents; i = state; t = year; and E = random error term.

This model is similar to the models used by Raman and Wilson (1990) and Marks and Raman (1988).

The study variable is UPO, or unfunded pension debt per $1,000 of personal income for all residents. This variable is operationalized as the unfunded pension benefit obligation, per GASB 5 requirements, divided by the states' aggregate income of all residents. The higher the ratio, the higher the unfunded pension obligation, resulting in increased default risk.

However, the increased risk is expected to be more strongly associated with bond issues with long-term maturities, as the unfunded pension debt is not expected to be funded until several years in the future. Also, states with overfunded plans will be able to decrease their contributions in future years. Therefore, we expect a positive relationship between UPO and YTM for long-term maturities but no relation for short-term maturities. The pension data for this variable were collected from the states' *Comprehensive Annual Financial Reports* while the aggregate income numbers were collected from *State Government Finances*, published by the U.S. Department of Commerce.

The control variables in the model are similar to those used by Raman and Wilson (1990). LMAT measures the term to maturity, in natural log form, and is expected to have a positive relationship with YTM. LPOP measures the states' population, in natural log form, and is expected to have a negative relationship with YTM. GODEBT measures the states' general obligation debt per $1,000 of personal income and is expected to have a positive relationship with YTM.[5] OWNREV measures the ratio of general revenues from states' own sources to their total general revenues and is expected to have a negative relationship with YTM.

The COUPON variable measures the coupon rate associated with the different maturities under a serial bond issue. Raman and Wilson (1990) predicted coupon rate would have a negative relationship with YTM, as it represented a measure of duration. However, Raman and Wilson (1990) used seasoned bond issues in their analysis.

We include COUPON in our model to facilitate comparison with Raman and Wilson (1990). However, the expected relationship to YTM is less clear. Because we examine new, rather than seasoned, bond issues, a positive relationship may exist. If states want to borrow close to the principal amount, they will set the coupon rate close to the expected borrowing rate. If this is true, then COUPON is a measure of default risk. Thus, higher coupon rates should be associated with higher borrowing costs, resulting in an expected positive relationship.

Table 1. Descriptive Statistics for a Sample of 42 State Serial Bond Issues Between 1990 and 1992 from 26 States with a Total of 720 Maturities

Variable	Mean	Standard Deviation	Minimum	Maximum
YTM[a]	5.8923	0.9125	2.30	10.00
LMAT[b]	2.1184	0.7714	0.00	3.40
COUPON[c]	5.9185	0.9297	2.60	10.00
IRATE[d]	6.7733	0.4310	5.88	7.53
LPOP[e]	8.5259	0.9328	6.33	10.30
PCINC[f]	15,656	2,721	11,040	21,830
STDR[g]	0.0037	0.0150	0.00	0.096
GODEBT[h]	441.21	424.07	12.20	2001.00
OWNREV[i]	0.7178	0.0532	.6073	.8311
UPO[j]	16.764	23.178	−12.42	70.10

Notes: a. YTM = yield to maturity on new state bond issues.
b. LMAT = term to maturity, natural log.
c. COUPON = coupon rate associated with each observation. d. IRATE = market interest rate for the week the bonds were issued.
e. LPOP = the states population, natural log.
f. PCINC = the states' per capita income.
g. STDR = short-term debt/general revenues.
h. GODEBT = general obligation debt per $1.000 of personal income.
i. OWNREV = ratio of general revenues from own sources to total general revenues.
j. UPO = unfunded pension debt per $1,000 of personal income for all residents.

Because the relative effects of COUPON are unclear, we do not predict the direction of its effect on YTM ex ante.[6]

The data for the MAT and COUPON variables were collected from Bloomberg's Financial Markets database. The data for LPOP, GODEBT, and OWNREV were collected from *State Government Finances* (U.S. Department of Commerce).

Three additional control variables were included in the model. IRATE measures the general level of interest rates at the time each bond was issued and is positively related to YTM. The rate used in our analysis is an arithmetic average of the yield-to-maturity of 15 high-grade municipal bonds, based on the mean of the weekly high-low prices. The data for IRATE was collected from Standard and Poor's Security Price Index Record.

PCINC measures median per capita income for each state. This variable controls for the wealth of each state, as states with higher incomes will have a larger tax base. The larger tax base should reduce the default risk on the bonds. Thus, we expect a negative relationship between PCINC and YTM. The data for PCINC were collected from *State Government Finances*.

Table 2. Correlation Matrix for the Explanatory Variables Included in the Regression Model

	LMAT	COUPON	IRATE	LPOP	PCINC	STDR	GODEBT	OWNREV	UPO
LMAT	1	.29	−.01	.02	.02	.00	−.02	.00	.01
COUPON	.29	1	.59	−.11	−.15	−.02	−.08	.02	.04
IRATE	−.01	.59	1	−.24	−.23	−.03	−.09	.07	.10
LPOP	.02	−.11	−.24	1	.36	−.30	−.21	.08	−.29
PCINC	.02	−.15	−.23	.36	1	.05	.36	.43	.04
STDR	.00	−.02	−.03	−.30	.05	1	.02	−.06	.33
GODEBT	−.02	−.08	−.09	−.21	.36	.02	1	.28	.05
OWNREV	.00	.02	.07	.08	.43	−.06	.28	1	.09
UPO	.01	.04	.10	−.29	.04	.33	.05	.09	1

Note: See Table 1 for a description of the variables.

STDR measures states' short-term debt divided by general revenues. Consistent with Marks and Raman (1985), we expect a positive relationship between STDR and net borrowing cost. The data for STDR were collected from *State Government Finances*. The descriptive statistics for all variables are presented in Table 1 and bivariate correlations in Table 2.[7]

IV. ANALYSIS OF THE DATA

Our objective is to determine if unfunded pension obligations are impounded in long-term borrowing costs differently than in short-term borrowing costs. We initially partitioned the sample into maturities of one to 10 years or greater than 10 years which yielded subsamples of roughly equal size, 342 and 378 observations respectively. We then calculated an F-statistic similar to a Chow test for differences in subsets of regression coefficients between independent samples (Copley 1993).[8] The resulting F-statistic is 4.879 (df = 1,710) with a p-value of .026, suggesting that a difference in the coefficient of the UPO variable exists between the model for bond issues with short-term maturities and the model for bond issues with long-term maturities.

Since the abovementioned difference exists, we next estimated models for the different maturity levels to examine the differences in coefficients across models.[9] We identified maturities of 10 years or less as short term and maturities greater than 10 years as long term. The significance of the UPO variable is compared across the models to determine if unfunded pension obligations are impounded in long-term borrowing costs but not in short-term borrowing costs.

Since we treat different maturities under the same bond issue as separate observations, the error terms are likely to be correlated across observations. To solve this problem we used Froot's (1989) technique to provide unbiased estimates of the significance of the explanatory variables.

Many studies in the accounting and finance literature use panel data, gathering data cross-sectionally for short time periods. These studies almost always have problems with cross-sectional dependence. In these cases it is often impractical to implement standard techniques for the entire cross section and correct for cross-sectional dependence. Even if standard techniques could be used, they often require homoscedasticity, a condition which is not met in many cases (Froot 1989).

While the severity of these problems has been addressed in the literature, Froot (1989) was the first to develop a technique to address both cross-sectional dependence and heteroscedasticity in the cross section as well as across time. Froot's technique combines elements of method-of-moments estimation pioneered by Hansen (1982) and the treatment of heteroscedasticity discussed by Eicker (1967) and White (1980a, 1980b) and is consistent and asymptotically efficient within the class of one-step estimators.

V. RESULTS OF THE ANALYSIS

Regression results appear in Table 3 and Table 4. UPO is significant and positive in the model for long-term maturities. Thus, our hypothesis of a positive relationship between unfunded pension obligations and borrowing costs for long-term maturities is supported. Also, there is an insignificant relationship for bonds with short-term maturities.

This result suggests that states currently underfunding their pension plans do not pay higher borrowing costs in the short term, but pay higher borrowing costs in the long term. This finding is consistent with our hypothesis in that, as the population ages and additional funding is required, these states pay higher borrowing costs.

Overall, all models are statistically significant as the adjusted R^2 ranged from .459 for the short-term model to .862 for the long-term model. All variables related to bond characteristics and market conditions have the anticipated relationship with states' borrowing costs,

Table 3. Regression Coefficients, *T*-statistics, (*P*-Values, two-tail), and Variance Inflation Factors of a Model of Yield to Maturity on a Sample of 42 State Government Bond Issues (720 maturities) between 1990 and 1992

Variable*		Coefficient	T-Statistic (P-Value)	VIF
Constant		.8183	.901 (.184)	
LMAT	(+)	.6097	−6.967 (.000)	2.21
Coupon	(?)	.7097	7.287 (.000)	8.72
IRATE	(+)	.5854	4.303 (.000)	5.67
LPOP	(−)	−.0763	−2.044 (.021)	0.89
PCINC	(−)	−.00004	−3.556 (.000)	1.42
STDR	(+)	1.2392	1.073 (.142)	1.08
GODEBT	(+)	.00039	3.938 (.000)	2.81
OWNREV	(−)	−2.103	−3.671 (.000)	1.43
UPO	(+)	−.0010	−.781 (.218)	3.74
N		720		
ADJ R^2		.478		

Notes: *Predicted signs appear in parenthesis.
See Table 1 for a description of the variables.

although LMAT was insignificant in the long-term model. Also, all variables relating a state's financial situation have the anticipated relationship. However in some cases the relationship is insignificant.

VI. IMPLICATIONS OF THE FINDINGS

This study has implications for future research examining the relationship between bond prices and unfunded pension obligations. The results emphasize the importance of examining and controlling for the term to maturity in determining the significance of variables in explaining bond prices, especially variables relating to a state's financial condition.

Table 4. Regression Coefficients, *T*-Statistics, and (*P*-Values, two-tail) of a Model of Yield to Maturity on a Sample of 42 State Government Bond Issues (720 maturities) between 1990 and 1992—Models Partitioned by Term to Maturity

		Term to Maturity			
		1-10 T-Stat.		11+ T-Stat.	
Variable*		Coeff.	(P-Value)	Coeff.	(P-Value)
Constant		.6994	.456 (.324)	−1.466	−1.653 (.049)
LMAT	(+)	.6758	5.950 (.000)	.1398	.742 (.229)
Coupon	(?)	.6262	5.655 (.000)	.5435	2.375 (.009)
IRATE	(+)	.8195	4.141 (.000)	.5460	2.165 (.015)
LPOP	(−)	−.0989	−1.516 (.065)	−.0583	−2.724 (.003)
PCINC	(−)	−.00009	−4.158 (.000)	−.00002	−.199 (.421)
STDR	(+)	1.9564	1.027 (.152)	.3568	.756 (.225)
GODEBT	(+)	.00069	4.395 (.000)	.00007	1.889 (.029)
OWNREV	(−)	−2.740	−2.609 (.005)	−.4638	−1.333 (.091)
UPO	(+)	−.0015	−.731 (.233)	.00076	1.824 (.030)
N		381		339	
Adj. R^2		.459		.862	

*Predicted signs appear in parenthesis. See Table 1 for a description of the variables.

The key finding from the study is that states currently underfunding their pension plans pay higher borrowing costs for issues with long-term maturities but not for bond issues with short-term maturities. We examine this issue by treating each maturity under a serial bond issue as a separate observation. The study also contributes to the literature by illustrating how Froot's (1989) technique can be used to control for cross-sectional dependence and heteroscedasticity, common problems in the accounting and finance literature.

APPENDIX

State/Year Combinations of New Bond Issues

State	Year
Alabama	1990
	1992
Arkansas	1990
	1992
California	1990
Connecticut	1992
Delaware	1991
Florida	1991
	1992
Georgia	1990
	1991
Illinois	1992
Louisiana	1990
Maryland	1990
	1991
	1992
Minnesota	1992
Mississippi	1990
	1991
	1992
Missouri	1991
	1992
Nevada	1991
New Jersey	1991
New Mexico	1991
New York	1990
	1991
	1992
Oregon	1990
	1992
Pennsylvania	1991
	1992
Rhode Island	1991
South Carolina	1991
	1992

Tennessee	1991
	1992
Texas	1992
Utah	1990
	1991
Vermont	1990
Washington	1991

ACKNOWLEDGMENT

The authors wish to thank the editor and two anonymous reviewers for their insightful comments on earlier versions of this manuscript. We also wish to thank Ken Gaver (University of Georgia) for his assistance with the Froot technique. Rob Ingram and Mary Stone (University of Alabama) also provided valuable insights at the beginning of this project.

NOTES

1. Froot (1989) cited examples where the failure to control for cross-sectional dependence significantly influenced the results. In our analysis the only differences between using Froot's technique and OLS are that LMAT is significant in the OLS long-term model and OWNREV is insignificant in the OLS long-term model.
2. The unfunded pension obligation in this study is based on the pension benefit obligation per GASB 5 requirements, using estimated future salaries.
3. The baby boom generation is usually defined as people born from 1946 to 1964. Since people in this age group are currently in or approaching their fifties, it is expected that they will start retiring in large numbers in approximately 10 years.
4. The pension ratios used were pension fund assets/benefits paid, benefits paid/pension contributions, and the number of active employees/number of retirees.
5. General obligation debt and unfunded pension debt also were scaled by general revenues, finding consistent results.
6. The interpretation of the other explanatory variables, including the UPO variable, remained the same when COUPON was omitted from the model.
7. We examined the distribution of the age of the workforce and found that it did not vary much among the states: mean of 38.5 years and standard deviation of .5 years. If it had proven to be highly variable, additional control would be warranted.
8. The test statistic is calculated as:

$$[(SSE_r - SSE_u) / MSE_u]$$

where SSE_u (MSE_u) represents the sums of squared errors, and mean squared errors, of an unrestricted regression which allows the coefficients to be different in the two samples and SSE_r represents the sums of squared errors of a restricted regression which is identical to the unrestricted regression except that the variable of interest (UPO) has one coefficient across both samples. The resulting statistic approximates an F-distribution with degrees of freedom $(1, df_u)$.

9. We examined the data for problems with multicollinearity for the complete sample as well as the subsamples. The highest variance inflation factor was 8.72 indicating that multicollinearity is not a problem (Belsley 1991). Since the variance inflation factors for the partitioned models are very similar for those of the combined model, we only present the variance inflation factors for the combined model (Table 3).

REFERENCES

Belsley, D. 1991. *Conditioning Diagnostics*. New York: John Wiley and Sons.

Bloomberg's Financial News Service. *Bloomberg's Financial Markets Electronic Data Base*. New York.

Copeland, R., and R. Ingram. 1983. Municipal bond market and recognition of pension reporting practices. *Journal of Accounting and Public Policy* (Fall): 147-166.

Copley, P. 1993. An assessment of the potential effect of Big Eight firm mergers on competition in the market for audit services. In *Advances in Accounting* 11, eds. B. Schwartz, P. Reckers, E. Chewning Jr., and J. Scheiner, 185-205. Greenwich, CT: JAI Press.

Eicker, F. 1967. Limit theorems for regressions with unequal and dependent errors. In *Proceedings of the Fifth Berkeley Symposium on Mathematical Statistics and Probability*, eds. L. Lecam and J. Neyman, 59-82. Berkeley, CA: University of California Press.

Froot, K. 1989. Consistent covariance matrix estimation with cross-sectional dependence and heteroskedasticity in financial data. *Journal of Financial and Quantitative Analysis* (September): 333-355.

General Accounting Office. 1979. *Funding of State and Local Government Pension Plans: A National Problem*. Washington, DC: General Accounting Office.

Governmental Accounting Standards Board. 1986. *Disclosure of Pension Information by Public Employee Retirement Ssystems and State and Local Government Employers*. Statement No. 5. Norwalk, CT: GASB.

———. 1987. *Objectives of Financial Reporting*. Concepts Statement No. 1. Norwalk, CT: GASB.

———. 1988. *Preliminary Views, State and Local Governmental Employers' Accounting for Pensions*. Norwalk, CT: GASB.

Hansen, L. 1982. Large sample properties of generalized method of moments estimators. *Econometrica* (July): 1029-1054.

Ives, M. 1988. Pension accounting—the controversy continues. *Government Finance Review* (December): 13-17.

Kotlikoff, L., and D. Smith. 1983. *Pensions in the American Economy*. Chicago: University of Chicago Press and the National Bureau of Economic Research.

Marks, B., and K. Raman. 1985. The importance of pension data for state and municipal creditor decisions. *Journal of Accounting Research* (Autumn): 878-887.

———. 1987. The information content of unfunded pension obligations for municipal bond ratings: An empirical evaluation. In *Advances in Accounting* 4, eds. B.

Schwartz, P. Reckers, J. Deitrick, and J. Scheiner, 33-42. Greenwich, CT: JAI Press.

———. 1988. The effect of unfunded accumulated and projected pension obligations on governmental borrowing costs. *Contemporary Accounting Research* (Spring): 595-608.

Munnell, A., and K. Keefe. 1982. PEPPRA: Do New England public pension systems need federal regulation? *New England Economic Review* (September-October): 5-24.

Raman, K., and E. Wilson. 1990. The debt equivalence of unfunded government pension obligations. *Journal of Accounting and Public Policy* (Spring): 37-56.

Standard and Poor's. 1996. *Security Price Index Record.* New York: McGraw-Hill.

U.S. Department of Commerce. 1990-1992. *State Government Finances.* Washington, DC: U.S. Printing Office.

White, H. 1980a. A heteroskedasticity-consistent covariance matrix estimator and a direct test for heteroskedasticity. *Econometrica* (May): 817-838.

———. 1980b. Nonlinear regression on cross-section data. *Econometrica* (April): 721-746.

Woodruff, T. 1983. *Dollars and Sense: The Case for State and Local Government Pension Reform.* Washington, DC: American Federation of State, County, and Municipal Employees.

Zorn, P. 1992. *Survey of State and Local Government Employee Retirement Systems.* Washington, DC: Government Finance Officers Association.

THE INFLUENCE OF AUDITOR CHANGE AND TYPE ON AUDIT FEES FOR MUNICIPALITIES

Bruce W. Chase

ABSTRACT

The purpose of this study is to further explore the relationship of auditor change and auditor type on local government audit fees. The study reports tentative evidence from a limited number of auditor changes for one type of municipality from one state. The findings indicate a price premium for Big 6 firms as well as a price discount for a non-Big 6 firm specializing in municipal audits. These findings suggest that some public sector markets may be segmented resulting in a discount from audit specialization. A time-series model, which includes control variables for a change in auditor type (regional specialist, Big 6 firm, and all other firms), is also used to test the effect of a change in auditor. The results for the variables used to control for change among auditor type provides preliminary evidence that failure to control for changes in auditor type may be obscuring the significance of an initial engagement in other public sector studies.

I. INTRODUCTION

Studies of corporate audit fees generally find a significant negative effect associated with initial audit engagements and significant positive effects associated with Big 6 firms (Francis and Simon 1987; Palmrose 1986; Ettredge and Greenberg 1990). Studies of public sector audit fees, however, yield mixed results for both the effects of initial audit engagements and auditor size (Rubin 1988; Baber, Brooks, and Ricks 1987; Copley 1989; Raman and Wilson 1992; Ward, Elder, and Kattelus 1994).

The differences in finding may be due to differences that exist between the corporate and public sector audit markets. One major difference is that accounting and reporting requirements are often set on a state-by-state basis, resulting in a reduced dominance by large national firms and the existence of regional specialists. Failure to control for auditor changes among different categories of auditing firms (regional specialist, Big 6 firm, and all other firms) may explain the inconclusive results for the effects of initial audit engagements observed in public sector studies. For example, if an organization changes auditors from a low-cost category to a high-cost category, any reduction in audit fees from a change in auditors may be offset from the change in category of auditors.

I address the problem of different categories of auditing firms by controlling for firm type in the models examined. This study examines the relationship of auditor change and type on audit fees for counties in Virginia—an audit market with a significant regional specialist. The results of this study are tentative because of the limited number of auditor changes, however, the results indicate a significant effect on audit fees for the variables used to control for changes among different categories of auditors.

II. FACTORS THAT INFLUENCE AUDIT FEES

Five public sector studies (Rubin 1988; Baber, Brooks, and Ricks 1987; Copley 1989; Raman and Wilson 1992; and Ward, Elder, and Kattelus 1994) form the basis for this study. These studies all employ a cross-sectional analysis to examine the determinants of audit fees. The studies use a model based on the natural log transformation of audit fees and certain other variables intended to proxy for size, audit risk, complexity, initial engagement, and auditor quality.

Additionally, Baber, Brooks, and Ricks (1987) examine the effect of initial audit engagement using both a cross-sectional analysis and a time-series analysis. The time-series analysis compares the mean percentage change in audit fees for counties (excluding initial engagements) to that of counties that had an initial audit engagement. The cross-sectional analysis finds no significant effect for the indicator variable used to represent an initial audit engagement, while the time-series results indicate a significant effect.

I employ both a cross-sectional and time-series analysis in this study and add variables to control for auditor type. The results are reported in Sections IV and V, respectively. The variables I used are discussed below.

A. Auditor Type

Prior research suggests that audit quality is associated with higher audit fees. A fee premium has been found in studies (Palmrose 1986; Francis and Simon 1987; Craswell, Francis and Taylor 1995) where "Big-6" firms are used to represent audit quality. In the public sector studies, Baber, Brooks, and Ricks (1987), Copley (1989), and Ward, Elder, and Kattelus (1994) find a significant fee premium for the large audit firms; however, Rubin (1988) does not report a significant difference. Raman and Wilson (1992) find a significant fee difference only for small cities and this difference diminished over the time period examined. They speculate that many of the lower price/lower quality firms withdrew from the market due to federal audit requirements.

Regional firms that specialize in public sector clients play a larger role in the market for audit service within a particular state. For example, a non-Big-6 firm audited 21 percent of the municipalities in the Ward and colleagues (1994) study. They suggest that industry experience represents audit quality and find a significant fee premium for these firms. However, Deis and Giroux (1992) do not find a significant difference in fees based on auditor experience. Further, Ettredge and Greenberg (1990), in a study of private sector, find a larger reduction in first-year fee when the change is made to a more experienced auditor, suggesting that the larger reduction is due to audit efficiency.

Currently, over half the counties in Virginia are audited by a single non-Big 6 accounting firm, referred to as a regional specialist (RS) in this study. Therefore, I use two indicator variables in the cross-sectional test to represent three possible classifications of auditor: RS, Big 6, and all others.

B. Auditor Change

Prior research provides conflicting results on the effects of changing auditors on audit fees. DeAngelo (1981) suggests that because of increased competition, auditors "low-ball" the audit fee on an initial engagement and then charge higher rates to recover costs. On the other hand, Simunic (1980) suggests that the start-up cost of a new engagement requires the audit firm to charge more for an initial engagement. Cost savings in later years resulting from audit efficiency would be passed on to the client. Johnson and Lys (1990) suggest that auditor changes are related to client-auditor realignments. Generally, audit firms achieve competitive advantages through specialization and clients purchase audit service from the least-cost supplier. Therefore, many of the auditor changes are the result of changing client characteristics and the resulting auditor realignment. For example, Johnson and Lys find that firms with increased external financing are positively associated with changes to larger audit firms.

In the public sector studies, Rubin (1988) and Raman and Wilson (1992) do not detect a significant effect on audit fees from an initial audit engagement. I use an indicator variable to test for the influence of an initial engagement on audit fees.

Baber and colleagues (1987) examine the effect of initial audit engagement by using a time-series analysis which compares the mean percentage change in audit fees for counties (excluding initial engagements) to that of counties that had an initial audit engagement. The results indicate a significant reduction in audit fees for an initial engagement, which is not completely recovered in the year subsequent to the change. I employ a similar time-series test; however, I add additional variables to control for change in auditor type.

C. Control Variables

Prior public sector studies find significant effects related to auditee size, debt levels, and report and entity complexity. I use the natural logarithm of population to represent size and debt per capita to represent debt level. I also use the number of funds to represent entity complexity.

All counties in Virginia must issue a Comprehensive Annual Financial Report (CAFR). However, certain counties go beyond the requirements of a CAFR in their financial reporting and receive a "Certificate of Achievement for Excellence in Financial Reporting" (Certificate) issued by the Governmental Financial Officers Association (GFOA). Evans and Patton (1993) suggest that managers voluntarily participate in this program because of lower borrowing costs and increased professional recognition. However, the certificate requires expanded disclosure of both financial and nonfinancial information which would increase audit costs. I include an indicator variable for certificate to represent report complexity.

Table 1. Explanatory Variables for Audit Fee Model, Empirical Measures, Expected Relationship to Audit Fee, and Data Source

Explanatory Variable	Measure	Variable Name	Expected Relationship to Audit Fee	Source
Auditee size	Natural log of population	LPOP	+	Comparative Report[1]
Debt level	Debt-per-capita	DEBT	+	Comparative Report
Report complexity	1 if received Certificate of achievement, 0 otherwise	CERT	+	1992 CAFRs[2]
Entity complexity	Number of funds	FUNDS	+	1992 CAFRs
Auditor change	1 if county changed auditor, 0 otherwise	CHANGE	?	Questionnaire
Auditor type	1 if Big 6 auditor, 0 otherwise	AUDBSIX	+	1992 CAFRs
Auditor type	1 if Regional Specialist (RS) auditor, 0 otherwise	AUDRS	?	1992 CAFRs

Sources: [1]Auditor of Public Accounting (1993).
[2]Comprehensive Annual Financial Reports.

III. SAMPLE AND DATA COLLECTION METHODOLOGY

The sample for this study is the 95 counties in Virginia. These counties receive a significant amount of funds from the state and, therefore, are required to follow certain state regulations. The Auditor of Public Accounts regulates and monitors the financial reports of the counties in Virginia. Because of this oversight, the accounting and reporting methods used are fairly homogeneous among the counties, which provide better control over extraneous factors that may influence audit fees among municipalities from different states.[1]

Table 1 reports the variables used in this study, their expected relationship to audit fees, and the source of the data. Audit fees and auditor changes were obtained from a questionnaire. Nonrespondents were contacted and the information collected by phone: complete 1992 data was obtained for all 95 counties.

IV. EMPIRICAL RESULTS FOR CROSS-SECTIONAL TESTS

Table 2 reports descriptive statistics for the variables in the study. The table reports that 14.7 percent of the counties receive a Certificate of Achievement in Financial Reporting. The table also reports that 12.6 percent use a Big 6 auditor, 57.9 percent use RS, and the remaining 29.5

Table 2. Descriptive Statistics for a Sample of 95 Virginia Counties for Fiscal Year 1991-1992

Variable	Continuous Variables		
	Mean	*Range*	*Std. Dev.*
Population (000)	43.312	2.6-837.5	92.367
DEBT	543.609	2.68-1869.89	440.031
FUNDS	9.642	2-54	7.60

	Categorical Variables	
	Number of Counties	*% of Total*
CERT	14	14.7
CHANGE	9	9.5
AUDBSIX	12	12.6
AUDRS	55	57.9

Note: See Table 1 for a description of all variables.

Table 3. OLS Regression Results for Cross-Sectional Audit Fee Model
$\text{LFEE} = b_0 + b_1(\text{LPOP}) + b_2(\text{DEBT}) + b_3(\text{CERT}) + b_4(\text{FUNDS}) + b_5(\text{CHANGE}) + b_6(\text{AUDBSIX}) + b_7(\text{AUDRS})$ for a Sample of 95 Virginia Counties for Fiscal Year 1991-1992

Variable	Expected Sign	Coefficient	t Statistic
INTERCEPT		6.109594	15.903*
LPOP	+	0.347448	8.492*
DEBT	+	0.000180	2.369**
CERT	+	0.219871	1.699**
FUNDS	+	0.008346	1.804**
CHANGE	?	0.080339	0.824
AUDRS	?	−0.153184	−2.315**[1]
AUDBSIX	+	0.273014	2.105**[1]

Notes: Level of significance (two-tail test for CHANGE and AUDRS, one-tail test for all other variables)
* $p < .01$
** $p < .05$
[1] A joint F test for the incremental explanatory value of all auditor type variables was significant (F Value 7.346; P value <.01).
$R^2 = .842$, adjusted $R^2 = .829$
LFEE = the natural log of audit fees. See Table 1 for a description of all variables.

percent use some other audit firm. Only nine counties (9.5%) changed auditors during the year. Because of the limited number of auditor changes, the results of this study should be considered tentative and caution should be taken in generalizing the results.

Consistent with prior research, I use an OLS regression model to test the influence of the identified variables on audit fees. Variance inflation factors indicate a low degree of collinearity (largest variance inflation factor is 3.05). A plot of the residual values and inspection of the hat diagonal values indicates that no outliers were significantly influencing the variables in the regression.

Table 3 reports the results of regressing the natural log of audit fees on the variables identified in Table 1. The regression model explains a significant portion of the variance in audit fees for the counties. The model is significant at the .01 level. The overall R^2 of the model is .842 and the adjusted R^2 is .829. Controlling for extraneous factors by using only counties from one state may explain the high level of R^2 achieved.

Consistent with previous public sector studies, the control variables used to represent size, debt level, report complexity, and entity complexity have a significant positive relation with audit fees. Categorical variables, AUDBSIX and AUDRS, are used to represent three possible auditor types, RS, Big 6, and all others. The joint effect of auditor type

Table 4. Auditor Type *P*-values for a Least Squares Means Test of Differences Among Auditor Type Parameter Estimates for a Sample of 95 Virginia Counties for Fiscal Year 1991-1992

	Big 6 n = 12	RS n = 55	All Others n = 28
Big 6			
RS	.0009		
All Others	.0382	.0230	

Note: See Table 1 for a description of all variables.

is significant at the .01 level (determined by employing a partial F test). The positive coefficient for AUDBSIX indicates that there is a fee premium for the Big 6 auditor compared to the other audit firms (excluding RS). The negative coefficient for AUDRS indicates the existence of a fee discount for the regional audit firm (RS) specializing in county audits. Table 4 reports the results of a least-squares means tests for the three auditor types. The tests report the probability of wrongly concluding a difference between a pair of means in the regression model and indicate that the means for the three classes of auditors are statistically different from one another.

The finding of a fee discount related to a regional audit firm specializing in county audits conflicts with the findings of Ward and colleagues (1994). Ward, Elder, and Kattelus find a fee premium for the regional firm that audited a significant number of municipalities. Ettredge and Greenberg (1990) suggest that industry expertise may be associated with technological efficiency resulting in lower fees in a competitive setting. They also suggest that such expertise may also be associated with a positive reputation effect for which clients will pay a premium.

One explanation for the findings of this study may be related to the level of competitiveness within different segments of the audit market for the municipalities. Evidence of audit market segmentation is provided by Francis and Simon (1987). Table 5 reports descriptive statistics by different auditor type. Client size for the RS and all other non-Big 6 firms is much smaller than for the Big 6 firms. It appears that competition for audit service among smaller counties is mainly between the RS and other non Big-6 firms. Smaller client markets contain more lower-quality/cost firms. In a review of the quality of audits of recipients of federal assistance, the General Accounting Office (GAO 1987) finds that smaller firms had a greater problem than larger firms in

Table 5. Summary of Descriptive Statistics by Auditor Type for a Sample of 95 Virginia Counties for Fiscal Year 1991-1992

Variable	Big 6 Firms n = 12		RS Firm n = 55		Other Firms n = 28	
	Mean/ Std. Dev.	Min./ Max.	Mean/ Std. Dev.	Min./ Max.	Mean/ Std. Dev.	Min./ Max.
Population	170,191/ 224,674	10,900/ 837,500	23,365/ 16,000	6,200/ 73,700	24,721/ 17,466	2,600/ 59,900
DEBT	1,183/ 514	326/1,870	455/338	45/1,714	444/362	3/1456
FUNDS	19/16	3/54	7/3	2/16	11/5	3/26
CERT (Number Only)	10 (83%)	n.a.	3 (5%)	n.a.	1 (4%)	n.a.

Note: See Table 1 for a description of all variables.

complying with standards. Copley, Doucet, and Gaver (1994) find that audit reports cited for unacceptable audit quality by the GAO were associated with smaller clients and audit fees. Also, smaller municipalities may be more likely to select auditors based primarily on price. In such an audit service market, an experienced firm can exploit its technological efficiency in winning audit contracts by charging lower fees.

Larger counties have different needs and characteristics than smaller counties. For example, large counties may need to raise capital in the national bond markets. Johnson and Lys (1990) suggest that audit relationships are based on clients' characteristics and auditors' specialization. Both Wallace (1981) and Wilson and Howard (1984) find bond ratings to be positively associated with national auditors. Table 5 reports that clients of Big 6 firms are larger and have higher debt levels than clients of non-Big 6 firms. In the market for audit services for large counties, a regional specialist is competing with the positive reputation of the Big 6 firms. To remain competitive, a regional specialist must again exploit its technological efficiency by charging a lower fee. Smaller firms generally would not have the positive reputation or technological experience needed to be competitive in this environment (Table 5 reports that the largest county audited by an OTHER firm had a population of 59,900).

The coefficient of the indicator variable used to represent an initial audit engagement, CHANGE, is positive, but not significant in the model (Table 3). Rubin (1988) and Raman and Wilson (1992) also find no significant audit fee effects for initial audit engagement, but the signs were negative. The effect of an initial audit engagement on audit

Table 6. Frequency of Types of Auditor Changes and Mean Percentage Change in Audit Fee for a Sample[1] of 94 Virginia Counties for Fiscal Year 1991-1992

Description	Number	% Mean Change in Fee
No Change	85	5.41
Change between Groups:		
RS to Other	4	21.45
Big 6 to RS	1	−29.79
Change within Group:		
Other to Other	3	−13.63
Big 6 to Big 6	1	−8.73

Notes: [1]Data on percentage change was not available for one county.
See Table 1 for a description of all variables.

fees may be difficult to detect if an organization moves from a low-cost auditor type (RS) to a high-cost auditor type (Big 6). Table 6 reports the frequency of types of auditor changes and the percentage change in audit fees. Again, only nine counties changed auditor and because of the limited number of observations (two types of changes had only one observation), caution should be taken in interpreting the results. However, counties that changed auditors within the same type grouping report a decrease in fees. Counties that changed from RS (the lowest cost type) to the other type grouping have an average 21.45 percent increase in fees and the county that changed from the Big 6 (the highest cost type) to RS has a 29.79 percent decrease in fees.

The data suggest that the effects from changes among auditor cost types may obscure the significance of an indicator variable representing an initial audit engagement in the cross-sectional studies. While Raman and Wilson (1992) and Baber, Brooks, and Ricks (1987), do not find a significant effect on audit fees from an initial engagement, both studies find some significant price premiums for Big 6 firms. My results suggest that if auditor changes are from non-Big 6 firms to Big 6 firms, the possible significance of the indicator variables used to represent initial engagement may be obscured.

V. EMPIRICAL RESULTS FROM TIME-SERIES TEST

Baber and colleagues (1987) suggest that the effect on audit fees from an initial audit engagement will only be detected in a cross-sectional analysis if the change in fees is substantial. Instead, a year-to-year

Table 7. Descriptive Statistics by Fiscal Year for the Variables Used in Time-Series Analysis of Audit Fees for a Sample of Virginia Counties from 1989 to 1993 ($n = 417$)

	1989	1990	1991	1992	1993	Total
Mean Percent Change in Audit Fees[1]:						
All observations	2.75	5.37	4.78	5.22	2.40	4.13
	$n = 73$	$n = 80$	$n = 82$	$n = 94$	$n = 88$	$n = 417$
Excluding initial	4.05	6.45	5.17	5.41	2.29	4.66
engagement	$n = 70$	$n = 74$	$n = 71$	$n = 85$	$n = 81$	$n = 381$
Auditor Changes:						
Big 6 to RS	0	0	0	1	0	1
Big 6 to other	0	0	0	0	0	0
RS to Big 6	0	0	0	0	0	0
RS to other	1	0	1	4	1	7
Other to Big 6	0	0	0	0	0	0
Other to RS	2	0	4	0	3	9
Changes in same Group	0	6	6	4	3	19
Total Changes	3	6	11	9	7	36

Notes: [1] Change in audit fee stated as a percentage of the county's mean audit fees.
See Table 1 for a description of all variables.

examination of changes in audit fees would better detect the influence of an initial engagement on audit fees. They examine the change in annual audit fees (computed as a percentage of mean audit fees for a four-year period) by regressing the change in fees on the following indicator variables; initial single audit, initial engagement, initial engagement last year, and initial engagement next year. The results of the time-series analysis indicate there is a significant relationship between audit fees and an initial engagement (negative), and an initial engagement last year (positive). Furthermore, the reduction in audit fees during an initial engagement is not offset in the year following the change in auditors.

The cross-sectional analysis presented in Table 3 indicates that auditor type is significant in explaining audit fees. Therefore, if a county changes auditor, the change in audit fees will also reflect the effects of any change in auditor type. Table 7 reports the distribution of counties changing auditors, the mean percentage change in audit fee for all observations, as well as the mean percentage change in audit fees for all observations excluding initial engagements. Data related to audit fees and auditor changes were gathered from a questionnaire: information was not available for all years for all counties.

The data in Table 7 reflects that, in all but one year, the mean percentage change in audit fees was higher when initial engagements were excluded from the sample, indicating that the change in audit fees were lower for initial engagements. There were a total of 417 audit fee observations, of which 36 represent initial audit engagements. Of these, 17 involve a change in auditor type and 19 involve a change to an auditor in the same grouping.

Table 8 reports the results of regressing the change in audit fees (stated as a percentage of mean audit fees) by the variables of interest (Model 1): initial engagement, initial engagement last year, initial engagement next year, and the change in auditor type; Big 6 to RS, RS to Other, and Other to RS^2. Table 8 also reports the results that does not control for changes in auditor type (Model 2) which is presented for comparative purposes.

Model 1 is significant at the .0018 level and the results indicate that the variables representing initial engagement, change from RS to Other and change from Other to RS, are significant in explaining the change in audit fee. The coefficient for initial engagement is negative which indicates a reduction in fees from changing auditors within the same group (expected mean change in audit fee of 4.279-10430 = −6.151%).

Table 8. Regression Result for Time-Series Regression Model for Percent Change in Audit Fee^1 = b_0 + b_1 (initial engagement) + b_2 (initial engagement last year) + b_3 (initial engagement next year) + b_4 (Big 6 to Other) + b_5 (RS to Other) + b_6 (Other to RS) for a Sample of Virginia Counties for 1989 to 1993 (n = 417)

	Model 1		Model 2	
Variable	Coefficient	t Statistic	Coefficient	t statistic
Intercept	4.279	6.282*	4.308	6.366*
Initial Engagement	−10.430	−3.851*	−5.885	−2.718*
Initial Engagement Last Year	3.118	1.400	3.005	1.337
Initial Engagement Next Year	0.238	0.106	1.138	0.506
Big 6 to RS	−2.580	−0.209		
RS to Other	15.675	3.069*		
Other to RS	6.862	1.741**		

Notes: Level of significance (two-tail test)
  * $p < .01$
  ** $p < .10$
  Model 1: R^2 = .050, adjusted R^2 = .036
  F-Value = 3.588, P = .0018
  Model 2: R^2 = .025, adjusted R^2 = .018
  F-Value = 3.489, P = .0158
  ^{1} Change in audit fee stated as a percentage of the county's mean audit fees.
  See Table 1 for a description of all variables.

Interestingly, the coefficients for the other significant variables (RS to Other and Other to RS) are positive. This indicates that the reduction in audit fees is higher for an initial engagement that retained an auditor from the same group than for an initial engagement that had a change between auditor type. A change from Other to RS results in a small increase in fees (expected mean change in audit fee of 4.279 −10.430 + 6.862 = .711%) while a change from Other to RS results in a much larger increase (expected mean change in audit fee of 4.279 −10.430 + 15.675 = 9.524%). The higher increase in fees for a change from Other to RS suggest a fee discount for the RS and is consistent with the cross-sectional results. There was only one observation for a Big 6 to RS change and this variable is not significant in the model. However, the coefficient is negative, indicating a fee premium for a Big 6 auditor.

Model 2 is also significant at .0158 level and the results indicate that the variable representing initial engagement is significant in explaining the change in audit fee. However, the Model had a lower adjusted R^2, F-value, and level of significance than Model 1. Also, the coefficient for initial engagement was lower. The lower coefficient for initial engagement also suggests that not controlling for changes among auditor type is reducing the effect of this variable in the model.

Model 1 (controlling for change in auditor type) was compared to Model 2 (not controlling for change in auditor type) using a partial F-test. The results (F value = 3.62) indicate that the models are significantly different at the .01 level, suggesting that change in auditor type is an important variable. Omitting this variable can lead to biased estimates and obscure the significance of an initial engagement.

VI. CONCLUSIONS

The intent of this study is to investigate the effects of auditor type and change on audit fees. In the cross-sectional model the results for the control variables used as proxy for size, audit risk, and complexity are consistent with other public sector research. However, unlike Ward, Elder, and Kattelus (1994), the non-Big 6 audit firm with the most municipal experience is associated with a fee discount. Perhaps there are differences among regional specialist audit firms as well as different levels of competition between small and large municipalities.

Data from the cross-sectional model also suggest that changes among auditor types may be obscuring the significance of indicator variables representing an initial engagement. The time-series model included control variables for a change in auditor type. The findings indicate a significant negative effect on audit fees from a change in auditor, which is consistent with Baber, Brooks, and Ricks (1987). The results for the variables used to control for the effects of making a change between auditor type are also significant. This suggests that future research examining the effects of initial engagements should control for changes between auditor type.

The major limitation of this study is that it is limited to one type of government from one state and further generalization may be limited. Additionally, the number of counties that changed auditor is small and the results may therefore be considered tentative. Additional research is needed to determine if the same results are achieved for larger and more diverse samples.

ACKNOWLEDGMENT

I am grateful for the helpful comments of the editor. In addition, the assistance of the Virginia Government Finance Officers Association and the Auditor of Public Accounts is gratefully acknowledged. Financial support of the Radford University Foundation and its Summer Research Grant Program is also acknowledged.

NOTES

1. Other public sector studies use samples of organizations from a single state. For example, Deis and Giroux (1992) examined Texas School Districts, Baber, Brooks, and Ricks (1987) examined North Carolina counties, and Ward, Elder, and Kattelus (1994) examined Michigan cities and towns.

2. Table 7 reports that there were several possible types of auditor changes with no observations. Specifically, there were no observations for the following types of auditor changes: Big 6 to Other, RS to Big 6, and other to Big 6. The regression model reported in Table 8 includes only auditor type changes with available observations.

REFERENCES

Auditor of Public Accounts. 1993. *Comparative Report of Local Government Revenues and Expenditures*. Commonwealth of Virginia.
Baber, W., E. Brooks, and W. Ricks. 1987. An empirical investigation of the market for audit services in the public sector. *Journal of Accounting Research* 25 (Autumn): 293-305.

Copley, P. A. 1989. The determinants of local government audit fees: Additional evidence. *Research in Governmental and Nonprofit Accounting*, Vol. 5, ed. J. L. Chan, 3-23. Greenwich, CT: JAI Press.

Copley, P. A., M. S. Doucet, and K. M. Gaver. 1994. A simultaneous equations analysis of quality control review outcomes and engagement fees for audit of recipients of federal financial assistance. *The Accounting Review* 69 (January): 244-256.

Craswell, A. T., J. R. Francis, and S. L. Taylor. 1995. Auditor brand name reputations and industry specializations. *Journal of Accounting and Economics* 20 (December): 297-322.

DeAngelo, L. E. 1981. Auditor independence, low-balling, and disclosure regulation. *Journal of Accounting and Economics* 3 (August): 113-127.

Deis, D. R., and G. A. Giroux. 1992. Determinants of audit quality in the public sector. *The Accounting Review* 67 (July): 462-479.

Ettredge, M., and R. Greenberg. 1990. Determinants of fee cutting on initial audit engagements. *Journal of Accounting Research* 28 (Spring): 198-210.

Evans, J. H., and J. M. Patton. 1993. An economic analysis of participation in the municipal finance officers association certification of conformance program. *Journal of Accounting and Economics* 14 (December): 375-99.

Francis, J., and D. Simon. 1987. A test of audit pricing in the small-client segment of the U.S. audit market. *The Accounting Review* 62 (January): 145-157.

General Accounting Office (GAO). 1986. *CPA Audit Quality: Many Governmental Audits Do Not Comply With Professional Standards*. Washington, DC: General Accounting Office.

Johnson, W. B., and T. Lys. 1990. The market for audit services—evidence from voluntary auditor changes. *Journal of Accounting and Economics* 12 (January): 281-308.

Palmrose, Z. 1986. Audit fees and auditor size: Further evidence. *Journal of Accounting Research* 24 (Spring): 97-110.

Raman, K. K., and E. R. Wilson. 1992. An empirical investigation of the market for "single audit" services. *Journal of Accounting and Public Policy* 11 (Winter): 271-295.

Rubin, M. A. 1988. Municipal audit fee determinants. *The Accounting Review* 63 (April): 219-36.

Simunic, D. A. 1980. The pricing of audit services: Theory and evidence. *Journal of Accounting Research* 18 (Spring): 161-90.

Wallace, W. 1981. The association between municipal market measures and selected financial reporting practices. *Journal of Accounting Research* 19 (Autumn): 502-520.

Ward, D., R. Elder, and S. Kattelus. 1994. Further evidence on the determinants of municipal audit fees. *The Accounting Review* 69 (April): 399-411.

Wilson, E. R., and T. P. Howard. 1994. The association between municipal market measures and selected financial reporting practices: Additional evidence. *Journal of Accounting Research* 22 (Spring): 207-224.

AUDIT FEES AND NONAUDIT FEES IN THE GOVERNMENTAL SECTOR
A SELF-SELECTION ANALYSIS

Randal J. Elder, Susan C. Kattelus, and
Edward B. Douthett, Jr.

ABSTRACT

We use a self-selection model to examine differences in audit fees between purchasers and non-purchasers of nonaudit services for a sample of 165 Michigan governmental units. Understanding the relationship between audit fees and nonaudit fees is important because nonaudit services potentially influence audit quality in the governmental sector, including fees and auditor selection. We find significant differences between purchasers and non-purchasers of additional services which influence audit fees. Purchasers of additional services have more audit adjustments and less experienced financial personnel than non-purchasers, suggesting that purchasers experience more accounting problems. Consistent with previous private sector research, we find a positive relationship between audit fees and nonaudit fees. Further analysis by auditor type suggests that the relationship between audit fees and nonaudit fees is negative for Big 6 auditors, but positive for other audit firms. This difference in the relationship between audit fees and nonaudit fees by auditor type may be due to differences in the nature of the consulting services demanded, or differences in the contractual arrangements for audit and nonaudit services.

I. INTRODUCTION

The relationship between audit and nonaudit or consulting fees is of interest to accounting researchers, in part fostered by the concern that such fees may influence auditor incentives, affecting auditor selection and audit quality. This is of particular concern in the governmental sector, where evidence exists of significant problems with audit quality (GAO 1986). In addition to increasing the total compensation to the audit firm, purchase of nonaudit services may strengthen the relationship between the auditor and client, decreasing the likelihood that the audit is bid. Auditor compensation and use of competitive bidding have both been linked to audit quality in the governmental sector (e.g., Deis and Giroux 1992; Copley and Doucet 1993; Brown and Raghunandan 1995). Understanding the relationship between audit and nonaudit services may also further our understanding of public sector audit procurement.

Several studies (e.g., Simunic 1984; Simon 1985; Palmrose 1986) find a significant positive relationship between audit and nonaudit fees in the private sector. In contrast, Rubin (1994) finds a negative relationship between accounting-related consulting services and audit fees for a sample of U.S. cities. Several explanations exist for the relationship between audit fees and nonaudit fees. Palmrose (1986) suggests that the positive relation between audit fees and consulting fees may be due to additional audit effort as a result of organizational changes attributed to the consulting engagement. Alternatively, Simunic (1984) suggests that clients that incur nonaudit services are those that have unusual problems. Davis, Ricchiute, and Trompeter (1993) provide support for this explanation, finding that audit hours, in addition to audit fees, are higher for engagements where the client is a purchaser of nonaudit services.

We investigate the relationship between audit and nonaudit fees for a sample of Michigan municipalities using a self-selection analysis similar to the model used by Abdel-khalik (1990). Our sample includes both Big 6 and non-Big 6 audit firms, providing new evidence on the relationship between audit fees and nonaudit fees in the public sector. Results indicate significant differences between purchasers and nonpurchasers of additional services. Both audit fees and nonaudit fees are positively associated with the number of audit adjustments, suggesting that clients purchasing additional services experience problems. Consistent with most private sector research, the overall relationship between audit fees and nonaudit fees is positive. However, when the analysis is restricted to government entities audited by the Big 6, the relationship between audit and nonaudit fees is negative, consistent with Rubin (1994).

II. SUMMARY OF EARLIER FINDINGS ON THE EFFECT OF NONAUDIT SERVICES ON AUDIT FEES

Research on private sector entities finds a positive relation between audit and nonaudit fees (e.g., Simunic 1984; Simon 1985; Palmrose 1986). However, in the only study addressing this question for governmental entities, Rubin (1994) reports a negative relationship between audit and nonaudit fees. Rubin's study is restricted to large cities (population > 50,000) audited by Big 6 audit firms. The focus on Big 6 firms is consistent with private sector research. However, except among large cities, most governmental units are not audited by Big 6 firms. The underlying concern in research examining the relation between audit and nonaudit fees is on the potential effects of nonaudit fees on independence and audit quality. This is of particular concern in the governmental sector, as audit quality is lower for governmental audits than for audits of private sector entities (Brown and Raghunandan 1995). However, most of the problems with audit quality relate to non-Big 6 firms (GAO 1986). Because Rubin's results are inconsistent with private sector studies, and relate only to Big 6 firms, additional study of the relationship between audit fees and nonaudit fees in the governmental sector is warranted. We provide further evidence on the relationship between audit fees and nonaudit fees for governmental entities by testing this relationship on a different sample of governmental entities which includes non-Big 6 firms.

Simunic (1984) provides a comprehensive set of conditions identifying plausible relationships between audit and nonaudit fees. He argues that the positive relation between audit and nonaudit fees is consistent with consulting services reducing the cost of auditing (i.e., knowledge spillovers) and relatively elastic audit demand such that the lower cost of auditing increases the amount of auditing demanded, or knowledge spillovers from auditing to consulting. Rubin (1994) suggests that audit demand is likely to be less elastic in the public sector than for private firms. As a result, he argues that knowledge spillovers that reduce the cost of the audit are more likely to result in lower audit fees.

Palmrose (1986) finds a positive relation between audit fees and consulting fees paid to nonincumbent audit firms. This is inconsistent with the existence of knowledge spillovers, since the consulting services are not being provided by the audit firm. Palmrose suggests that consulting services may result in increased auditing, an outcome consistent with Simunic's alternative argument that purchasers of nonaudit services are experiencing problems.

Abdel-khalik (1990) argues that the positive relationship between audit and nonaudit fees for private sector firms is counterintuitive, and that a client should not pay more for the joint acquisition of two products, compared to the cost of acquiring them separately. An alternative explanation is that there are underlying differences in auditee characteristics between clients purchasing nonaudit services from incumbent auditors compared to non-incumbent auditors. Abdel-khalik uses the Heckman-Lee method of switching regressions to control for the self-selection bias of purchasers of consulting services. After controlling for this self-selection bias, he does not find significant costs or benefits to clients who select incumbent auditors to provide nonaudit services. This result is not consistent with the existence of knowledge spillovers, but is consistent with the argument that purchasers of nonaudit services are experiencing problems.

A subsequent study, which examines both audit fees and hours, provides support for Abdel-khalik's findings. Davis and colleagues (1993) find that nonaudit services are associated with increased audit hours.[1] After controlling for audit hours, they do not find a significant relationship between audit fees and nonaudit fees. This suggests that the provision of nonaudit services does not result in economic rents to the auditor. However, the additional audit effort is consistent with several interpretations, including knowledge spillovers with elastic demand,

Table 1. Comparison of Previous Nonaudit Fee Research

Author	Private/ Government	Audit/Nonaudit Fee Relation	Interpretation
Simunic (1984)	Private	Positive	Knowledge spillover with elastic audit demand [1]
Palmrose (1986)	Private	Positive	Nonaudit services increase required audit effort
Abdel-khalik (1990)	Private	Positive	No significant differences between purchases from incumbent auditors compared to non-incumbent auditors
Davis et al. (1993)	Private	Positive	Nonaudit services are associated with increased audit effort
Rubin (1994)	Government	Negative	Knowledge spillover with inelastic demand

Note: [1] Alternative explanations are that auditing generates knowledge useful in the production of nonaudit services, or that the client is experiencing unusual problems.

increased auditing of changes brought about by the nonaudit services, or problems increasing audit effort and the demand for auditing. Davis and colleagues (1993) also find that the positive relationship between audit fees and nonaudit fees is strongest for tax and accounting-related nonaudit services. Since these services are frequently purchased on a recurring basis, this finding is more consistent with the argument that higher audit effort arises from problems, and less consistent with the argument that additional audit effort results from audit changes brought about as a result of the consulting services.

A summary of the results of previous studies is included in Table 1. Existing private sector research fails to verify the existence of knowledge spillovers from consulting to auditing.[2] Instead, the results support a positive relationship between audit fees and nonaudit fees, where the increase in audit fees is related to additional audit effort (Davis et al. 1993). Based on the nature of the services in Davis and colleagues (1993) and Palmrose (1986), as well as the results in Abdel-khalik (1990), it appears that the positive relation between audit and nonaudit fees is due to common client factors, rather than increased audit effort arising from the provision of the nonaudit services. In contrast, Rubin finds a negative relationship between audit fees and nonaudit fees among city governments. He attributes this negative relationship to knowledge spillovers with an inelastic audit demand. However, Rubin fails to address whether differences exist between governmental purchasers and non-purchasers of additional services which may be affecting audit fees. A method for assessing the effect of self-selection on audit fees is described in the following section.

III. RESEARCH DESIGN

We first develop a model of the governmental entity's decision to purchase nonaudit services from the audit firm. The estimates from the nonaudit services demand model are then used to measure whether self-selectivity arising from the decision to purchase nonaudit services is present in a model of audit fees. Determining whether self-selection is present is important because the observed relation between nonaudit fees and audit fees may reflect differences between purchasers and non-purchasers of additional services which cause clients to self-select into these two groups. Constructing a model based on the factors underlying the client's choice of whether to purchase nonaudit services provides a way to empirically examine whether that choice affects audit fees, even for clients that do not choose to purchase nonaudit services.

A. Self-selection Model of Audit Fees

We use a self-selectivity model similar to that used by Abdel-khalik (1990) to correct for self-selection bias arising from the client's decision to purchase additional nonaudit services from their auditor. If we assume that clients make cost-minimizing choices when deciding to jointly purchase audit and nonaudit services, then the fees for all audit services purchased are from a truncated distribution (i.e., we assume that clients do not make cost-maximizing choices, and so all choices observed are assumed to be "correct"). Regressions performed on observations from a truncated distribution are biased (Maddala 1983; Hogan 1997). If we can effectively model the probability of purchasing nonaudit services, then as Maddala (1983) demonstrates, we can reduce the self-selection bias for the observed truncated distribution of fees. The self-selection analysis also allows for a comparison of differential effects for purchasers and non-purchasers of nonaudit services.

Estimation of the self-selection model is done in two stages. In the first stage a binary probit model is used to estimate the probability of purchasing nonaudit services. The independent variables in this estimation proxy for client attributes that are hypothesized to influence the demand for nonaudit services. Predicted values ($\beta'Z$) from the first stage, which represent the difference in audit fees between purchasers and non-purchasers, are transformed into a probability function (λ_i) for the purchasing decision, which is then used as the self-selection variable in the second-stage regression. In the second-stage regression, the sample is partitioned between purchasers and non-purchasers and audit fees are regressed on fee determinants and the self-selection variable, λ_i. The significance, direction, and difference between λ_0 and λ_1 in each partition indicate the presence and nature of the client's inclination to purchase nonaudit services, where λ_0 and λ_1 are the self-selection variable for non-purchasers and purchasers, respectively.

In addition to Abdel-khalik's (1990) examination of nonaudit services, other examples of accounting issues for which self-selection analysis has been applied include the choice of accounting for research and development (Shehata 1991) and selection of auditor for initial public offerings (Hogan 1997). Our model differs from Abdel-khalik's in that we compare purchasers to non-purchasers of nonaudit services, while Abdel-khalik examines purchasers of consulting services from incumbent and nonincumbent auditors. Our model is similar to Hogan's (1997) model in that we assume the client makes cost-minimizing choices relative to the purchase of nonaudit services. For example, a client who "incorrectly" chooses to source nonaudit services internally instead of externally would incur higher total costs (audit fee plus internal service costs). Therefore, if the characteristics of the client give rise to differences in the demand for jointly provided audit and nonaudit services, then this should result in differences in audit fees as clients self-select into the purchaser or non-purchaser group. The first research hypothesis predicts the existence of self-selection bias in the client's decision to purchase nonaudit services which affects audit fees.

Hypothesis 1. Self-selection bias exists in the client's decision to purchase nonaudit services which affects audit fees.

If audit fees vary depending on whether or not the auditor provides nonaudit services, then the tendency of clients to select the cost-effective mix of audit and nonaudit services results in the observed distribution of audit fees being truncated (i.e., only the cost-minimized choices are observed). Significant coefficients on the self-selection variables, λ_0 and λ_1, in the fee regressions indicate the presence of selectivity bias. Estimation of the fee regressions without correcting for selectivity bias produces inconsistent estimates of the parameters. As in Hogan's (1997) model, if self-selection is based on cost-minimization, then $\theta_0 - \theta_1 < 0$ in the fee regressions, where θ_0 and θ_1 are the regression coefficients for the self-selection variable for non-purchasers and purchasers of nonaudit services.[3] This leads to the second hypothesis:

> **Hypothesis 2.** Clients decide to purchase or not purchase nonaudit services to minimize the total of audit and nonaudit fees ($\lambda_0 < \lambda_1$).

First-Stage Model: The Demand for Nonaudit Services

Simunic (1984) suggests that clients purchasing nonaudit services may be those that experience problems. We use two proxies for the presence of audit problems. The first is the number of audit adjustments, which represents errors uncovered and detected by the auditor. The second is the existence of an audit qualification. A qualification indicates that a problem could not be corrected with a reasonable amount of audit effort, or in some cases, an unwillingness by the client to address the problem.

The argument that entities purchasing nonaudit services are experiencing problems has not been directly tested for either public or private sector entities. One reason is that it is difficult to measure the extent to which the governmental unit is experiencing "problems." Although the number of audit adjustments is an imperfect proxy, we believe it at least partially reflects problems experienced by the client, and the ability of the client to address those problems.[4]

Abdel-khalik (1990) includes client-related variables, demand-related variables, and auditor-related variables as explanatory variables in a model of the decision to purchase nonaudit services. The size of the governmental unit measured by total revenues may capture both the ability to purchase nonaudit services, and a range of activities that are likely to increase the demand for nonaudit services. We also include the number of funds as a measure of the range of client activities. Additional client-related variables for a city manager, the tenure of the finance officer, and whether the finance officer is a CPA are designed to control for internal management capabilities. More professionally run cities and those with more experienced finance officers are expected to be less likely to require additional services from the auditor.

The demand-related variables in Abdel-khalik (1990) were collected by survey and addressed the cost of searching for and adapting to a new auditor, as well as tolerance for fee increases. We use a variable indicating whether the audit was bid as a proxy for the willingness of the client to change auditors.

Auditor-related variables included in the model are auditor tenure and auditor classification variables indicating Big 6 firms and a regional firm with a large share of the Michigan governmental audit market. The auditor tenure variable is included since the decision to purchase additional services may be affected by the length of the client-auditor relationship. An indicator variable is included for Big 6 firms since they offer a range of services in addition to auditing that may be demanded by government units. An indicator variable is also included for a regional firm since previous research indicated this firm has a large share of the Michigan government audit market and receives higher fees in this market (Ward, Elder, and Kattelus 1994). Governments may be more likely to purchase additional services from this firm because of the firm's governmental experience.

These variables are used in the following probit model of the demand for nonaudit services:

$$\text{Nonaudit} = \alpha + \beta_1 \ln\text{Rev} + \beta_2 \text{Funds} + \beta_3 \text{Mgr} + \beta_4 \text{Finten} + \beta_5 \text{CPA} + \beta_6 \text{AJE} + \beta_7 \text{Opinqual} + \beta_8 \text{Bid} + \beta_9 \text{Audten} + \beta_{10} \text{Big6} + \beta_{11} \text{Expaud} + \varepsilon \qquad (1)$$

where (expected sign in parentheses):

Nonaudit	=	one if municipality acquired nonaudit services; zero otherwise
$\ln$Rev (+)	=	natural log of total entity revenues
Funds (+)	=	number of funds
Mgr (-)	=	one if government has a city manager; zero otherwise
Finten (-)	=	finance officer tenure in years
CPA (-)	=	one if finance officer is a CPA; zero otherwise
AJE (+)	=	categorical measure of the number of audit adjustments

Opinqual (+) = one if municipality receives an audit qualification; zero otherwise
Bid (-) = one if audit was awarded by bid; zero otherwise
Audten (+) = auditor tenure in years
Big6 (+) = one if auditor is Big 6 firm; zero otherwise
Expaud (+) = one if auditor is a regional firm with a large government audit practice; zero otherwise

The probit model is used to estimate the likelihood that a client purchases additional services. Estimates from this model are used in the audit fee model to control for self-selection bias between purchasers and non-purchasers of nonaudit services in an audit fee model.

Second-Stage Model: Determinants of Audit Fees

A model of municipal audit fees based on Ward, Elder, and Kattelus (1994) is used to test for the existence of a self-selection bias arising from the purchase of nonaudit services.[5] Additional data include whether the municipality acquired additional services from the auditor, and the dollar amount of the services.[6] Control variables in the model include total revenue, number of funds, number of audit adjustments, auditor reputation, and whether the audit was bid.[7] These variables are designed to control for client size, client complexity, audit complexity, the audit production function, and competition. Logarithmic transformations are used for the audit fee and total revenue variables to improve the linear fit of the data, consistent with previous research. The audit fee model is as follows (hypothesized sign in parentheses):[8]

$$\ell n \text{Audit Fee} = \alpha + \beta_1 \ell n \text{Rev} + \beta_2 \text{Funds} + \beta_3 \text{Big6} + \beta_4 \text{Expaud} + \beta_5 \text{Bid} + \beta_6 \text{AJE} + \theta \lambda + \varepsilon \qquad (2)$$

where:

ℓnAudit Fee = natural log of the audit fee
ℓnRev (+) = natural log of total entity revenues
Funds (+) = total number of funds
Big6 (+) = one if auditor is Big 6 firm; zero otherwise
Expaud (+) = one if auditor is a regional firm with a large government audit practice; zero otherwise

Bid (−) = one if audit was awarded by bid; zero otherwise
AJE (+) = categorical measure of the number of audit adjustments
λ = self-selection variable that corrects for estimation bias on observations drawn from a truncated normal distribution.
λ_1 = $-\phi(\beta'Z)/\Phi(\beta'Z)$ for purchasers of nonaudit services
λ_0 = $\phi(\beta'Z)/(1-\Phi(\beta'Z))$ for non-purchasers where $\phi(\bullet)$ and $\Phi(\bullet)$ are the standard normal density and distribution functions, and $(\beta'Z)$ is the prediction from the probit model. $\beta'Z$ is an estimate of the difference in audit fees between purchasers and non-purchasers.

The control variables are expected to have a positive relationship with audit fees, except for the variable indicating the awarding of the audit by competitive bid, which is expected to be negatively related to audit fees. If the unexplained audit fees are significantly different for clients purchasing nonaudit services, the estimated coefficients for θ_1 and θ_0 will be significantly different, where θ_1 and θ_0 are the estimated coefficients on the self-selection variable for purchasers and non-purchasers.

B. Data Description

Audit fees, nonaudit fees, and other explanatory variables for the year 1988 were collected by survey from a sample of 165 Michigan municipalities. Financial data were collected directly from copies of the municipalities' financial statements on file with the state of Michigan Bureau of Local Government Audits. Descriptive statistics for the sample are presented in Table 2. The sample is partitioned into purchasers and non-purchasers of nonaudit services; approximately 60 percent of the municipalities purchased nonaudit services.

Based on univariate analysis, purchasers of nonaudit services have greater revenues, and incur larger audit fees. They are more likely to hire an industry experienced auditor, but are less likely to use a Big 6 auditor. Purchasers of nonaudit services are also less likely to purchase the audit by competitive bid. Perhaps as a result, audit tenure is higher for purchasers of nonaudit services. These results suggest that bidding and auditor tenure are related to the provision of nonaudit services.

Table 2. Descriptive Statistics for a Sample of 165 Michigan Municipalities for the Year 1988

Variable	Label	Mean (std. deviation)			P-Value[1]
		(n = 165) Total Sample	(n = 97) Purchasers	(n = 68) Non-Purchasers	
Audit fees ($)	Audit fee	19,147 (28,018)	22,706 (34,420)	14,170 (13,255)	.03
Nonaudit fees ($)	Nonaudit fee	3,235 (10,725)	5,502 (13,562)	–	–
Revenues ($ millions)	Rev	12.50 (25.55)	14.08 (29.18)	10.42 (19.35)	.33
Number of Funds	Funds	16.38 (12.70)	15.95 (11.90)	17.00 (13.90)	.61
City Manager (1/0)	Mgr	.52 (.50)	.48 (.50)	.56 (.50)	.35
Finance officer tenure (years)	Finten	8.57 (6.88)	7.62 (6.52)	9.92 (7.18)	.03
Finance officer is CPA (1/0)	CPA	.20 (1.02)	.16 (.94)	.25 (1.12)	.58
Audit adjustments (Categorical values 1-6)	AJE	3.40 (1.90)	3.72 (1.85)	2.96 (1.89)	.01
Audit qualification (1/0)	Opinqual	.29 (.46)	.24 (.43)	.38 (.49)	.04
Audit awarded by bid (1/0)	Bid	.31 (.46)	.25 (.43)	.40 (.49)	.04
Auditor tenure (years)	Audten	10.44 (8.37)	11.62 (8.59)	8.74 (7.82)	.03
Big 6 auditor (1/0)	Big6	.08 (.28)	.05 (.22)	.13 (.34)	.07
Regional CPA firm with large governmental audit practice (1/0)	Expaud	.21 (.41)	.27 (.45)	.13 (.34)	.04

Note: [1] *t*-test of mean difference between purchasers and non-purchasers of nonaudit services for continuous and categorical variables; chi-squared test of independence for dichotomous variables.

Purchasers of nonaudit services have more audit adjustments, consistent with the existence of greater audit complexity, although they have fewer audit qualifications.[9]

Table 3 presents a matrix of the bivariate correlations between variables. Both the decision to purchase nonaudit services and the amount of nonaudit services are significantly correlated with the audit fee. Audit complexity, as measured by the number of audit adjustments, is significantly correlated with both the audit fee and nonaudit fee. Most of the remaining independent variables are significantly correlated with

Table 3. Pearson Correlations Coefficients for a Sample of 165 Michigan Municipalities for the Year 1988

	ln Audit fee	Nonaudit fee (1/0)	ln Non-audit fee	ln Rev	Funds	Mgr	Finten	CPA	AJE	Opinqual	Bid	Audten	Big6	Expaud
ln Audit fee														
Nonaudit fee (1/0)	.15**													
ln Non-audit fee	.36***	.78***												
ln Rev	.83***	.01	.23***											
Funds	.49***	-.04	.04	.64**										
Mgr	.27***	-.07	.00	.35***	.21***									
Finten	-.12	-.17**	-.21***	-.04	.00	.08								
CPA	.15*	-.04	.02	.10	.06	.16**	-.10							
AJE	.25***	.20**	.26***	.05	.02	.08	-.12	-.07						
Opinqual	.03	-.16**	-.14*	.06	.08	.15*	-.05	-.09	.09					
Bid	-.10	-.18**	-.11	.12	.12	.18**	-.03	-.10	-.06	.25***				
Audten	.18**	.18**	.13*	.07	.01	.03	.13	.12	.05	-.23***	-.48***			
Big6	.28***	-.14*	-.04	.34***	.23***	.12	.01	.09	-.14*	.04	-.01	.11		
Expaud	.46***	.16**	.22***	.24***	.06	.06	-.14*	.25***	.14*	.05	-.08	-.04	-.16**	

Note: *,(**),(***) - Significant at the (.10),(.05),(.01) level based on two-tailed test.

Table 4. Self-Selection Analysis of a Model of the Decision to Purchase Nonaudit Services for a Sample of 165 Michigan Municipalities for the Year 1988
Probit model of demand for nonaudit services:

$$\text{Nonaudit} = \alpha + \beta_1 \ell n \text{Rev} + \beta_2 \text{Funds} + \beta_3 \text{Mgr} + \beta_4 \text{Finten} + \beta_5 \text{CPA} + \beta_6 \text{AJE} + \beta_7 \text{Opinqual} + \beta_8 \text{Bid} + \beta_9 \text{Audten} + \beta_{10} \text{Big6} + \beta_{11} \text{Expaud} + \varepsilon \quad (1)$$

Variable	Pred. Sign	(n = 165) Coefficient (t-value)
Constant		−0.520 (−0.65)
ℓnRev	+	0.060 (0.57)
Funds	+	−0.003 (−0.32)
Mgr	−	−0.108 (−0.46)
Finten	−	−0.038 (−2.34)***
CPA	−	−0.145 (−1.38)*
AJE	+	0.113 (1.93)**
Opinqual	+	−0.440 (−1.821)
Bid	−	−0.100 (−0.343)
Audten	+	0.056 (2.04)**
Big 6	+	−0.564 (−1.317)
Expaud	+	0.436 (1.406)*
Log-Likelihood		96.882**
Correctly classified		69 %

Note: *,(**),(***) - Significant at the (.10),(.05),(.01) level based on one-tailed test.

the audit fee. Finance officer tenure, auditor tenure, and the industry-experienced audit firm are significantly correlated with nonaudit services, suggesting the importance of client and auditor variables.

IV. RESULTS

A. Self-selection Analysis

The results for the demand model for nonaudit services are reported in Table 4. The probit model is significant, and correctly classifies 69 percent of the observations. There is a significant association between nonaudit services and the number of audit adjustments, consistent with greater audit complexity for purchasers of nonaudit services. We also ran an OLS regression using the level of nonaudit fees (not reported) as the dependent variable. Audit adjustments are significantly associated with the magnitude of nonaudit fees. These results are consistent with the proposition that problems or other entity factors increase both audit and nonaudit fees.

Several audit firm and client variables are also significantly associated with the decision to acquire nonaudit services. The decision to purchase nonaudit services is decreasing with finance officer tenure, and is less likely if the finance officer is a CPA. These results suggest that more financially sophisticated clients are less likely to require additional services from their audit firm. The decision to purchase nonaudit services is increasing in auditor tenure, but is not significantly related to whether the audit was bid. The greater auditor tenure for purchasers of nonaudit services suggests that the audit contracting is related to the purchase of nonaudit services.[10] Consistent with the descriptive results reported in Table 2, purchase of additional services is more likely if the audit firm specialized in governmental auditing, and less likely if the auditor is a member of the Big 6.[11]

Table 5 reports the results of the audit fee regression for purchasers and non-purchasers of nonaudit services. The last column of the table reports the difference in coefficients between purchasers and non-purchasers. The control variables are generally significant with the hypothesized signs, except for the number of funds which is insignificant. The variable for the number of adjustments is significant for purchasers, but not for non-purchasers.

Of particular interest is the self-selection variable (λ), which is significantly negative for non-purchasers, and is positive and insignificant for purchasers. A Wald test of the difference between the two coefficients is significant ($\theta_0 - \theta_1 < 0, p < .05$), indicating the presence of self-selectivity bias in the audit fee model. The signs on the selection variables

Table 5. Self-Selection Analysis of a Model of Audit Fees for a Sample of 165 Michigan Municipalities for the Year 1988
Audit Fee Model:

$$\ell n\text{Audit Fee} = \alpha + \beta_1 \ell n\text{Rev} + \beta_2\text{Funds} + \beta_3\text{Big6} + \beta_4\text{Expaud} + \beta_5\text{Bid} + \beta_6\text{AJE} + \theta\lambda + \varepsilon \quad (2)$$

		Coefficient (t-statistic)		
Variable	Pred. Sign	(n = 97) Purchasers of Nonaudit Services	(n = 68) Non-purchasers of Nonaudit Services	Differential Coefficient
Intercept		4.821 (13.11)***	4.917 (11.83)***	0.096 (.17)
ℓnRevenues	+	0.492 (12.21)***	0.442 (8.01)***	−0.050 (−.72)
Funds	+	−0.002 (−.37)	0.005 (.90)	0.007 (.92)
Big6	+	0.340 (1.52)*	0.434 (2.04)**	0.094 (.31)
Expaud	+	0.603 (6.38)***	0.563 (3.36)***	−0.040 (−.20)
Bid	−	−0.268 (−2.24)**	−0.235 (−1.72)**	0.033 (.18)
AJE	+	0.116 (4.28)***	0.031 (.95)	−0.085 (−1.99)**
λ	?	0.079 (.37)	−0.478 (−2.02)**	−0.557 (−1.75)**
Adjusted R-Squared		.819	.802	

Notes: *,(**),(***) -Significant at the (.10),(.05),(.01) level based on one-tailed test, except for self-selection variable λ, which is two-tailed. Tests of the differential coefficients are two-tailed, except for λ, which is one-tailed.
λ = Self-selection variable measuring likelihood that client purchases nonaudit services based on the probit model prediction.
$\lambda_1 = -\phi(\beta'Z)/\Phi(\beta'Z)$ for purchasers of nonaudit services
$\lambda_0 = \phi(\beta'Z)/(1-\Phi(\beta'Z))$ for non-purchasers where $\phi(\bullet)$ and $\Phi(\bullet)$ are the standard normal density and distribution functions, and $(\beta'Z)$ is the prediction from the probit model. $\beta'Z$ is an estimate of the difference in audit fees between purchasers and non-purchasers.
See Table 2 for description of remaining variables.

($\theta_0 < 0$, $\theta_1 > 0$) are also consistent with self-selection based on cost-minimization. A selection process based on cost-minimization is rational and consistent with theory (Maddala 1983), suggesting that the first-stage probit estimation for the demand of nonaudit services is an appropriate model. Additionally, the significant differential coefficients on the λ suggest that client attributes which explain the decision to purchase nonaudit services jointly explain audit fees. The significant difference in coefficients on AJE further supports the notion that client attributes, including the underlying problems of the client, jointly determine the choice of services purchased from the auditor, as well as the related fees.

B. Relation Between Audit and Nonaudit Fees and Auditor Type

The self-selection analysis indicates that audit fees are significantly higher for purchasers of nonaudit services. These results are not consistent with the negative relationship between governmental audit fees and nonaudit fees in Rubin (1994). However, Rubin's sample includes only cities with populations over 50,000 that were audited by Big 6 audit firms. We partitioned our sample into three groups based on auditor reputation. Results for the fee model for each auditor type and for all observations for the continuous measure of nonaudit fees are reported in Table 6.[12]

Although based on a limited number of observations, the coefficient for nonaudit services for municipalities audited by Big 6 firms is negative

Table 6. Audit Fee Model Partitioned by Auditor Type for a Sample of 165 Michigan Municipalities for the Year 1988

Model: ℓnAudit Fee = α + $\beta_1 \ell n$Revenues + $\beta_2 \ell n$(1+Nonaudit fee) + β_3Funds + β_4Bid + β_5AJE + ε

	Coefficient (t-statistic)			
Variable	$(n = 14)^1$ Big 6 Firms	$(n = 35)$ Regional Firm	$(n = 116)$ Other audit Firms	$(n = 165)$ All Observations
Intercept	2.837 (2.69)**	5.688 (14.26)***	5.208 (18.33)***	4.623 (18.86)***
ℓnRev	0.748 (5.69)***	0.493 (9.46)***	0.443 (11.29)***	0.538 (16.22)***
ℓn(1 + Nonaudit fee)	−0.106 (−2.10)*	0.013 (0.96)	0.018 (1.69)*	(0.025) (2.565)**
Funds	−0.024 (−1.88)*	−0.003 (−0.44)	0.003 (0.68)	−0.001 (−0.30)
Bid	0.701 (1.91)*	−0.201 (−1.46)*	−0.366 (−4.14)***	−0.371 (−4.60)***
AJE	0.285 (2.92)***	0.029 (0.99)	0.090 (4.16)***	0.088 (4.44)***
Adjusted R^2	.857	.831	.690	.765

Notes: *,(**),(***) -Significant at the (.10),(.05),(.01) level based on one-tailed test, except for nonaudit fee variable, which is two-tailed.
(1)Sample size for municipalities audited by Big 6 firms is small and results should not be regarded as statistically reliable.
See Table 2 for description of variables.

and statistically significant, consistent with the results in Rubin (1994).[13] The coefficient for nonaudit services for the sample audited by the regional firm is positive, but not significant. The coefficient on nonaudit services is positive and significant for municipalities audited by other firms, and for the overall sample.

We performed separate analyses partitioning the entire sample at population cutoffs of 50,000 and 25,000. There is a positive and significant association between audit fees and nonaudit fees for the smaller governmental units. The association is positive and insignificant for the larger population partitions. These results suggest the negative association between audit fees and nonaudit fees for municipalities audited by the Big 6 is not driven solely by differences in client size.

To further analyze these differences by auditor type, we computed the nonaudit fee for each sample partition based on auditor type. This information is reported in Table 7. Municipalities audited by Big 6 firms are less likely to use their audit firm for additional services. Approximately 36 percent of municipalities audited by Big 6 firms also use the firm for nonaudit services, compared to 75 percent of the municipalities audited by the regional firm and 58 percent for municipalities audited by other audit firms. The dollar magnitude of the additional services provided by Big 6 firms is much larger, but is not significantly larger as a percentage of the audit fee.

There are several interpretations for these results. The lower percentage of nonaudit fees for municipalities audited by Big 6 firms is consistent with larger municipalities requiring fewer consulting services. An alternative explanation is that some nonaudit services are included in the audit fee.[14] Big 6 firms tend to provide larger consulting services,

Table 7. Descriptive Statistics for Nonaudit Fees by Auditor Type for a Sample of 165 Michigan Municipalities for the Year 1988

	Mean (std. dev.)		
	(n = 14) Big 6 Auditor	(n = 35) Regional Auditor	(n = 116) Other Auditor
Percentage with nonaudit fee	.357 (.497)	.750 (.439)	.580 (.496)
Mean nonaudit fee—purchasers ($)	25,314 (31,952)	8,657 (18,485)	2,758 (5,964)
Nonaudit fee as percentage of audit fee	.261 (.152)	.211 (.331)	.222 (.270)

which may generate knowledge spillovers or other cost savings that are reflected in the audit fee. However, the sample size for the municipalities audited by the Big 6 is small and the results should be interpreted with caution.

V. CONCLUSIONS

This study finds self-selectivity differences in audit fees for purchasers and non-purchasers of nonaudit services. Evidence that self-selection is present is important because it suggests that the observed effect of nonaudit fees on audit fees is the result of differences between purchasers and non-purchasers of additional services which cause clients to self-select into these two groups. Our results suggest that purchasers of nonaudit services experience reporting problems and have less experienced and qualified finance officials, and it is these factors, not knowledge spillover effects, that cause the observed relations between audit and nonaudit fees.

The purchase of additional services is associated with the number of audit adjustments, as well as measures of the competence of finance personnel, consistent with the explanation that purchasers of nonaudit services are experiencing problems. The positive relation between audit fees and nonaudit fees is consistent with previous research in the private sector. However, when the analysis is restricted to the small number of municipalities audited by Big 6 firms, the association between audit fees and consulting fees is negative, consistent with the finding in Rubin (1994). These results suggest that the nature of nonaudit services and how they are priced in conjunction with the audit fee may vary by audit firm or audit market segment.

A. Limitations

This study was limited to Michigan municipalities, and did not consider the nature of the nonaudit services rendered. Future research should also consider whether the nonaudit services were provided by auditors or consultants, since the effects on auditor effort and compensation may depend upon the provider of the services. This research also assumed that audit services and nonaudit services are priced separately. Some nonaudit services may be jointly priced with audit services, depending on the nature of the services, the contracting arrangement, and client and auditor characteristics. Further research is necessary into the nature and demand for nonaudit services by governmental entities.

ACKNOWLEDGMENT

The authors wish to express their appreciation to the Michigan Municipal Finance Officers Association and the Michigan Township Association for their assistance in eliciting member responses. Helpful comments were received from the editor, Paul Copley, two anonymous reviewers, Chris Hogan, and participants at the 1996 AAA Annual and Midwest Regional Meetings.

NOTES

1. O'Keefe, Simunic, and Stein (1994) tested for a relationship between nonaudit services and the disaggregated staff level components of audit hours and did not find a significant relationship.

2. Although existing research fails to support the existence of knowledge spillover, it may still exist. Research has identified higher fees and audit hours associated with the provision of nonaudit services. However, these higher fees and hours could be attributed to additional problems which obscure any potential knowledge spillovers. It is also important to note that spillovers can also occur from auditing to consulting, but variation in the type and cost of nonaudit services make it difficult to test for such spillovers.

3. The reader is referred to Hogan (1997) for the derivation of this result. Our cost minimization problem is similar in that we assume the mean total costs of a client correctly choosing to purchase nonaudit services are $E(TC_1|TC_1<TC_0) = \mu_1 - \sigma_1(\lambda_1)$ and the mean total costs of client correctly choosing not to purchase nonaudit services are $E(TC_0|TC_0<TC_1) = \mu_0 - \sigma_0(\lambda_0)$, where σ_i is the covariance of the disturbance. θ, the coefficient on λ in the fee regression, is an estimate of σ_i.

4. There are many types of nonaudit services which may be provided to clients, and many of them will not be directly associated with problems which result in audit adjustments. However, nonaudit services will be positively associated with audit adjustments to the extent they both capture the need for outside assistance in addressing problems.

5. See Ward and colleagues (1994) for a review of governmental audit fee research and further description of the model used in this study.

6. Data on nonaudit services were collected as part of the original Ward and colleagues (1994) fee study to help insure the audit fee variable did not include nonaudit services, but the nonaudit fee variable was not tested in the original fee model.

7. The model is a simplified version of the model in Ward and colleagues (1994) to focus on the relation between audit and nonaudit fees. Excluded variables which were significant in the original fee model include auditor tenure, bond rating, percentage of revenues from property taxes, and the property tax rate. Exclusion of additional

variables did not significantly alter the reported results, and as reported in Table 5, the model has high explanatory power.

8. The audit fee models used in this study are single-equation fee functions that incorporate supply and demand characteristics. See Copley, Gaver, and Gaver (1995) for a discussion of the limitations of single-equation models.

9. The most common qualification for the municipalities in our sample is for a failure to record general fixed assets. As a result, qualifications may not be strongly related to the purchase of nonaudit services. However, we are unable to explain why purchasers have fewer qualifications than non-purchasers.

10. There are a number of plausible explanations for the relationship between auditor tenure and nonaudit services. Increased auditor tenure may allow the identification of services which could be provided by the auditor. The positive relationship is also consistent with spillovers from auditing to nonauditing services where auditor familiarity with the client allows for the provision of nonaudit services at lower cost.

11. Differences in the acquisition of nonaudit services by auditor type do not appear related to the audit acquisition process. There were no significant differences in auditor tenure or the use of bidding to award the audit across auditor types.

12. Similar results to those reported were obtained using the dichotomous measure of nonaudit services.

13. The model for the Big 6 firms includes only 14 observations and has eight degrees of freedom, which is insufficient to generate reliable statistical estimates. However, the results are consistent with the results reported by Rubin (1994).

14. Davis and colleagues (1993) provide evidence that nonaudit services are sometimes included in the audit fee. In their study, 44 of 176 observations were deleted because the client was not billed separately for audit and nonaudit services. Davis and colleagues do not provide information on the types of nonaudit services or contracting arrangements associated with combined billing of audit and nonaudit services.

REFERENCES

Abdel-khalik, A.R. 1990. The jointness of audit fees and demand for MAS: A self-selection analysis. *Contemporary Accounting Research* 7 (Spring): 295-322.

Brown, D., and K. Raghunandan. 1995. Audit quality in audits of federal programs by non-federal auditors. *Accounting Horizons* 9 (September): 1-10.

Copley, P., and M. Doucet. 1993. The impact of competition on the quality of governmental audits. *Auditing: A Journal of Practice and Theory* 12 (Spring): 88-98.

Copley, P., J. Gaver, and K. Gaver. 1995. Simultaneous estimation of the supply and demand of differentiated audits: Evidence from the municipal audit market. *Journal of Accounting Research* 33 (Spring): 137-155.

Davis, L., D. Ricchiute, and G. Trompeter. 1993. Audit effort, audit fees, and the provision of nonaudit services to audit clients. *The Accounting Review* 68 (January): 135-150.

Deis, D., and G. Giroux. 1992. Determinants of audit quality in the public sector. *The Accounting Review* 67 (July): 462-479.

Hogan, C. 1997. Costs and benefits of audit quality in the IPO market: A self-selection analysis. *The Accounting Review* 72 (January): 67-86.

Maddala, G. 1983. *Limited Dependent and Qualitative Variables in Economics.* Econometric Society Monographs in Quantitative Economics No. 3. New York: Cambridge University Press.

O'Keefe, T., D. Simunic, and M. Stein. 1994. The production of audit services: Evidence from a major public accounting firm. *Journal of Accounting Research* 32 (Autumn): 241-261.

Palmrose, Z. 1986. The effect of nonaudit services on the pricing of audit services. *Journal of Accounting Research* 24 (Autumn): 405-411.

Rubin, M. 1994. The pricing relationship of audits and related services in municipal governments. *Public Budgeting and Financial Management* 6 (3): 422-443.

Shehata, M. 1991. Self-selection bias and the economic consequences of accounting regulation: An application of two-stage switching regression to SFAS No. 2. *The Accounting Review* 66 (October): 768-787.

Simon, D. 1985. The audit services market: Additional empirical evidence. *Auditing: A Journal of Practice & Theory* 5 (Fall): 71-78.

Simunic, D. 1984. Auditing, consulting and auditor independence. *Journal of Accounting Research* 22 (Autumn): 679-702.

U.S. General Accounting Office. 1986. CPA Audit Quality: Many Governmental Audits Do Not Comply with Professional Standards. Washington, DC: GAO.

Ward, D., R. Elder, and S. Kattelus. 1994. Further evidence on the determinants of municipal audit fees. *The Accounting Review* 69 (April): 399-411.

A COMPARISON OF ALTERNATIVE MODELS OF BUDGETARY BEHAVIOR: EVIDENCE FROM CALIFORNIA CITY DEPARTMENTS

Alberto M. Bento and Lourdes F. White

ABSTRACT

Varying empirical models exist in the public administration, political economics, and accounting literatures to describe budgetary behavior. The purpose of this study is to compare the descriptive ability of three alternative models of budgetary behavior: bureaucratic, ecological, and analytical. The empirical tests are based on actual and budgeted figures collected directly from city budget documents for a sample of 91 municipal departments from 13 cities. Shift-point analysis and linearity tests are used to investigate patterns of budgetary behavior, departing from the usual assumptions of linear budgetary functions. The results indicate that the bureaucratic model best explains budgetary decisions in 60 percent of the departments, followed by the ecological model (28%) and analytical model (12%). Furthermore, the results offer evidence that different types of activities performed by city departments (e.g., general government, public safety, culture and recreation, and infrastructure) may be associated with different budgetary styles.

I. BUDGETARY DECISION-MAKING STYLES

We examine three competing models of budgetary decision-making styles, focusing on city governments at the departmental level. Budgets are the result of a complex decision-making process, and in the context of public organizations, constitute the instrument by which society establishes priorities and enacts policies to meet a set of public needs. At the level of city departments, those needs are clearly evident due to the proximity of voters who exert influence on local officials. City governments must make difficult resource allocation decisions to cope with conflicting social needs while facing financial constraints.

Despite much research and debate during the last three decades, there is still a lack of descriptive model that can adequately link policy-making and budgetary decisions at the city level (Rubin 1990). The budgeting literature comes from disciplines such as management accounting, public administration, economics, and political science, with sometimes conflicting views on how allocation decisions are reached in the budgetary process (Caiden 1985). Our review of the literature led us to integrate these views into three major models of budgetary behavior: bureaucratic model, ecological model, and analytical model. A direct comparison among these models has been difficult to date, since previous studies typically rely on only one of the models, without considering competing explanations based on other models.

In order to compare these competing models, we develop a methodology to represent each model by a set of functions and corresponding functional forms. The same data are used to test which functional form best explains how city departments make budgetary decisions. The empirical tests are based on actual and budgeted figures collected directly from city budget documents for a sample of 91 municipal departments. The 91 departments in the sample are the seven largest departments of 13 cities selected via a stratified, proportional, random sampling procedure among departments in California cities with populations greater than 50,000.

The empirical evidence in this paper helps to reconcile contradictory evidence in the budgeting literature supporting the bureaucratic, ecological, or analytical models of budgeting. It shows that there are significant cross-sectional differences in budgetary styles among city departments, and that neither the bureaucratic, the ecological, nor the analytical view can be universally applied.

The next three sections will describe each competing budgetary model and its corresponding classes of functions. These sections are followed by a description of the specific functional forms and variables used in the empirical tests. Next, data collection methods, shift points, and linearity tests are discussed. Finally, a summary of the results and their implications is presented.

II. BUREAUCRATIC MODEL

In the management accounting and public administration literatures, the bureaucratic model of budgeting opposed traditional normative views of budgetary behavior by proposing that budgets are the product of a complex set of organizational routines that occur within large bureaucracies (Wildavsky 1964; Crecine 1969; Larkey 1979). Bureaucracies are perceived as having their own strong internal dynamics, with their budgetary decisions scarcely influenced by the uncertainties of the external environment (Weber 1946). Rather, each year, small changes to the previous year's budgets are decided on the basis of a relatively stable distribution of power among internal constituencies (as in the interest group politics theory described by Downs and Rocke 1984).

Incremental functions are frequently used in the public administration literature to apply the bureaucratic model to budgeting. Incremental budgeting assumes that an agency's budget "is based on last year's budget with special attention to a narrow range of increases or decreases" (Wildavsky 1964, 15). Incrementalism introduces the concept of *base*, representing expenditures necessary to carry out existing programs (which are expected to continue and therefore do not require further consideration), and of *increments* that are negotiated each year. After budget proposals for the base and increments are prepared and justified, the determination of final budgetary allocations becomes a matter of internal politics within the bureaucracy. Empirical evidence in support of incrementalism led to a normative discussion (particularly heated in the public administration literature) about whether budgeting *should* be incremental (see discussion in Rubin 1989).

Even though the bureaucratic model has been in the public administration literature since the 1960s, it was only in the 1980s that its focus on the interplay between politics and budgeting became an "emergent theory" in the accounting literature (Covaleski et al. 1985). Accounting studies conducted in the public sector (e.g., Covaleski and Dirsmith 1988; Giroux et al. 1986; Hofstede 1981) call attention to the symbolic and political nature of budget negotiations, motivating a debate about whether budgets simply reflect economic activity (as proposed by traditional normative budgetary theory) or whether they help create social reality (as indicated by the bureaucratic model).

Incremental budgeting assumes only a few changes in policy and no comparisons among alternatives for spending within the budgeting process (Rubin 1990). Therefore, incremental budgeting is represented in this study by linear functions, whereby the previous year's budgeted or actual expenditures become the largest determining factor of both the size and the content of current budgets.

III. ECOLOGICAL MODEL

In the political science and economics literatures, another budgetary model has challenged the traditional normative view of comprehensive budgetary decisions by proposing that budget allocations are continuously revised in response to changes in the environment or in "collectively exercised demands" (Conte and Darrat 1993, 20). This model is known by different names in different contexts; we labeled it "ecological" to highlight the influence of many aspects of the environment (political, economic, social) on budgetary decisions. According to this model, resource allocation decisions are based on social and economic factors (such as income, degree of industrialization, urbanization), and influenced by political process variables (such as party competition and equity). Constrained by limited resources, budgeters can at best "satisfice" (satisfy and suffice, as proposed by Simon 1957), instead of maximize, complex public demands.

Several determinant studies attempt to sort out, empirically, whether social, economic, or political factors prevail in determining public expenditures. Those determinant studies are widely criticized, due to their lack of underlying theory (Inman 1979). Other studies based on the ecological model focus on specifying the demand for public services, such as those employing the median voter model (as reviewed by Duncombe 1996) or group decision-making models (e.g., Behrman and Craig 1987). Contrary to the bureaucratic view of budgeting, these studies report that environmental factors (such as changes in demand for public services, and in outcomes) are more relevant to budgetary decisions than past budgetary allocations or inputs (Todd and Ramanathan 1994).

In order to allow a direct comparison with linear incremental formulations of the bureaucratic model, a nonlinear function is needed to represent the satisficing approach to budgeting based on the ecological model. For example, Giroux and Shields (1993) find a very good fit for their log-linear models relating public expenditures to monitoring, political, and demographic variables. According to the ecological model, city departments adjust their supply of public services in response to shifts in their environment which reflect the nonlinear patterns of changing needs of their constituencies. Therefore a nonlinear function is more suitable for representing public budgetary decisions. We chose the semilog function to represent the satisficing approach to budgeting based on two conditions for human satisfaction: (a) diminishing rate of substitution—the satisfaction derived from consumption of a good increases rapidly at lower initial levels, but later increases at decreasing rates; and (b) no upper bound exists, inasmuch as public needs are unlimited.

IV. ANALYTICAL MODEL

In the accounting and information systems literature we find a third budgetary model we label "analytical." Based on a rational world view, it assumes that accounting information is a rational description of economic reality, and proposes that managers use accounting information to perform a comprehensive examination of all existing programs. These programs are compared to all possible alternative uses of resources in order to maximize the attainment of ex ante organizational goals in accordance with the organization's strategies and policies (Anthony 1965). Consistent with this top-down perspective on budgeting, policies and strategic objectives are formulated at higher levels to devise a global solution to identified goals; at lower levels, these policies and strategies are implemented through local budgets.

The analytical model is represented in the accounting and systems literatures by the rational approach to budgeting (Churchman 1968; Salanick and Pfeffer 1977). According to this approach, the budgeting process follows two stages: first, organizations conduct a thorough environmental scanning, and perform a rational analysis of societal problems; and second, to accomplish a comprehensive resource allocation, they evaluate alternatives and resources available to the organization for coping with diagnosed public needs. When demand for a specific public service changes, the problem is reevaluated and a new budget level is established. Such changes produce distinct leaps in budget levels, either above or below the previous year's levels. The new levels are expected to remain almost constant (assuming relatively stable, formalized objectives as described in Hofstede 1981) until another change in social needs occurs. This rational approach has influenced several trends in public budgeting, such as program planning budgeting systems, zero base budgeting, and management by objectives. Empirical studies on budgeting based on an analytical model provide evidence that accounting information both reflects and helps to shape the environment facing the organization (e.g., Cooper et al. 1981; Boland and Pondy 1983).

In this comparative study, we chose the step function to represent the rational approach to budgeting because it meets the following conditions required by the analytical model: (a) relative independence of budgets from internal factors; (b) shifts in budgetary decisions due to changes in the environment; and (c) stability of the budgetary levels, once these levels have been rationally established.

V. FUNCTIONAL FORMS AND VARIABLES

Previous studies based on the ecological and analytical models use methodologies and produce results that do not allow a direct comparison with studies using the bureaucratic model. In summary, we find three competing models that are used to explain budgetary behavior, and all three have substantial empirical support. Downs and Rocke (1984) provide some insight into how this condition might occur:

Alternative Models of Budgetary Behavior

> One of the chief reasons why progress in resolving theoretical differences takes place slowly in social science is that critical tests capable of evaluating two or more competing theories are so difficult to conduct. Nowhere are the effects of this difficulty more keenly felt than in the area of budgetary decision-making...(Downs and Rocke 1984, 329).

In order to test which of the competing models described in the previous sections best explains budgetary behavior, we selected linear functional forms to represent the bureaucratic model based on existing literature, and specified nonlinear formulations to represent the ecological and analytical models. A summary of the functional forms used in this study appears in Appendix A.[1] The incremental, satisficing and rational functions used to apply the three competing budgetary models are illustrated in Figure 1, based on expenditure data from the departments of public utilities and transportation, fire, and building and safety in the city of Los Angeles.

A. Bureaucratic Model

We selected three functional forms to represent the bureaucratic model, each one using a different linear function to describe budgetary decisions made according to the incremental approach.

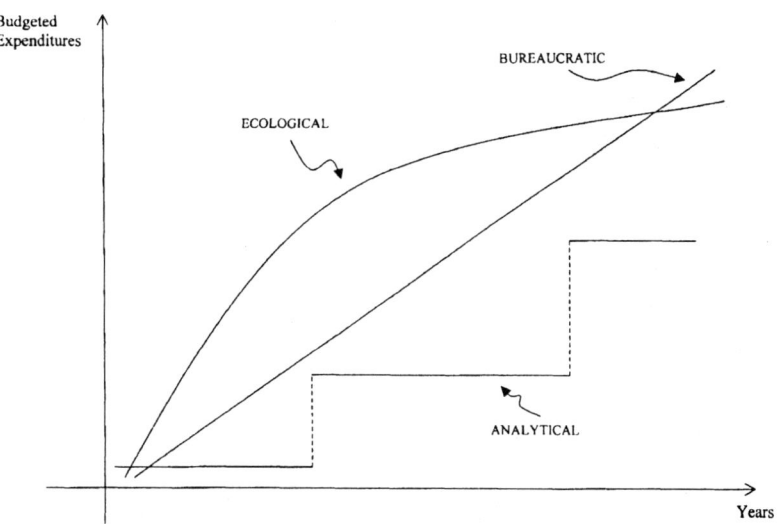

Figure 1. Budgetary Model Illustration

Davis, Dempster, and Wildavsky (DDW)

Davis, Dempster, and Wildavsky (1966, 532-533) proposed that departments set new budgets as if they followed a simple linear function of the previous year's budgeted expenditures (we used actual, rather than budgeted, expenditures).

DDW: $\quad y^*_t = b_1 + b_2 y_{t-1}$ \quad (1)

where: $\quad y^*_t$ is the budgeted expenditure for year t
y_{t-1} is the previous year's actual expenditures.

Wanat Basis for Incrementalism (WBI)

Wanat (1974, 1124-1226) proposed that departments set new budgets as if they followed a linear function of the previous year's budgeted expenditures and the change in actual expenditures during the previous year.

WBI: $\quad y^*_t = b_1 + b_2 y^*_{t-1} + b_3 \Delta y_{t-1}$ \quad (2)

where: $\quad y_{t-1}$ is the previous year's budgeted expenditures
Δy_{t-1} is the increment in actual expenditures from year $t-2$ to year $t-1$.

Constant Growth Revenue Increment (CGRI)

Larkey (1975, 269-271) proposed that departments set new budgets as if they followed a linear function of the previous year's actual expenditures and the expected increment in revenue.

CGRI: $\quad y^*_t = b_1 + b_2 y_{t-1} + b_3 \Delta x^*_t$ \quad (3)

where: $\quad \Delta x^*_t$ is the increment in estimated revenue in year t over actual revenue in year $t-1$

B. Ecological Model

We chose one functional form to represent the ecological model, using the semilog function to describe budgetary decisions made according to the satisficing approach.

Satisficing Bento-White (SBW)

We propose that departments set new budgets as if they followed a nonlinear function of past actual expenditures. Past expenditures are expected to have met some of the social needs in previous years, and those needs are expected to increase at decreasing rates during the following years.

SBW: $\quad y^*_t = b_1 + b_2 \ln y_{t-1}$ (4)

where: $\ln y_{t-1}$ is the Napierian logarithm of actual expenditures of the previous year.

C. Analytical Model

We chose one functional form to represent the analytical model, using the step function to describe budgetary decisions made according to the rational approach.

Rational Bento-White (RBW)

We propose that departments set stable budgets, reflecting policies that have been enacted during a certain period of time, until a change in policy warrants a budgetary change. As described in the methodology section, the step-function formulation used in this study allows for only two shifts in policies in order to facilitate analysis.

RBW: $\quad y^*_t = b_1 p_1 + b_2 p_2 + b_3 p_3$ (5)

where:
p_1 is the policy in effect from year 1 to shift point 1
p_2 is the policy in effect from shift point 1 to shift point 2
p_3 is the policy in effect from shift point 2 to the last year studied.

VI. DATA AND METHODOLOGY

A. Data

Cities in one state (California) were chosen to reduce data collection costs and ensure a certain level of homogeneity in the preparation of budget documents. A total of 68 California cities had populations greater than 50,000, and their governments had 468 departments for which budgetary data were disclosed. A stratified, proportional, random sample of those city departments yielded a total of 91 departments located in 13 cities, representing the seven largest departments in each of these cities.

The departments selected for this study met two criteria: (a) they had no sources of revenue other than the city budget; and (b) excluding mandatory programs and capital expenditure funds, they accounted for most of the city budget (the departments chosen account for over 75% of the total operating funds in the sample cities). These criteria allowed us to focus on the most important departments in each city (the ones with largest budgets), and helped ensure that the selected departments were in existence during the entire study period. A list of departments in the final sample is provided in Appendix B.

Data were collected directly from official adopted budget documents published by the cities (primary sources). For each department in the sample, budget documents were reviewed over the period 1944-1980. Annual data were collected on the amount of budgeted and actual expenditures for each of the 91 departments, and the total amount of budgeted and actual operating funds (revenues) for each of the 13 cities.[2]

B. Methodology

As noted earlier, most empirical studies on public sector budgeting have employed only linear incremental functions to fit the budgetary data. For this study we develop a methodology to test whether the budgetary time series is best explained by a linear or nonlinear function and to identify which particular functional form (among equations (1) through (5) described in the previous section) best fits each department's budgetary decisions. Our methodology is summarized in Figure 2 and explained below.

As Kmenta (1971, 468-469) shows, the hypothesis that a function is linear can be tested by dividing the sample into a number (three should be sufficient) of nonoverlapping subsamples, and then testing whether the slope and intercept estimated for each subsample are significantly different from one subsample to another. The function is assumed linear if the slope and intercepts are essentially the same; and nonlinear otherwise. Davis, Dempster, and Wildavsky's (1966) pioneering study

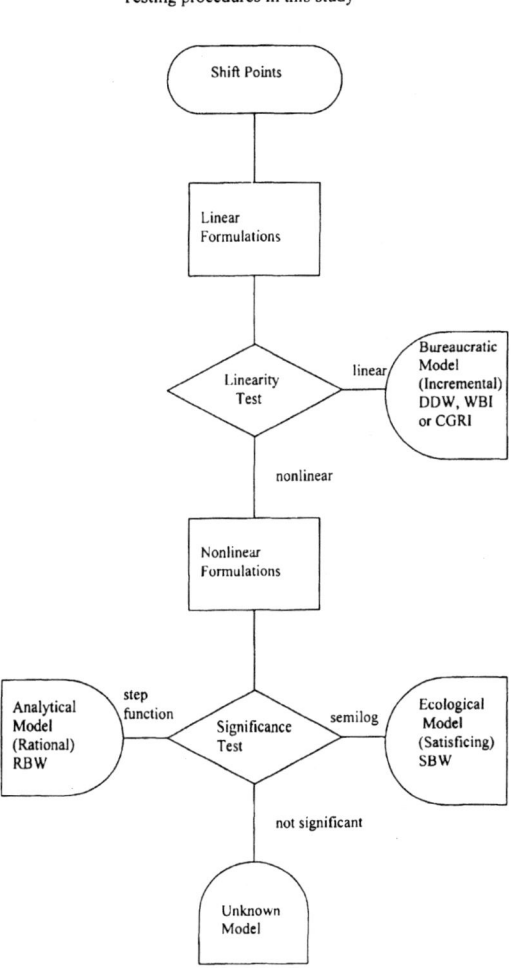

Figure 2. Methodology Flowchart

followed this procedure to test the linearity of budgetary functions, but they used arbitrary points to split the observations into subsamples. Later works disregarded the implications of this procedure until Dempster and Wildavsky applied it again (1986). Given the limited scope of their study (based on data from 53 federal agencies spanning 15 years), it was only possible to find one meaningful shift point in their time series.

One drawback of using arbitrary shift points is that the linearity hypothesis may be rejected when it is true (error Type I), or it may fail to be rejected when the function is actually nonlinear (error Type II). The shift-point method developed for this study addresses this limitation and is described below.

Identifying Shift Points

To find out whether or not a department followed a linear budgetary style we first searched for the most likely points of discontinuity in the time series of budgetary decisions. A shift point is defined here as a point of discontinuity resulting from a major change in public policy. We searched for shift points by moving along the budgetary time series and comparing a local regression line estimated for each observation, with a global regression estimated by using all observations. The local regression line included five observations: the one under consideration as a shift point, and the four observations that preceded it. A confidence interval was constructed around the slope of the global regression line and an observation was considered a potential shift point if the slope of its local regression line was not contained within that confidence interval.

We found that, in a given city, the shift points of the individual departments tended to occur in concentrated periods of time, suggesting that shift points corresponded to years of significant policy changes for that city. For this reason, and given the need to simplify the analysis due to the large volume of data, we identified overall shift points that fit approximately all departments within each city. Following Malinvaud (1964, 270) and Kmenta (1971, 470), two shift points were selected for each city.

Estimating Linear Formulations and Testing for Linearity

The next step involved the estimation of the three linear regression equations—DDW, WBI, and CGRI—for each of the 91 departments. In addition, extended regression equations were estimated for each department (based on Malinvaud 1964, 233-234 and Kmenta 1971, 468-469), to test whether the department's budgetary style is best explained by a linear function. For example, the following extended regression was used to test the linearity of the DDW equations estimated for all departments:

$$y^*_t = b_1 + b_2 y_{t-1} + b_3 z_1 + b_4(z_1 y_{t-1}) + b_5 z_2 + b_6(z_2 y_{t-1}) \qquad (6)$$

where: $z_1 = 1$ if the observation belongs to subsample 1, $= 0$ otherwise;
$z_2 = 1$ if the observation belongs to subsample 2, $= 0$ otherwise;
z_1 and z_2 determined by the shift-point method described above.

Autoregression problems were corrected via second-order autoregressive scheme, which was selected after experimenting with lags ranging from one to five years. F-tests were then performed to compare the explanatory power of the extended regressions with the original linear functional forms DDW, WBI, and CGRI.[3] If the results of the extended regression were significantly different, the department's budgetary style was classified as nonlinear. Otherwise, the department's budgetary style was classified as linear.

Selecting the Best-fitting Linear Functional Forms (DDW, WBI, or CGRI)

In cases where the department's budgetary style was classified as linear, F-tests were used to measure the significance of the estimated linear functional forms (DDW, WBI, and CGRI). For each department, the significant functional form with the highest adjusted R-square was then selected as the best-fitting functional form for that department.

Estimating and Selecting the Best-fitting Nonlinear Functional Forms (SBW, RBW)

In cases where the department's budgetary style was classified as nonlinear, the two nonlinear functional forms (SBW, RBW) were estimated as intrinsically linear formulations by applying the transformations described in Kmenta (1971, 451). The best-fitting nonlinear functional form for each department was selected on the basis of the same criteria used for the linear functions: significant F statistics and the highest adjusted R-squares (after the necessary autoregression transformations had been performed).

Table 1. Frequency Distribution of Budgetary Models Exhibiting the Highest Explanatory Power for a Sample of 91 Departments from 13 California Cities over the Period 1944 to 1980

	Linear				Nonlinear		
	Bureaucratic Model				Ecological Model	Analytical Model	
City	DDW[a]	WBI[b]	CGRI[c]	Total Linear	SBW[d]	RBW[e]	Total Nonlinear
Alameda	0	0	5	5	2	0	2
Alhambra	1	1	1	3	3	1	4
Berkeley	1	1	3	5	1	1	2
Compton	0	1	1	2	3	2	5
Long Beach	2	1	2	5	2	0	2
Los Angeles	0	0	3	3	2	2	4
Oakland	1	0	4	5	2	0	2
Sacramento	0	3	4	7	0	0	0
San Diego	0	1	3	4	2	1	3
San Francisco	1	1	2	4	3	0	3
San Jose	1	1	5	7	0	0	0
Santa Ana	0	0	1	1	4	2	6
Whittier	1	0	3	4	1	2	3
TOTAL	8	10	37	55	25	11	36
% of Total	8.8	11	40.6	60.4	27.5	12.1	39.6

Notes: [a]Davis, Dempster, and Wildavsky : Current budgets are simply a linear function of previous year's actual expenditures.
[b]Wanat Basis for Incrementalism: Current budgets are linear function of previous year's budgeted expenditures and the change in actual expenditures in the previous year.
[c]Constant Growth Revenue Increment: Current budgets are a linear function of previous year's actual expenditures and increases in estimated revenue.
[d]Satisficing Bento - White: Current budgets are a nonlinear (semilog) function of previous year's actual expenditures.
[e]Rational Bento - White: Current budgets remain stable until policies change (step function).

VII. RESULTS

Earlier we proposed that city departments may have significantly different budgetary decision-making styles. This proposition is strongly supported by the results in Table 1, which show that CGRI was the best-fitting functional form in 40.6 percent of the city departments, followed by SBW (27.5%), RBW (12.1%), WBI (11%), and DDW (8.8%).

Overall, 60.4 percent of the departments exhibited budgetary behavior consistent with bureaucratic model, 27.5 percent with the ecological model, and 12.1 percent with the analytical model. To measure the significance of these results, a series of counter-hypotheses were considered and tested against the hypothesis that the three types of budgetary models apply in practice. These counter-hypotheses were then translated into expected frequencies. Using Chi-square tests, we were able to reject all counter-hypotheses at the .001 level of significance.[4]

Table 2. Frequency Distribution of Adjusted R^2 Obtained for Three Best-Fitting Linear Functional Forms Estimated for the 55 City Departments Found to Have a Linear Budgetary Style from a Sample of 91 Departments from 13 California Cities over the Period 1944 to 1980[a]

Range of Adjusted R^2	DDW[b] n	%	WBI[c] n	%	CGRI[d] n	%
0.991 - 1.00	17	31	18	32.7	25	45.5
0.951 - 0.99	21	38.2	22		4015	27.3
0.901 - 0.95	9	16.4	8	14.6	10	18.2
0.851 - 0.90	2	3.6	3	5.5	2	3.6
0.801 - 0.85	2		3.61	1.8	0	–
0.751 - 0.80	2		3.61	1.8	1	1.8
≤ 0.75	2	3.6	2	3.6	2	3.6
TOTALS	55	100%	55	100%	55	100%

Notes: [a]The linearity tests revealed that 55 out of the sample of 91 departments followed a linear budgetary style, as shown in Table 1.
[b]Davis, Dempster, and Wildavsky:
Current budgets are simply a linear function of previous year's actual expenditures.
[c]Wanat Basis for Incrementalism:
Current budgets are linear function of previous year's budgeted expenditures and the change in actual expenditures in the previous year.
[d]Constant Growth Revenue Increment:
Current budgets are a linear function of previous year's actual expenditures and increases in estimated revenue.

As indicated in Table 1, 55 departments were found to have a bureaucratic, linear budgetary style. But the results also indicate that there were significant differences in budgetary behavior, even among those departments that have a linear (incremental) budgetary style.

Table 2 shows the frequency distribution of the adjusted R-square values obtained for the three best-fitting linear functional forms estimated for the 55 departments found to have a linear budgetary style. In over 85 percent of the cases the adjusted R-square is above 0.9, consistent with a very good fit.[5]

A total of 36 city departments were found to have nonlinear budgetary decision-making styles, consistent with either the ecological or analytical models. The results in Table 1 indicate that SBW was the best-fitting nonlinear functional form in 22 of the 36 departments following a nonlinear budgetary style, and provided the second best fit among all functional forms; RBW had the third best fit overall, followed by WBI and DDW.

Table 3 shows the frequency distribution of adjusted R-square values obtained for the SBW and RBW functional forms estimated for the 36 departments which have a nonlinear budgetary style. Unlike the results in Table 2, where the adjusted R-squares were mostly well above 0.9,

Table 3. Frequency Distribution of Adjusted R^2 Obtained for Two Best-Fitting Nonlinear Functional Forms Estimated for the 36 City Departments Found to Have a Nonlinear Budgetary Style from a Sample of 91 Departments from 13 California Cities over the Period 1944 to 1980[a]

Range of Adjusted R^2	SBW[b]		RBW[c]	
	n	%	n	%
0.801 - 0.85	5	13.9	3	8.3
0.751 - 0.80	4	11.1	1	2.8
0.701 - 0.75	2	5.5	–	–
0.651 - 0.70	9	25.0	6	16.8
0.601 - 0.65	2	5.5	2	5.5
0.551 - 0.60	6	16.8	5	13.9
≤ 0.55	8	22.2	19	52.7
TOTALS	36	100%	36	100%

Notes: [a]The linearity tests revealed that 36 out of the sample of 91 departments followed a nonlinear budgetary style, as shown in Table 1.
[b]Satisficing Bento - White:
Current budgets are a nonlinear (semilog) function of previous year's actual expenditures.
[c]Rational Bento - White:
Current budgets remain stable until policies change (step function).

the adjusted R-square values for the nonlinear functional forms did not reach the same levels of goodness of fit. Here, one functional form seemed to be significant for some departments (with adjusted R-squares over 0.8), and clearly not significant for other departments, even within the same city.

Overall, the evidence presented here contradicts results from studies that find that budgetary behavior follows linear (incremental) models. This difference in results may be explained by several factors: (a) unlike previous studies, we use a common methodology to represent each competing budgetary model which allows for a direct test of competing models; (b) we follow extensive procedures to determine potential shift points and to test for linearity; and (c) the scope of our study is much larger than other studies which focus on either a smaller sample of agencies, or a limited test period. The results of this research, however, are consistent with the conclusions reached by Wildavsky (1992), that not all change in policy is incremental and that several budgetary models may apply in practice at any point in time.

Further tests were performed to investigate whether the types of activities performed by the city departments were related to particular models of budgetary behavior. For this analysis, the departments were grouped according to four types of activities: general government (including buildings and city manager), public safety (police, fire), culture and recreation (parks and recreation, library), and infrastructure (public works, health, and sanitation).

The data were analyzed using the best-fitting functional forms obtained for the 91 departments and by pooling those results according to the four types of activities. Table 4 shows that, on average, 60 percent

Table 4. Percentage of City Departments Performing Each Type of Activity Found to Have either a Linear or Nonlinear Budgetary Style for a Sample of 91 Departments from 13 California Cities over the Period 1944 to 1980

Activities	Linear %	Nonlinear %
General Government	68%	32%
Public Safety	43	57
Culture and Recreation	64	36
Infrastructure	74	26
Total: All Departments	60	40

of all departments follow a linear style, and 40 percent follow a nonlinear style. Departments involved with culture and recreation activities tend to fit this average distribution of linear (64%) and nonlinear (36%) styles.

General government and infrastructure departments show more frequent use of linear budgetary styles (68 and 74%, respectively), while public safety departments show a reverse tendency with almost 60 percent following a nonlinear budgetary style and about 40 percent following a linear style.

Some examples can illustrate those differences. In the city of Sacramento the department of public works showed linear budgetary behavior, consistent with functional form WBI, which is based solely on past year's budgeted and actual expenditures, with limited influence from demographic or other environmental changes. On the other hand, the fire department in the city of San Diego, which has experienced explosive population growth in the last decades and the consequent increased risks of fire accidents, has maintained a budgetary style consistent with the RBW functional form (analytical model). According to that model, no new equipment, employees, or facilities are added to the budget until a major change in public needs makes a budgetary change imperative.

VIII. IMPLICATIONS FOR RESEARCH AND PRACTICE

Our results have several theoretical implications. First, the cross-sectional differences in budgetary styles reported in this study raise the question of which factors determine such differences. This research focused on budgetary decisions made within city departments, but further research is needed to investigate the complex relationships between those decisions and the types of environments (social, economic, and political) that influence them.

As discussed earlier, previous studies show that certain environmental factors influence budgetary decisions. Those studies stress the limitations of incrementalism, which focuses solely on budgetary variables and downplays environmental influences. Our results help to reconcile those seemingly conflicting views. On the one hand, the results show that budgetary variables can explain budgetary decisions and help identify particular budgetary styles. On the other hand, the finding that cross-sectional differences in budgetary styles exist, even when based only on budgetary variables, is consistent with the argument that the environment influences budgetary decisions.

Another implication of this study concerns explanations of how budgets are prepared at the local government level, as evidenced by the best-fitting functional forms identified in this research. Functional form CGRI suggests that city departments budget expenditures while taking into consideration the incremental change in revenues, emphasizing that revenues serve as a limiting factor, even for city departments that set budgets incrementally. Functional form CGRI also suggests that city departments consider past actual expenditures when setting new budgets. This may imply a control orientation, which acknowledges that city departments must justify new budgets in light of the actual expenditures necessary to carry out activities in the previous year. This control orientation did not exist in all cities, however. Through interviews during the data collection stage, we found that some cities did not even collect information on actual expenditures for some departments, *because their managers felt that past actual data were simply irrelevant for their budgetary decisions.* Finally, functional form SBW suggests that city departments consider their task to be the satisfaction of public needs. In extreme cases, cities that focus primarily on meeting public needs during times of consistently declining revenues eventually face serious financial difficulties.

While all these explanations of budgetary behavior exist at any point in time, other environmental influences determine which will prevail for each public organization and how the same organization will change budgetary styles in response to major events such as tax reform, demographic shifts, or elections. A budgetary style chosen under certain conditions, for example, continuous revenue growth, may not lead to the desired performance outcomes once conditions change.

Our results also have practical implications for the training of budgeters in the public sector. For decades, the dominance of incrementalism in the budgeting literature directed the attention of practitioners and students of budgeting to the political aspects of budget negotiations, and steered them away from other concerns, such as forecasting revenues, analyzing budget variances, and measuring policy outcomes. We provide further evidence that city governments cannot rely exclusively on an incremental framework for budgetary decisions. For example, in cities with legal requirements for balanced budgets, public officials must address conflicting public needs within the constraints of previous levels of expenditures and expected revenues.

APPENDIX A

Summary of Budgetary Models and Their Corresponding Functions and Functional Forms

Budgetary Model	Function	Functional Forms		
Bureaucratic	Incremental	Linear	1.	DDW (Davis, Dempster and Wildavsky): $y_t^* = b_1 + b_2 y_{t-1}$
		Linear	2.	WBI (Wanat Basis for Incrementalism): $y_t^* = b_1 + b_2 y_{t-1}^* + b_3 \Delta y_{t-1}$
		Linear	3.	CGRI (Constant Growth Revenue Increment): $y_t^* = b_1 + b_2 y_{t-1} + b_3 \Delta x_t^*$
Ecological	Satisficing	Nonlinear (Semilog)	4.	SBW (Satisficing Bento - White): $y_t^* = b_1 + b_2 \ln y_{t-1}$
Analytical	Rational	Nonlinear (Step Function)	5.	RBW (Rational Bento - White): $y_t^* = b_1 p_1 + b_2 p_2 + b_3 p_3$

Where:
y_t^* = Budgeted expenditures for year t.
y_{t-1}^* = Budgeted expenditures for year $t-1$.
y_{t-1} = Actual expenditures for year $t-1$.
Δy_{t-1} = Increment in actual expenditures from year $t-2$ to $t-1$.
Δx_t^* = Increment in estimated revenue of year t over actual revenue in year $t-1$
$\ln y_{t-1}$ = Napierian logarithm of actual expenditures in year $t-1$.
p_1 = Policy in effect from year 1 to shift point 1.
p_2 = Policy in effect from shift point 1 to shift point 2.
p_3 = Policy in effect from shift point 2 to last year studied.

APPENDIX B

Description of Sample: Departments Studied by City

Cities	General Government	Public Safety	Culture and Recreation	Infrastructure
Alameda	Buildings	Police, Fire	Parks & Recreation, Library, Golf	Streets
Alhambra	Buildings	Police, Fire	Parks & Recreation, Library	Streets, Sanitation
Berkeley	City Manager	Police, Fire	Parks & Recreation, Library	Public Works, Health
Compton	Buildings, City Manager	Police, Fire, City Attorney	Parks & Recreation	Public Works
Long Beach	Buildings	Police, Fire	Parks & Recreation, Library	Public Services, Health
Los Angeles	Buildings, Personnel	Police, Fire	Parks & Recreation	Public Works, Public Utilities & Transportaion
Oakland	Buildings, Finance	Police, Fire	Parks & Recreation, Library	Public Works
Sacramento	Buildings, City Manager	Police, Fire	Parks & Recreation, Library	Public Works
San Diego	Buildings	Police, Fire	Parks & Recreation, Library	Streets, Solid Waste
San Francisco		Police, Fire, City Attorney	Parks & Recreation, Library	Public Works, Health
San Jose	Buildings, City Manager	Police, Fire	Parks & Recreation, Library	Public Works
Santa Ana	Buildings, Finance	Police, Fire	Parks & Recreation, Library	Public Works
Whittier	Buildings, City Manager	Police, Fire	Parks & Recreation, Library	Public Works

NOTES

1. Three additional functional forms were tested relating budgetary *changes*, rather than budgetary *levels*, to expected changes in revenues and changes in actual expenditures. These functional forms were either not significant or had adjusted R-squares well below the values obtained for the functional forms reported in this paper.

2. The study period was chosen to ensure that both budgeted and actual data on expenditures were available for all 91 departments and to preserve consistency in budgetary practices through time. We used historical dollar levels because inflation

should *not* be controlled in a comparative study of budgetary decision-making styles, as inflation significantly impacts budgetary decisions by influencing revenues and expenditures differently (Wanat 1974, 1227).

3. The extended regressions and the test statistic used were defined as in Kmenta (1971, 370-371 and 468-470).

4. The following counter-hypotheses were tested: all departments are bureaucratic; all departments are ecological; the results could have been obtained from random numbers chosen between one and three; and all departments have either a bureaucratic or ecological budgetary style, so that the results obtained for the analytical style are due to random error.

5. Given the volume of results generated by approximately 2,000 regressions estimated to perform all the tests, the results are reported as frequency distributions of adjusted R-square values.

REFERENCES

Anthony, R. 1965. *Planning and Control Systems: A Framework for Analysis.* Boston, MA: Harvard University Press.

Behrman, J. R., and S. G. Craig. 1987. The distribution of public services: An exploration of local government preferences. *The American Economic Review* 77: 37-49.

Boland, R., and L. Pondy. 1983. Accounting in organizations: A union of natural and rational perspectives. *Accounting, Organizations and Society* 8: 223-234.

Caiden, N. 1985. The boundaries of public budgeting: Issues for education in tumultuous times. *Public Administration Review*: 495-502.

Churchman, C. 1968. *The Systems Approach.* New York: Dell Publishing.

Conte, A. M., and A. F. Darrat. 1993. Testing alternative views of government budgeting. *Review of Financial Economics* 3 (Fall): 19-40.

Cooper, D. J., D. Hayes, and F. Wolf. 1981. Accounting in organized anarchies: Understanding and designing accounting systems in ambiguous situations. *Accounting, Organizations and Society* 6: 175-191.

Covaleski, M. A., M. W. Dirsmith, and S. Jablonsky. 1985. Traditional and emergent theories of budgeting: An empirical analysis. *Journal of Accounting and Public Policy*: 277-300.

Covaleski, M, A., and M. W. Dirsmith. 1988. The use of budgetary symbols in the political arena: An historically informed field study. *Accounting, Organizations and Society* 13: 1-24.

Crecine, J. P. 1969. *Governmental Problem-Solving: A Computer Simulation of Municipal Budgeting.* Chicago: Rand McNally.

Davis, O., A. Dempster, and A. Wildavsky. 1966. A theory of the budgetary process. *American Political Science Review* 60: 529-547.

Dempster, M. A. H., and A. Wildavsky. 1986. From qualitative to quantitative models. *In Budgeting: A Comparative Theory of Budgetary Processes*, ed. A. Wildavsky, 55-88. New Brunswick NJ; Transaction, Inc.

Downs, W.G., and D. M. Rocke. 1984. Theories of budgetary decisionmaking and revenue decline. *Policy Sciences* 16: 329-347.

Duncombe, W. 1996. Public expenditure research: What have we learned? *Public Budgeting & Finance* 16 (Summer): 26-59.

Giroux, G., A. Mayper, and R. Daft. 1986. Organization size, budget cycle, and budget related influence in city governments: An empirical study. *Accounting, Organizations and Society* 11: 47-64.

Giroux, G., and D. Shields. 1993. Accounting control and bureaucratic strategies in municipal government. *Journal of Accounting and Public Policy* 12: 239-262.

Hofstede. 1981. Management control of public and not-for-profit activities. *Accounting, Organizations and Society* 6: 193-211.

Inman, R. 1979. The fiscal performance of local governments: An interpretive review. *In Current Issues in Urban Economics*, eds. P. Mieszkowski and M. Straszheim, 270-321. Baltimore MD; John Hopkins University Press.

Kmenta, J. 1971. *Elements of Econometrics*. New York: Macmillan.

Larkey, P. D. 1975. Process models and program evaluation: The impact of the general revenue sharing on municipal fiscal behavior. Ph.D. dissertation, University of Michigan.

———. 1979. *Evaluating Public Programs*. Princeton, N.J.: Princeton University Press.

Malinvaud, E. 1964. *Methods Statistiques de l'Econometrie*. Paris: Dunod.

Rubin, S. I. 1989. Aaron Wildavsky and the demise of incrementalism. *Public Administration Review* 49: 78-81.

———. 1990. Budget theory and budget practice: How good the fit? *Public Administration Review* 50 (March/April): 179-189.

Salanick, G., and J. Pfeffer. 1977. Constraints on administrator discretion. *Urban Affairs Quarterly* 12 (4)

Simon, H. 1957. *Administrative Behavior*. New York: Free Press.

Todd, R., and K. V. Ramanathan. 1994. Perceived social needs, outcomes measurement, and budgetary responsiveness in a not-for-profit setting: Some empirical evidence. *The Accounting Review* 69 (January): 122-137.

Wanat, J. 1974. Bases of budgetary incrementalism. *American Political Science Review* 68: 1221-1228.

Weber, M. 1946. *From Max Weber, Essays in Sociology*, trans and eds. by H. H. Gerth and C. W. Mills, 196-264. New York: Oxford University Press.

Wildavsky, A. 1964. *The Politics of the Budgetary Process*. Boston,MA: Little Brown.

———. 1992. Political implications of budget reform: A retrospective. *Public Administration Review* 52: 594-603.

AN ANALYSIS OF CROSS-SECTIONAL VARIATION IN THE RATE OF FINANCIAL RATIO ADJUSTMENT BY CITY GOVERNMENTS

Paul A. Copley and Sharon S. Seay

ABSTRACT

We analyze operating ratios for a comprehensive sample of city governments for the period 1973 to 1991 for the purpose of determining whether municipal governments adjust their financial ratios to governmental norms. Using a partial adjustment model we estimate the extent to which each municipality adjusts its ratios to national averages. Our analysis indicates that, similar to private sector corporations, municipal governments adjust their ratios toward predetermined levels based on industry norms. Also similar to the private sector, governments vary (cross-sectionally) in the degree to which they adjust financial ratios (i.e., the rate of adjustment). Using the coefficients estimated from the partial adjustment model, we examine the relation between these rates of adjustment and city-specific factors which previous research indicates are associated with public sector financial reporting practices. Our results suggest that factors such as regulation, political competition, and growth in debt financing contribute to the observed variations in the rates of adjustment.

I. INTRODUCTION

Within the private sector, empirical evidence by Lev (1969), Frecka and Lee (1983), Lee and Wu (1988), Fieldsend, Longford, and McLeay (1987), and Tippett (1990) generally indicates that firms adjust their financial ratios to industry norms. The mechanisms used to effect this adjustment are attributable to passive industry-wide effects operating on the firm as well as active attempts by management (Frecka and Lee 1983). Ratio adjustment is relevant to accounting policy setters because accounting standards affect many of the mechanisms available to management to adjust ratios (Lev 1969). These include discretionary accruals, accounting estimates, and the choice of accounting procedures from available alternatives.

Bond analysts and rating agencies, commercial investors, legislative and oversight bodies, and others (e.g., interests groups and political rivals) use financial ratios computed from governmental financial reports. Recognizing the importance of these ratios, incentives exist for government officials to manage the levels of ratios through a variety of fiscal and financial policies. In contrast to the private sector, few empirical studies examine ratio adjustment by governmental entities, particularly using large samples. The first objective of our study is to determine whether the ratios of municipal governments adjust to national norms. This analysis is performed on a comprehensive sample of U.S. city governments over a 19-year period beginning in 1973.

Lev (1969) is the earliest study to examine whether firms adjust their financial ratios to predetermined targets. Subsequent studies by Frecka and Lee (1983), Lee and Wu (1988), and Tung and Crowe (1993) focus on methodological issues regarding model estimation.

Two outcomes are common to all of these studies. First, there is empirical evidence that firms adjust a variety of ratios to industry averages. Second, cross-sectional variation exists among firms in the rate of adjustment.[1] In response to the presence of this cross-sectional variation, Lee and Wu (1988, 306) suggest that future research "...examine whether firm-specific factors...contribute to the variations in adaptation." This is the second objective of our study. Specifically, we examine the relation between the ratio adjustment coefficients and city-specific factors which previous research indicates are important determinants of governmental financial reporting practices and which reflect cross-sectional differences in the incentives and ability of government officials to adjust performance measures. This is the first study, in either the public or private sector, to evaluate the determinants of the rate of adjustment.

We find that city government financial ratios adjust toward national norms. Additionally, we find that city specific factors, such as regulation, political competition, growth in debt financing, and size are related to the rate of adjustment. Together our findings have important implications for research into public sector accounting issues. Historically, governmental accounting research is hindered by the absence of performance measures (such as net income in the private sector) suitable for evaluating the incentives of management in accounting choice decisions. Our results suggest that government financial ratios and the extent to which they deviate from national norms may provide a basis from which to evaluate management incentives related to specific accounting choices.

In the following section we describe the processes by which governmental managers might adjust financial ratios. Additionally, we propose that the lack of widely accepted financial performance measures provides a reasonable expectation for government officials to use governmental norms as targets. Section three describes a longitudinal model related to our first objective, determining whether municipal ratios adjust to governmental norms. Section four describes a cross-sectional model related to our second objective, examining factors relating to differences between governments in the rate adjustment. The final three sections present our empirical findings and conclusions.

II. GOVERNMENTAL NORMS AS TARGETS

A. Existing Evidence

Evidence, primarily from surveys, exists that government managers actively adjust financial performance measures. Peterson (1990) surveyed city governments to determine the mechanisms used to correct budget imbalances. Raising fees and charges was the most frequently employed action. Additional measures included raising property tax rates, reducing the growth rate of operating expenditures, and contracting out services.

In addition to these fiscal adjustment mechanisms, governmental accounting practices provide considerable opportunity for manipulation of operating ratios. Unlike the private sector, governments receive significant resources in non-exchange transactions (e.g., taxes, grants, and donations). The absence of an identifiable exchange introduces ambiguity into the appropriate timing of the recognition of revenue items. Additionally, significant latitude exists within current governmental accounting standards in the recognition of expenditures. For example, pension expenditures are determined by the amount funded, rather that by the increase in the estimated liability. Hence, governments can reduce reported expenditures by cutting pension funding.[2]

Evidence exists to suggest that government officials opportunistically recognize revenues and expenditures to comply with predetermined targets. However, most of the existing evidence deals with state rather than local governments. For example, the U.S. General Accounting Office reports that:

- During the 1982-1983 biennium, Minnesota changed the method used to recognize property tax revenues, providing earlier recognition (GAO 1985, 76).
- In 1981 the Michigan legislature approved a law allowing the state to remain on a cash accounting basis for state Medicaid accounts, reducing the reported budget imbalance by $120 million (GAO 1985, 72).

Chaney, Copley, and Stone (1998) find evidence that states underfund their pensions to comply with predetermined budgetary targets. Additionally they find that these governments select accounting estimates (i.e., discount rates) which reduce the appearance of underfunding.

To our knowledge, Marks and Raman (1996) is the only study to examine whether local (i.e., city) governments adjust their ratios to industry averages. They examine financial ratios of the 40 largest U.S. cities and compute rates of adjustment to average values for the sample. Their results indicate that governments adjust their ratios to industry norms and that the rate of adjustment is higher for ratios reflecting operating activities. Our study represents a replication of Marks and Raman to a larger sample of governments. Additionally, we extend earlier ratio adjustment studies by examining the relations between entity characteristics and the rate of ratio adjustment.

B. Choice of Ratios

We select two operating ratios for consideration: Total Revenue/General Expenditures (TR/GE) and Local Revenue/General Expenditures (LR/GE). Total revenues are revenues from all sources, but do not include the proceeds from issuance of long-term debt. Local revenues are total revenues less intergovernmental revenue (revenue received from the federal and state government) and include property taxes, sales taxes, and service fees. General expenditures are all expenditures other than capital expenditures and payment of principal on long-term debt. Values less than 1.0 for TR/GE suggest that the government is financing a portion of current operations from prior surpluses or the issuance of debt. Values greater than 1.0 are necessary if capital expenditures are to be at least partially funded from current revenues. LR/GE provides a measure of the extent to which general expenditures are funded by locally derived (rather than intergovernmental) revenue.

A characteristic of the governmental sector is that the desired levels for these ratios are determined by balancing the opposing interests of different parties. High values for either of these two ratios are likely to be viewed negatively by current taxpayers who may feel they are paying too large a portion of the costs of government services and capital expenditures. Politicians, seeking to appease voters, have an incentive to defer the cost of current services to future periods (Epple and Schipper 1981). However, operating deficits, the use of long-term debt for operating purposes, and a decline in funding for capital expenditures indicate potential financial difficulties (Municipal Finance Officers

Association 1978) and are viewed negatively by bond analysts, commercial investors, and oversight agencies. Similarly, investors are likely to view reliance on intergovernmental revenues to fund current operations with concern, particularly as state and federal resources become constrained.

It is also apparent that the average levels for these ratios are likely to change with economic and political conditions. In periods of economic decline, local revenues fall while the demand for government services increases (Esser 1992). Variation in interest rates affects the costs of financing operating deficits and capital expenditures with debt. Changing political conditions at the state and federal level can affect the availability of intergovernmental grants. Given the lack of widely accepted financial performance guidelines and the effect of changing conditions, governmental norms may serve as reasonable targets for government officials. In the next section we describe a model which estimates the extent to which city governments adjust performance ratios to national averages.

III. LONGITUDINAL ANALYSIS: PARTIAL ADJUSTMENT MODEL

The partial adjustment model shown below depicts the ratio adjustment process:

$$y_t - y_{t-1} = \alpha + \lambda(y_t^* - y_{t-1}) + e \qquad 0 \leq \lambda \leq 1 \qquad (1)$$

where:
- y_t = a municipal government's financial ratio in period t,
- y_{t-1} = a municipal government's financial ratio in period $t-1$,
- y_t^* = the target level of a particular ratio, and
- λ = the speed of adjustment coefficient.

Equation (1) states that the current level of a financial ratio, y_t, will move partially from its previous position, y_{t-1}, to the desired target level, y_t^*. The amount of adjustment between the two time periods, t and $t-1$, is equal to $\lambda(y_t^* - y_{t-1})$, where the fraction λ measures the speed of adjustment. Lev (1969), and Frecka and Lee (1983) apply the partial adjustment model to the adjustment of financial ratios.[3] They assume y_t^* is the industry norm (mean) of a particular financial ratio.

Applying this model to the public sector, we propose that government officials observe the extent of deviations between the level of their municipality's financial ratios and national norms ($y_t^*-y_{t-1}$). In response to such deviations, officials adjust the municipality's ratio in the period t so that the observed deviation will be partially eliminated. We use the current year's mean as the target. This assumes that while the current year's average cannot be known in advance, managers are able to anticipate changes in average levels. Empirical support for this is provided by Lev (1969) and Marks and Raman (1996) who find higher R-squares for partial adjustment models using current year averages (rather than previous year averages) as targets. The speed of adjustment is represented by λ; the closer λ is to 1, the faster the periodic adjustment. The size of λ reflects the limitations to the periodic adjustment of y caused by institutional constraints.

Economists (Cagan 1956; Friedman 1957; Nerlove 1958) rationalize the extent of partial adjustment in terms of two opposing costs: (a) the cost of adjustment and (b) the cost of being out of equilibrium. The former often results from the technological, institutional, and psychological inertia, as well as the increasing cost of rapid change. The cost of adjustment reflects the degree of difficulty in a quick adjustment of the financial ratio to a predetermined target. The cost of being out of equilibrium reflects the importance to the government of the conformity of a ratio with a target. These costs vary across governments with differing financial, political and regulatory characteristics. Consequently, the speed of adjustment (λ) of a ratio to a target level will depend on the relative significance of these two costs and is expected to vary cross-sectionally.

IV. CROSS-SECTIONAL ANALYSIS: RATE OF ADJUSTMENT MODEL

In this section we develop a model which relates the rate of ratio adjustment to factors reflecting a government's competitive (political) and regulatory environment, form of government, and size of the municipality. In doing so, we consider the incentives of government officials to adjust financial ratios toward national norms. We also consider differences in the ability of officials to adjust financial ratios. These are reflected in the following conceptual model:

$$\text{Rate of Adjustment} = f(\text{Competition, Form of Government, State Regulation, Size}). \quad (2)$$

Arguments supporting the conceptual model relate to the signaling and monitoring paradigm applied to public sector accounting and reporting issues by Evans and Patton (1987). Empirical evidence of the determinants of local government reporting practices also supports the model (see Baber 1994 for a summary of the empirical evidence).

A. Competition

It is assumed that politicians maximize their wealth by enhancing the likelihood of election and advancement. Baber (1983) argues that elected officials seek the support of interest groups to win elections and provide monitoring (accounting and auditing) to demonstrate their execution of preelection promises. Further, the incentives to seek and retain the support of interest groups through financial reporting increase with political competition.

In addition to the monitoring role of accounting information, Evans and Patton (1987) argue that financial information is used to communicate (signal) efficiency to parties outside the government who provide resources to finance government activities. Evans and Patton focus on the debt market, but Baber (1994) argues that the signaling incentives relate to other resource providers including commercial investors and mobile taxpayers (Tiebout 1956). Government efficiency is a concern to commercial enterprises who provide large amounts of taxes and whose operations are affected by the cost and quality of public services. Yinger (1982) argues that government performance is also a concern to homeowners since local government fiscal variables are capitalized into local property values. Epple and Schipper (1981) provide some evidence of this in their finding that unfunded pension obligations are capitalized into housing values. If property values reflect fiscal performance, then the incentives to monitor governmental performance should increase with the average home value, since owners of high-value property have relatively more at stake.

Baber (1994) categorizes political competition into: (1) intra-coalition competition, competition arising from within the governing coalition, (2) inter-coalition competition, competition between incumbent and challenging coalitions, and (3) intergovernmental competition, competition among governments for lenders and investors. Election outcomes, as proxies for intra-coalition and inter-coalition competition, are significantly related to the financial reporting practices of governments (Baber and Sen 1984; Ingram 1984; Carpenter 1991). To date, existing investigations of the effects of intergovernmental competition are largely confined to measures of outstanding debt (Baber and Sen 1984; Evans and Patton 1987; Carpenter 1991) and report significant relations between debt and governmental reporting practices. Financial ratios provide information which may be used to evaluate the performance of elected officials. Deviation from expectations (e.g., national norms) imposes costs on politicians because it increases the likelihood that the elected official will lose the support of taxpayer groups or fail to attract and retain prospective and current resource providers. Either outcome increases the likelihood that political rivals will enter the election and commit the resources that are required to effectively compete for election (Baber 1990). Therefore, elected officials have incentives to adjust performance measures toward expectations and these incentives increase with political competition.

Ingram and Copeland (1981) provide empirical support for this in their finding that city government financial ratios are associated with voting decisions in mayoral elections. While bond analysts and commercial investors have the expertise to obtain and analyze municipal financial reports, it is doubtful whether the same is true of individual voters (Copley et al. 1997). However, voters have a variety of means of becoming informed. The press, together with taxpayer advocacy and other interest groups, provide information on government performance. Additionally, voters become aware of the consequences of elected officials' fiscal policies in the level of services received, taxes paid, and impact on property values.

In summary, we propose that government officials adjust performance ratios toward national norms to signal efficiency to present and potential taxpayers, commercial employers, and bond investors. Governments with relatively high political competition, governments with relatively high property values, and governments issuing relatively more debt will adjust their ratios more rapidly.

B. State Regulation

State governments transfer funds to local municipalities and impose specific restrictions as to how these funds are to be used. Local officials have incentives to use the funds in a manner that benefits their constituency but which may be inconsistent with the preferences of state officials. One way that states restrict the ability of local officials to misuse these funds is to regulate local government accounting and reporting practices (Ingram and DeJong 1987).

The nature of these regulations vary from state to state. Frequently, these requirements are intended to separate current appropriates from those of other periods and involve policies affecting the recognition of revenues, expenditures, and encumbrances (Ingram and DeJong 1987, 252). While many states require compliance with GAAP principles, others require local governments to report on the cash basis. Since the choice of accounting procedures is a mechanism that managers can use to adjust financial ratios, regulation which restricts choice will reduce the ability of managers to adjust to target levels.[4] Accordingly, we predict that municipalities in states which regulate local government accounting will adjust less rapidly to government norms.

C. Form of Government

Municipal governments operate under two forms of administration; the mayoral form where an elected official has day-to-day control over the operations of the government and the city manager form where this responsibility is delegated to a professional manager who reports to the elected council. Being elected officials, mayors are more likely to be concerned with the political consequences of deviating from performance expectations. Because of this difference in incentives and the fact that under the mayoral form elected officials have greater control over the financial operations, we predict that cities operating under a mayoral form of government will adjust to national norms more rapidly than cities operating under a city manager.

D. Size of Government

Size of the government is included primarily as a control variable since large entities require adjustments of greater magnitude to affect ratio levels. It is also conceivable that larger entities have less incentive to adjust to industry norms. Large municipalities receive more attention from the business press, bond analysts, and oversight bodies. Additionally, larger entities have greater resources available to generate and provide financial information. In such an environment, industry norms are relatively less important as target levels for performance evaluation, since performance can be effectively communicated by other means. Consequently, we expect that larger municipalities will adjust ratios less rapidly to national norms.

Conceptually, the rate of partial adjustment is determined by the cost of adjustment and the cost of being out of equilibrium. The factors we identify above reflect these two costs. Specifically, the importance (cost of being out of equilibrium) to the political manager of the conformity of a ratio with a target increases with political competition. State regulation increases the cost of adjustment since in imposes institutional constraints on the mechanisms available for adjustment. Size and form of the government have elements relating to both these costs.

V. EMPIRICAL RESULTS: LONGITUDINAL ANALYSIS

Revenue and expenditure amounts are obtained from the U.S. Bureau of Census *Annual Survey of Governments: Finance Statistics* for the years 1973 to 1991. The *Annual Survey of Governments* provides financial information for all U.S. cities with populations greater than 25,000.[5] Descriptive statistics for the two ratios appear in Table 1. A *t*-test for differences in mean values of consecutive years for these ratios is significant (p-value < .05) for both ratios in 12 of the 18 pairings, indicating that national norms change over time, possibly with changes in economic and political conditions.

We apply the partial adjustment model using the Marquardt nonlinear least squares regression method to estimate the structural parameters, α and λ. This method combines the features of both the Gauss-Newton and steepest descent nonlinear least-squares procedures and often reaches convergence when Gauss-Newton may not. The Marquardt method considers both direction and distance in computing parameter estimates.

While Lev (1969) and Frecka and Lee (1983) apply the partial adjustment model to the adjustment of financial ratios, Lee and Wu (1988) introduce adaptive expectations into the partial adjustment model. Their model estimates two parameters: λ, the speed of adjustment, and δ, the proportion of the change in the target considered to be permanent rather than transitory. However the coefficients (λ and δ) occur

Table 1. Descriptive Statistics: Operating Ratios During the Period 1973 to 1991 for Samples of City Governments with Populations Greater than 25,000

Year	Total Revenues^a/General Expenditures^b		Local Revenues^c/General Expenditures^b	
	Mean (n = 746)	Standard Deviation	Mean (n = 754)	Standard Deviation
1973	1.481	.30	1.093	.40
1974	1.556*	.33	1.076*	.28
1975	1.486*	.29	1.032*	.25
1976	1.486	.29	1.020	.24
1977	1.343*	.28	0.973*	.52
1978	1.432*	.31	1.038*	.55
1979	1.407	.29	0.991*	.25
1980	1.377*	.26	1.001*	.25
1981	1.349*	.28	0.990*	.27
1982	1.254*	.26	0.939*	.26
1983	1.257	.22	0.969	.24
1984	1.263	25	0.993	.36
1985	1.293*	.21	0.983	.25
1986	1.264*	.22	0.956*	.24
1987	1.235*	.19	0.971*	.23
1988	1.203*	.17	0.965*	.21
1989	1.212	.16	0.978	.22
1990	1.211	.16	0.978	.21
1991	1.191*	.15	0.957*	.20
All Years	1.332	.27	0.995	.31

Notes: * Indicates that value is significantly different from previous year's mean ($p < .05$, t-test).
^{a} Total revenues are revenues from all sources, but do not include the proceeds from issuance of long-term debt.
^{b} General expenditures are all expenditures other than capital expenditures and payment of principal on long-term debt.
^{c} Local revenues are total revenues less revenue received from the federal and state government.

symmetrically in this model producing ambiguity in the parameter estimates (Maddala 1988). Lee and Wu (1988) and Tung and Crowe (1993) report weak results regarding the presence of expectation adjustment lag, suggesting that firms either do not adjust target levels or adjust targets to their industry averages instantly, in which case, financial ratio adjustment follows a simple partial adjustment process. For this reason, we chose to utilize the less complex partial adjustment model.[6]

We obtained estimates of the rates of adjustment ($\hat{\lambda}$) over this 18-year period for the two ratios using equation (1). These are summarized in Table 2. The magnitude of $\hat{\lambda}$ reflects the speed of adjustment

Table 2. Estimated Financial Ratio Adjustment Coefficients for Samples of City Governments with Populations Greater than 25,000, Estimated Over the Period 1973 to 1991 using the Partial Adjustment Model

	Intercept α		Rate of Adjustment (λ)[a]	
Ratio:	Estm.	t-stat.[b]	Estm.	t-stat.[b]
Panel A Total Revenues/General Expenditures				
Mean ($n = 746$)	−0.0026	−0.3657	0.6783	3.2831
Standard Deviation	0.1007	1.8399	0.2680	1.2510
Means by Decile of λ:				
First	−0.0162	−0.5863	0.2242	1.3753
Second	0.0023	−0.2310	0.4030	2.2479
Third	0.0033	−0.2448	0.4888	2.5489
Fourth	0.0097	−0.3994	0.5744	2.8467
Fifth	0.0026	−0.4086	0.6362	3.1528
Sixth	−0.0056	−0.4254	0.7079	3.2736
Seventh	0.0111	−0.2452	0.7803	3.7240
Eighth	−0.0139	−0.5671	0.8628	4.0417
Ninth	0.0039	−0.3268	0.9764	4.3766
Tenth	0.0041	−0.1796	1.1606	5.4460
Panel B Local Revenues/General Expenditures:				
Mean ($n = 754$)	0.0050	−0.1038	0.6142	3.0445
Standard Deviation	0.1326	2.1691	0.2737	3.4845
Means by Decile of λ:				
First	−0.0179	−0.3968	0.1827	1.2526
Second	−0.0071	−0.2763	0.3091	1.8239
Third	−0.0053	−0.1762	0.4027	2.1883
Fourth	−0.0060	−0.2492	0.4842	2.4818
Fifth	0.0037	−0.1892	0.5650	2.8106
Sixth	−0.0032	−0.1868	0.6452	3.0436
Seventh	0.0293	0.5545	0.7297	3.3271
Eighth	0.0149	0.0366	0.8182	3.6568
Ninth	0.0117	0.1211	0.9202	5.2082
Tenth	0.0402	−0.1600	1.1006	5.8795

Notes: a. The rate of adjustment (to the sample mean) is the coefficient, λ, from the partial adjustment model. Both λ and the intercept are estimated from equation (1) over the period 1973 to 1991.
b. T-statistics greater than 1.753 are significant at $p < .05$ (two-tail).

to the target (mean) ratio. The closer $\hat{\lambda}$ is to 1.0, the faster the rate of adjustment. A $\hat{\lambda}$ of 1.0 implies complete adjustment to the target. When $\hat{\lambda}$ is less than 1.0, a partial adjustment to the desired target is achieved. We find that the estimated coefficients of partial adjustment, $\hat{\lambda}$, fall into the theoretical range of 0 to 1.0 for 86 percent of the sample for the ratio: Total Revenues/General Expenditures (panel

A) and for 90 percent of the sample for the ratio: Local Revenues/ General Expenditures (panel B).[7]

For comparative purposes we calculated $\hat{\lambda}$ for a ratio in which there is less expectation that governmental managers will adjust to national norms.[8] It is difficult to identify a ratio that perfectly meets this characteristic and is likely to be meaningful. However, we selected the ratio of property tax revenue to total revenues. While this ratio can be adjusted, it is very likely that *national* norms are not viewed as the appropriate target. This is because property tax rates are regulated by state law.[9] Estimates for the rate of adjustment for this ratio were computed in the same manner as before. Interestingly, nearly 30 percent of the coefficients of the rate of adjustment ($\hat{\lambda}$) for the ratio, property taxes/total revenues, were not significantly different than zero at the .05 level. This compares with only 8 percent for TR/GE and 16 percent for LR/GE.

In summary, the results of our longitudinal analysis indicate that municipalities adjust their ratios to the national average (target), supporting the findings of Marks and Raman (1996). Additionally, we observe significant cross-sectional variation among the sample municipalities in the rate of adjustment. In the next section we examine whether this variation in the rate of adjustment is related to city-specific characteristics.

VI. EMPIRICAL RESULTS: CROSS-SECTIONAL ANALYSIS

In this section we operationalize the conceptual model presented in equation (2) and present the empirical findings. Specifically we test the following model:

$$\text{RATE OF ADJUSTMENT} = \beta_0 + \beta_1 \text{ MAYOR\_TURN} +$$
$$(+)$$
$$\beta_2 \ln(\text{HOME\_VALUE}) + \beta_3 \text{ DEBT\_GROWTH} +$$
$$(+) \qquad\qquad (+)$$
$$\beta_4 \text{ MAYOR} + \beta_5 \text{ STATE\_REGUL} + \beta_6 \ln(\text{POPULATION}) + \varepsilon$$
$$(+) \qquad\qquad (-) \qquad\qquad (-) \qquad\qquad (3)$$

The dependent variable, RATE OF ADJUSTMENT, is the estimated coefficient, $\hat{\lambda}$, from the partial adjustment model (equation (1)). MAYOR_TURN is a discrete variable indicating the number of times between 1973 and 1991 that the mayor failed to be reelected in the subsequent election; ln(HOME_VALUE) is the natural logarithm of the median value of owner-occupied housing; DEBT_GROWTH is long-term debt outstanding at the end of 1991 divided by long-term debt outstanding at the beginning of 1974; MAYOR is a dichotomous variable assuming the value of one for a mayoral form of government and zero for a city manager form; STATE_REGUL is a dichotomous variable assuming the value of one if the state regulates local government accounting practices (zero otherwise); and Ln(POPULATION) is the natural logarithm of the city's population (1982). The hypothesized directions of the relations between the rate of adjustment and the independent variables appear in parentheses under the variables in equation (3).

While the rate of adjustment is estimated over a period of 19 years, the independent variables represent characteristics of a government which are subject to change over time. MAYOR_TURN and DEBT_GROWTH could be effectively measured over the entire time period. For the remaining variables, our approach is to measure these variables as close to the midpoint (1982) as possible, given data availability. DEBT_GROWTH and Ln(POPULATION) are computed from data available in the *Annual Survey of Governments*. Median value of owner occupied housing is found in *County and City Data Book* (U.S. Bureau of Census 1982). The form of government (MAYOR) and existence of state regulations (STATE_REGUL) are taken from surveys: Ingram and Robbins (1985) and the National Association of State Auditors, Comptrollers, and Treasurers (1986), respectively.[10] We proxy political competition with turnover of the chief elected official (Copley, Gaver, and Gaver 1995). While such a measure is likely to be correlated with the level of political competition within a given government, it does not distinguish between intra-coalition and inter-coalition competition (Baber 1994).[11] Turnover is determined through comparisons of directories of city policy officials (National League of Cities 1973-1991). Similar to other studies (Baber 1994), incentives related to intergovernmental competition for financial resources are proxied by growth in outstanding debt.

Complete information is available for 178 and 179 city governments (respectively for the two ratios), all of which have populations in excess

Table 3. Descriptive Statistics for a Sample of 179 City Governments with Populations Greater than 50,000 between 1973 and 1991

Continuous Measures	Mean	Standard Deviation	Minimum	Maximum
MAYOR_TURN[a] (#)	3.17	1.23	0	5
HOME_VALUE[b]	55,600	31,400	15,800	200,000
DEBT_GROWTH[c] (%)	8.80	17.35	0	206.78
POPULATION[d]	206,000	302,000	50,000	2,992,000
RATE OF ADJUSTMENT[e], λ_a	0.674	0.258	−0.029	1.331
RATE OF ADJUSTMENT[f], λ_b	0.594	0.282	0.020	1.219
Categorical Measures	Frequency	Percentage		
STATE_REGUL[g]	131	73.2		
MAYOR[h]	104	58.1		

Notes: a A discrete variable indicating the number of times the incumbent mayor failed to be re-elected in the subsequent election during the period 1973 to 1991.

b Logarithm of the median value of owner occupied housing (1982).

c A quantitative variable (Long-term Debt Outstanding 1991/Long-term Debt Outstanding 1973).

d Logarithm of the population of the municipality (1982).

e Estimated coefficient, $\hat{\lambda}$, from the partial adjustment model (equation (1)) representing the rate of adjustment of the ratio, (total revenues/general expenditures), to the mean value for all U.S. municipalities with populations in excess of 50,000. ($n = 178$)

f Estimated coefficient, $\hat{\lambda}$, from the partial adjustment model (equation (1)) representing the rate of adjustment of the ratio, (local revenues/general expenditures), to the mean value for all U.S. municipalities with populations in excess of 50,000.

g A qualitative variable indicating whether the form of government is mayoral (1) or city manager (0).

h. A qualitative variable indicating that the state government regulates local government accounting practices.

of 50,000. For this reason, we reestimate the ratio means and rates of adjustment based on the 427 cities in the *Annual Survey of Governments* with populations greater than 50,000. The estimated rate of adjustment coefficients, $\hat{\lambda}$, from this sample are used as the dependent variable in equation (3).[12] Table 3 presents descriptive statistics for the variables in equation (3).

A. Regression Results

Ordinary least-squares estimates of equation (3), test statistics, and the related two-tailed probabilities appear in Table 4. Regression diagnostics (Belsley, Kuh, and Welsch 1980) suggest that the results are not affected by influential observations or linear dependencies among the variables. In panel A we examine the rate of adjustment for the ratio of

Table 4. OLS Parameter Estimates of a Model of the Rate of Financial Ratio Adjustment[a] During the Period 1973 to 1991 for Samples of City Governments with Populations Greater than 50,000

Predictor Variables	Expected Sign	Coefficient	Std. Error	t-statistic	P-Value (two-tail)
Panel A (n = 178) Ratio: Total Revenues/General Expenditures					
Intercept		1.2402	0.538	2.306	0.0223
MAYOR_TURN[b]	+	−0.0009	0.016	−0.053	0.9580
ln(HOME_VALUE)[c]	+	0.0002	0.042	0.005	0.9957
DEBT_GROWTH[d]	+	0.0025	0.001	2.236	0.0267
MAYOR[e]	+	0.0292	0.042	0.698	0.4861
STATE_REGUL[f]	−	−0.0978	0.044	−2.221	0.0277
ln(POPULATION)[g]	−	−0.0453	0.024	−1.923	0.0561
Model F-statistic (p-value): 2.937 (0.0143) Adjusted R-square: 0.0712					
Panel B (n = 179) Ratio: Local Revenues/General Expenditures					
Intercept		−0.0402	0.579	−0.069	0.9448
MAYOR_TURN[b]	+	0.0293	0.018	1.674	0.0960
ln(HOME_VALUE)[c]	+	0.0940	0.045	2.069	0.0400
DEBT_GROWTH[d]	+	0.0024	0.001	1.967	0.0508
MAYOR[e]	+	0.0708	0.045	1.575	0.1172
STATE_REGUL[f]	−	−0.0488	0.048	−1.027	0.3059
ln(POPULATION)[g]	−	−0.0424	0.025	−1.673	0.0962
Model F-statistic (p-value): 3.058 (0.0113) Adjusted R-square: 0.0984					

Notes: a The dependent variable, RATE OF ADJUSTMENT is the estimated coefficient, $\hat{\lambda}$, from the partial adjustment model (equation 1).
b A discrete variable indicating the number of times the incumbent mayor failed to be reelected in the subsequent election during the period 1973 to 1991.
c Logarithm of the median value of owner occupied housing (1982).
d A quantitative variable (Long-term Debt Outstanding 1991/Long-term Debt Outstanding 1973).
e A qualitative variable indicating whether the form of government is mayoral (1) or city manager (0).
f A qualitative variable indicating that the state government regulates local government accounting practices.
g Logarithm of the population of the municipality (1982).

total revenues to general expenditures. Panel B presents the results for the rate of adjustment for the ratio of local revenues to general expenditures. All variables have coefficients of the predicted sign, except for MAYOR_TURN which is negative and insignificant in panel A.

For both ratios, we find that cities issuing more long-term debt adjust their financial ratios more rapidly than cities with lower growth in long-term debt.[13] The implication is that managers of governments issuing bonds adjust operating ratios to governmental norms to signal efficiency to the capital market. Additionally, the size of the municipality (population) is significant with a negative sign for both ratios. We found no significant evidence to suggest that municipalities operating under a city manager adjust ratios at a different rate than those operating under the mayoral form of administration.

A comparison of panels A and B shows mixed results for three variables, STATE_REGUL, MAYOR_TURN, and HOME_VALUE. The variable indicating that local government accounting practices are regulated by state law is significant with the expected negative sign for the ratio of total revenues to general expenditures (TR/GE), but insignificant for the ratio of local revenues to general expenditures (LR/GE).[14] The difference between these two ratios is that intergovernmental grants are included in the numerator of TR/GE, but are not included in LR/GE. The differing results are perhaps not surprising, given that the regulation is intended to assure compliance with restrictions as to how intergovernmental grants are to be expended (Ingram and DeJong 1987). That is, state regulation of local government accounting practices presents less of an obstacle to adjusting ratios which involve only local revenues.

We find that cities experiencing frequent turnover in the chief elected official adjust the ratio of local revenues to general expenditures more rapidly than cities with less frequent turnover. This result suggests that elected officials facing greater political competition react more quickly to deviations from expectations, since such deviations impose relatively higher political costs. Finally, we find that cities with higher home property values exhibit a higher rate of ratio adjustment for the ratio of local revenues to general expenditures. We interpret this as indirect evidence that the incentive to monitor governmental performance increases with property values and political managers in high-value cities respond to increased citizen concerns by adjusting more rapidly to governmental norms. The lack of consistent results for these competition variables between the two ratios suggests that the effects of political competition are more pronounced when the financial ratio reflects only revenues from local sources.

B. Sensitivity Tests

We ran additional analyses (not presented) to evaluate the sensitivity of our results to various conditions. For example, national averages and individual coefficients of adjustment were calculated after we excluded cities with populations greater than .5 million from the sample. The results were qualitatively similar to those reported earlier.

Additionally, we examined whether the rate of adjustment differed for those cities which were predominantly above the norm and those that were predominantly below the norm. For purposes of these tests we divided the sample into three partitions: (1) cities whose ratio exceeded the norm at least two-thirds of the time, (2) cities whose ratio was less than the norm at least two-thirds of the time, and (3) all other cities. No significant differences were noted among these partitions in the slope coefficients of equation (3). However, a 0:1 variable indicating that the city was predominantly above the norm was associated with a significant positive coefficient in some of the models, suggesting that these cities adjust more rapidly. Our intuition for this outcome is that these cities find it easier to adjust toward the norm since this can be accomplished by either increasing expenditures or reducing taxes. Cities below the norm face the politically more challenging task of increasing revenues or cutting expenditures.

VII. CONCLUSION AND DISCUSSION

Similar to the private sector, bond analysts, rating agencies, and others use financial ratios computed from governmental financial reports. Recognizing the importance of these ratios, we argue that incentives exist for government officials to manage the levels of ratios through a variety of fiscal and financial policies. We collect financial ratios for a comprehensive sample of city governments for the period 1973 to 1991 and determine yearly averages. Using a partial adjustment model, we estimate the extent to which each government in our sample adjusts its ratios to these averages. Our analysis indicates that, similar to private sector corporations, municipal governments adjust their ratios toward predetermined levels based on industry norms. Also similar to the private sector, public entities vary (cross-sectionally) in the degree to which they adjust financial ratios.

Our second objective is to determine whether this variation in the rate of adjustment is systematically related to characteristics of the municipality. The extent of partial adjustment is determined by two opposing costs: (a) the cost of adjustment and (b) the cost of being out of equilibrium. Using the estimated rate of adjustment coefficients, we examine the association between the rate of ratio adjustment and city-specific factors which affect government officials' ability and incentive to adjust ratios. Our results suggest that entity-specific factors, such as regulation, political competition, growth in debt financing, and size may directly contribute to the observed variations in the rates of adjustment.

Our study represents both a replication and extension of previous research. The longitudinal analysis of ratio adjustment is similar to earlier studies by Lev (1969) and Tippett (1990) and indicates that their results are generalizable to public sector entities. This is the first study to examine the relation between these rates of adjustment and entity-specific factors, answering a call for future research presented by Lee and Wu (1988).

Our results, based on a substantially larger sample of city governments, confirm the findings of Marks and Raman (1996) that public sector entities adjust financial ratios to national averages. Future research should address the question of whether accounting estimates and procedures are the mechanism through which this adjustment is accomplished. We provide indirect evidence that this may be the case. A variable indicating that local government accounting practices are regulated by the state is associated with significantly lower rates of adjustment for one of the two ratios tested. This finding suggests that such regulation restricts the ability of managers to adjust to target levels.

Previous studies of the financial reporting practices of local governments tend to focus on overall disclosure levels, rather than specific accounting treatments (Robbins and Austin 1986; Copley 1991). In contrast, studies of corporate financial reporting practices examine the choice of accounting procedures among alternative methods for the purpose of determining the existence of earnings management. Contributing to this divergence in focus between public and private sector research is the lack of identifiable measures of government performance which can serve an equivalent role to earnings in the private sector. Without suitable performance measures, it is difficult to evaluate management incentives and relate these incentives to accounting policy choices. We believe our results suggest that government financial ratios and the extent to which they deviate from national norms may provide future researchers with a frame of reference from which to evaluate management incentives related to specific accounting choices.

ACKNOWLEDGMENT

We appreciate the helpful comments of two anonymous reviewers and the Associate Editor, George Sanders. We would also like to thank Michael Bamber, Barbara Chaney, James Kurtenbach, George Sanders, and participants of the Southeast Summer Accounting Research Colloquium for suggestions on early drafts of this manuscript.

NOTES

1. The partial adjustment coefficients estimated by Lev (1969) have a theoretical range of 0.0 (no adjustment) to 1.0 (complete adjustment to the norm). Estimates obtained by Lev for the *quick ratio* varied considerably, with 25 percent of the sample firms having estimated adjustment coefficients of less than .29 and 25 percent of the sample firms having estimated adjustment coefficients in excess of .72. Similar results are reported for other ratios.

2. Additionally, governments vary in the extent to which they apply governmental accounting standards. Thus, even though a given practice may be required by GASB statements (such as accrual of sick and vacation pay), some governments choose not to comply with the standards (see Ingram and Robbins 1987, for examples of the extent of variation among governments in financial reporting practices and disclosures). Some evidence exists (Allen and Sanders 1994) that this variation has decreased in recent years.

3. The partial adjustment model is also applied empirically by Zarembka (1968) to the money demand function, by Lee (1976) to dividend policy, and by Kau and Lee (1976) to urban structure.

4. Historically, governmental accounting practices have been subject to considerable management discretion. Until recently, governments had little guidance concerning recognition of compensated absences (GASB 1992), the accrual of sales and income taxes (GASB 1993), and the reporting of pass-through grants of cash and food stamps (GASB 1994). Additionally, governments had latitude governing which activities of a government (i.e., component units) were included in the government's financial report (GASB 1991).

5. There were 848 city governments with populations greater than 25,000 for all 19 years. Missing data reduced the sample by 92 and 84 for the ratios, TR/GE and LR/GE, respectively. Additionally, we reduced the samples by an additional 19 and 10 observations due to probable data errors, evidenced by an abnormally high value for the ratios (> 7.0) in one year.

6. For comparative purposes we ran the longitudinal analysis using the adaptive expectations adjustment model used by Lee and Wu (1988). In a substantial number of cases the model was not able to converge.

7. The intercept estimates are generally small and insignificant as expected (Lev 1969). In our sample, 77 percent of the intercepts for TR/GE and 88 percent for LR/GE are not significant at the .05 level.

8. We are indebted to an anonymous reviewer for this suggestion.

9. We observed significant variation between states in the levels of this ratio. Future research might be directed to the appropriateness of state norms for the adjustment of certain ratios.

10. In this survey the existence of state regulation over local government accounting practices is determined by state comptrollers.

11. Measuring political competition at the local government level is problematic (see Baber 1994). Our approach is to count the number of mayoral changes that occurred between 1973 and 1991. Admittedly, there is the potential for measurement error, but we have no reason to expect this measurement error would bias the results in favor of rejection of the null hypothesis.

12. Regression results using estimated coefficients obtained from the full sample of cities (populations > 25,000) are comparable, with slightly lower R-squares than those using target values (means) calculated from the reduced sample of cities with populations > 50,000.

13. An alternative measure considering population growth (debt per capita 1991/ debt per capita 1973) yields qualitatively similar results.

14. Similar results are obtained for a variable indicating that the state required local governments to comply with GAAP standards.

REFERENCES

Allen, A., and G. Sanders. 1994. Financial disclosure in U.S. municipalities—Has the governmental accounting standards board made a difference? *Financial Accountability and Management* 10(August): 175-193.

Baber, W. R. 1983. Toward understanding the role of auditing in the public sector. *Journal of Accounting and Economics* 5(December): 213-227.

———. 1990. Toward a framework for evaluating the role of accounting and auditing in political markets: The influence of political competition. *Journal of Accounting and Public Policy* 9(Spring): 57-73.

———. 1994. The influence of political competition on governmental reporting and auditing. *Research in Governmental and Nonprofit Accounting*, Vol. 5, ed. J. L. Chan, 27-56. Greenwich, CT: JAI Press Inc.

Baber, W. R., and P. Sen. 1984. The role of generally accepted reporting methods in the public sector: An empirical investigation. *Journal of Accounting and Public Policy* 3(Summer): 293-305.

Belsley, D. A., E. Kuh, and R. E. Welsch. 1980. *Regression Diagnostics: Identifying Influential Data Points and Sources of Collinearity*. New York: John Wiley and Sons.

Cagan, P. 1956. The monetary dynamics of hyper-inflations. *Studies in the Quantity Theory of Money*, ed. M. Friedman, 25-117. Chicago: The University of Chicago Press.

Carpenter, V. 1991. The influence of political competition on the decision to adopt GAAP. *Journal of Accounting and Public Policy* 10(Summer): 105-134.

Chaney, B., P. Copley, and M. Stone. 1998. The effect of fiscal stress and balanced budget requirements on the funding and measurement of state pension obligations. Working paper, The University of Georgia.

Copley, P. A. 1991. The association between municipal disclosure practices and audit quality. *Journal of Accounting and Public Policy* 10(Winter): 245-66.

Copley, P. A., J. J. Gaver, and K. M. Gaver. 1995. Simultaneous estimation of the supply and demand of differentiated audits: evidence from the municipal audit market. *Journal of Accounting Research* 33(Spring):137-156.

Copley, P. A., R. H. Cheng, J. E. Harris, R. C. Icerman, W. L. Johnson, G. R. Smith, K. A. Smith, W. T. Wrege, and R. Yahr. 1997. The new governmental reporting model: Is it a "field of dreams?" *Accounting Horizons* 11(Sept.): 91-101.

Epple, D., and K. Schipper. 1981. Municipal pension funding: A theory and some evidence. *Public Choice* 37: 141-178.

Esser, J. 1992. As the economy goes, so goes state-local finance? *Government Finance Review* (February): 3.

Evans, J. H., and J.M. Patton. 1987. Signaling and monitoring in public sector accounting. *Journal of Accounting Research* 25 (Supplement): 130-158.

Fieldsend, S., N. Longford, and S. McLeay. 1987. Ratio analysis: A variance component analysis. *Journal of Business, Finance and Accounting* 14(Winter): 497-517.

Frecka, T. J., and C. F. Lee. 1983. Generalized financial ratio adjustment processes and their implications. *Journal of Accounting Research* 21(Spring): 308-316.

Friedman, M. 1957. *Theory of the Consumption Function*. Princeton, NJ: Princeton University Press.

Governmental Accounting Standards Board. 1991. *Statement No. 14: The Financial Reporting Entity*. Norwalk, CT: GASB.

———. 1992. *Statement No. 16: Accounting for Compensated Absences*. Norwalk, CT: GASB.

———. 1993. *Statement No. 22: Accounting for Taxpayer-Assessed Tax Revenues in Governmental Funds*. Norwalk, CT: GASB.

———. 1994. *Statement No. 24: Accounting and Financial Reporting for Certain Grants and Other Financial Assistance*. Norwalk, CT: GASB.

Ingram, R. W. 1984. Economic incentives and the choice of state government accounting practices. *Journal of Accounting Research* 22(Spring): 126- 144.

Ingram, R. W,. and R. M. Copeland. 1981. Municipal accounting information and voting behavior. *The Accounting Review* 56(October): 830-842.

Ingram, R. W., and D. V. DeJong. 1987. The effect of regulation on local government disclosure practices. *Journal of Accounting and Public Policy* 6(Winter): 245-270.

Ingram, R. W., and W. A. Robbins. 1987. *Research Report: Financial Reporting Practices of Local Governments*. Norwalk, CT: GASB.

Kau, J. B., and C. F. Lee. 1976. The functional form in estimating the density gradient: An empirical investigation. *Journal of the American Statistical Association* 71(June): 326-327.

Lee, C. F. 1976. Functional form and the dividend effect in the electric utility industry. *Journal of Finance* 31(December): 1481-1486.

Lee, C. F., and C. Wu. 1988. Expectation formation and financial ratio adjustment processes. *The Accounting Review* 63(April): 292-306.

Lev, B. 1969. Industry averages as targets for financial ratios. *Journal of Accounting Research* 7(Autumn): 290-299.

Maddala, G. S. 1988. *Introduction to Econometrics*. New York: Macmillan.

Marks, B. R., and K. K. Raman. 1996. The behavior of interperiod equity-related performance measures over time. *Accounting Horizons* 10(December): 52-66.

Municipal Finance Officers Association. 1978. *Is Your City Heading for Financial Difficulty: A Guidebook for Small Cities and Other Governmental Units*. Chicago: MFOA.

National Association of State Auditors, Comptrollers, and Treasurers. 1986. *State Comptrollers: Technical Activities and Functions*. Washington, DC: NASACT.

National League of Cities. 1983-1991. *Directory of City Policy Officials*. Washington, DC: National League of Cities.

Nerlove, M. 1958. Adaptive expectations and cobweb phenomena. *Quarterly Journal of Economics* 72(May): 227-240.

Peterson, D. 1990. How local officials adjust to bring in a balanced budget. *Cities Weekly* (July 2): 7.

Robbins, W. A., and K. R. Austin. 1986. Disclosure quality in governmental financial reports: An assessment of the appropriateness of a compound measure. *Journal of Accounting Research* 24(Autumn): 412-426.

Tiebout, C. 1956. A pure theory of local expenditures. *Journal of Political Economy* 64(October): 416-424.

Tippett, M. 1990. An induced theory of financial ratios. *Accounting and Business Research* 21(Winter): 77-85.

Tung, S., and J. Crowe. 1993. Expectation formation and financial ratio adjustment processes: A comment and an extension. *The Accounting Review* 68(October): 942-955.

U.S. Bureau of Census. 1982. *County and City Data Book*. Washington, DC: U.S. Government Printing Offices.

———. 1973-1991. *Survey of Governments: Annual Financial Statistics*. Washington, DC: U.S. Government Printing Offices.

United States General Accounting Office. 1985. *Budget Issues: State Balanced Budget Practices*. Washington, DC: U.S. Government Printing Office.

Yinger, J. 1982. Capitalization and the theory of local public finance. *Journal of Political Economy* 90(October): 917-943.

Zarembka, P. 1968. Functional form in the demand for money. *Journal of the American Statistical Association* 63(June): 502-511.

FACTORS AFFECTING THE RELATION BETWEEN DONATIONS TO NOT-FOR-PROFIT ORGANIZATIONS AND AN EFFICIENCY RATIO

Daniel Tinkelman

ABSTRACT

Accounting standard-setters assume that donors use financial information to allocate donations among nonprofit organizations. Using regression analysis on a sample of approximately 6,500 nonprofit organizations' state regulatory filings, I find that greater reported efficiency is generally associated with higher subsequent donations, and identify several factors related to the efficiency measure's relevance or reliability that affect the strength of the relationship. In addition, I compare the performance of two different models of the price elasticity of donations and the sensitivity of donations to fund-raising share.

I. INTRODUCTION

An important objective of financial reporting for nonprofit organizations is to inform financial statement users about organizations' service efforts and accomplishments (FASB 1980b). While accomplishments are relatively difficult to capture in nonprofit financial statements, efforts are measured by reported expenses and categorized as program, fund-raising, or administrative. Industry monitors, such as the Council of Better Business Bureaus, use expense ratios to help judge the efficiency of these organizations (CBBB 1994). There is also evidence that such ratios are considered by United Way personnel in allocating funds to member organizations (Stout 1997). However, to date, research on the usefulness to donors of financial statement-based efficiency measures is inconclusive.

The FASB asserts that "relevance and reliability are the two primary qualities that make accounting information useful for decision making" (FASB 1980a). The major contribution of this study is its identification of several factors related to the relevance and reliability of accounting information (such as organization type, size, data plausibility, organizational age, geographic location, and relative dependence on donated funds). Additionally, it tests their effects on the efficiency/donations association. I find that general factors such as data plausibility and the organization's degree of dependence on contributions are important in explaining differences in the sensitivity of donations to reported efficiency. These factors help explain differences in sensitivity across various types of organizations.

Prior research into the relation of accounting ratios and donations yields mixed results. Steinberg (1983, 1986a, 1986b) finds no evidence that donors use accounting ratios, while Weisbrod and Dominguez (1986), Posnett and Sandler (1989), and Callen (1994) find significant associations between donations and measures based on reported expense ratios. The results presented here indicate that donations are affected by accounting expense data when it is relevant and reliable. Further, they suggest that conflicting prior results may be due to an inappropriate use of a first-difference specification.

The remainder of this paper is organized as follows. I briefly summarize related prior research in Section II, which also defines "price," the efficiency variable. Section III discusses various organizational characteristics posited to affect the reliability or relevance of price data. The sample is described in Section IV. Sections V, VI, and VII contain the empirical testing. Section VIII details the conclusions based on the analysis.

II. RELATED LITERATURE

Existing empirical studies of the relationship between donations and various explanatory variables, including accounting information, employ either a first difference or a log-linear regression model. Because the studies use different models and different samples, it is hard to compare their results.

Steinberg (1983, 1986a, 1986b) is skeptical of the usefulness of reported expense ratios to donors. Among other limitations, financial statements do not provide marginal cost or revenue data. Using a sample of IRS data between 1974 and 1976, he regresses the first difference in donations (the change in donations from one period to the next) on the first and second difference in the three major expense categories (fund-raising, administrative, and program) and on the ratio of program expenses to donations. A first-difference specification is used to control for variables that are constant across time (Steinberg 1983). Steinberg finds the expense ratio is not significant in any of the six industries tested.

Weisbrod and Dominguez (1986), Posnett and Sandler (1989), and Callen (1994) follow a different approach. Weisbrod and Dominguez "postulate that the market demand function for a particular type of collective-good output depends—as in the case of purely private goods—on price, quality, and the information about both price and quality available to the buyer." Quality is difficult to measure, and these three studies use the age of an organization as a quality proxy.[1] Total reported fund-raising expenses are used as a proxy for the information available to donors.

These models all attempt to measure the perceived price to the donor of obtaining a dollar of charitable output from an organization. The perceived price depends on both the amount of any tax deduction available to the donor and on the organization's efficiency in putting donations to use in programs, rather than fund-raising or administration. Following Posnett and Sandler (1989), I define price as follows:

$$Price = \frac{1-t}{1-f-a}$$

where t is the donor's tax rate, and f and a are the fractions of total expenses represented by fund-raising and administrative costs, respectively.[2] If the donor's tax rate is ignored, because it is uniform across all organizations, the price simplifies to the ratio of total expenses to program expenses.[3] Thus, price can be seen as simply the inverse of the ratio of program expenses to total expenses. It has a lower bound of $1.00 and no upper bound. A high (low) price is equivalent to spending a low (high) proportion of total expenses on programs. An organization that spends 90 percent of its funds on programs has a price of $1.11, while one that spends only 10 percent of funds on programs has a price of $10.00.

These three studies use log-linear regression models, where donations are a function of age, price, fund-raising costs, and alternative revenue sources. The price coefficients are consistently negative and statistically significant. Fund-raising is strongly positively correlated with donations, but age generally has a minor effect. These regression models differ from the first-difference model used by Steinberg in both functional form and in the choice of included variables.

III. ORGANIZATIONAL CHARACTERISTICS POSITED TO AFFECT THE DECISION-USEFULNESS OF EXPENSE RATIOS

Measuring the effectiveness of nonprofit organizations is problematic.[4] The profit measure used by business enterprises is inappropriate, and, as the FASB has noted, "the ability to measure service accomplishments, particularly program results, is generally undeveloped" (FASB 1980b).

Price and related expense ratios measure the relationship of program expenses to total expenses and serve to indicate the relative degree of effort the organization devotes to program activity. If efforts are correlated with accomplishments, such ratios may signal efficiency. The use donors make of such measures is hypothesized to be affected by the following organizational factors, which affect either relevance or reliability:

1. Organizational size—I predict lower price sensitivity for smaller organizations, due to lesser accessibility and reliability of expense ratios for smaller organizations. Cost allocations are likely to be relatively more difficult in smaller organizations, where the same key people perform multiple tasks. Small organizations may also have less access to professional accounting expertise in preparing financial statements. In addition to reliability issues, small organizations are less likely to receive media attention, reducing data availability.
2. Organization age—I predict lower price sensitivity for new organizations. Bennett and DiLorenzo (1994) suggest that donors recognize that new organizations have not yet achieved economies of scale, and may need to advertise heavily to develop name recognition. Grimes (1977) finds that young organizations often exhibit very high fund-raising percentages. Thus, expense ratios in the early years may not be reliable indicators of long-term performance.
3. Degree of dependence on donations—I expect lower price sensitivity for organizations with relatively low dependence on donations. Overall organizational expense ratios may be uninformative for organizations that depend primarily on program fees or other revenues. The total expenses of such organizations reflect primarily the program and administrative costs funded by fees, not their contribution-supported operations, so the relevance of price data is reduced. For example, colleges are more heavily dependent on program revenues than donations. Engstrom (1988) finds that donors to colleges did not use financial statements "in a significant way" for "the evaluation of institutional performance, either for efficiency or effectiveness."
4. Degree of dependence on United Way or other indirect donations—An entity's reported fund-raising costs only relate to its own activities. If a large part of the organization's funds are received indirectly, net of the costs of support organizations, reported fund-raising costs are likely to be low, and the ratio of fund-raising expenses to total expenses is less relevant to judging the organization's overall fund-raising efficiency. Therefore, I predict lower price sensitivity for organizations that receive major funding from indirect donations.

5. Location—Donors may have alternate means of monitoring local organizations, as their service efforts may be more visible, thus reducing the need to rely on financial statements. Therefore, I expect lower price sensitivity for local organizations
6. Data limitations—A recent guide to 35,000 large, publicly supported charities notes that 62 percent report zero fund-raising expenses in their latest Form 990 filing (*Guidestar Directory of American Charities, 1996 Index*), suggesting the possibility of classification errors. Unreliable data are predicted to have lower decision-usefulness.

   Under-reporting of fund-raising may arise from several causes. Preparers may consciously shift fund-raising expenses into other categories (Froelich and Knoepfle 1996). In some organizations fund-raising costs may be judged immaterial, too small to merit separate reporting. Costs of unconsolidated affiliates are absent in data prepared on a legal entity basis, so, while the reported contributions of a national headquarters unit might include contributions shared with it by separately incorporated regional affiliates, the headquarter's expenses would not include the related fund-raising expenses. [5]
7. Organizational type—It is possible that donors to different types of organizations (e.g., arts or health organizations) differ in their concern for efficiency. Weisbrod and Dominguez (1986) and Steinberg (1986b) separately report results by organization type. However, these studies do not present any theory to explain why donors or managers might behave differently across types of organizations. I propose that, after controlling for other effects, price elasticity does not depend on organization type.

IV. DATA SELECTION AND DESCRIPTIVE STATISTICS

I obtained copies of New York State's Charities Database as of December 1994, November 1995, and June 1996, and combined the information. The database contains summaries of state regulatory filings, which are required for all organizations soliciting more than $25,000 annually in New York, unless they qualify for exemption. (Religious organizations and many schools are exempt.) The reports generally must follow

Table 1. Application of Sample Selection Criteria on Data Contained in New York State's Database of Regulatory Filings for Fiscal Years Ending 1992 to 1994[a]

Number of organizations listed in New York State's Charities Database in Dec. 1994, Nov. 1995, or June 1996 that reported nonzero total income in at least one of the years 1992-1994 Less organizations which:	11,213
A. Had missing or implausible registration dates	−740
B. Had apparent decimal point errors in total assets	−184
C. Are schools	−362
D. Are hospitals	−302
Total meeting criteria in any year	9,625
Organizations meeting criteria in 1993	8,719
Organizations meeting criteria in 1994	9,287
Organizations meeting criteria in both 1992 and 1993	6,470
Organizations meeting criteria in both 1993 and 1994	6,559

Notes: [a]The samples were selected from copies of the Charities Database maintained by the New York State Department of State as of the dates listed above. Organizations were eliminated from the sample if they were inactive, as indicated by zero reported total income, or if the registration dates or total assets had apparent errors. Schools and hospitals are also excluded. Finally, the regression models require data for two consecutive years, eliminating a number of observations.

Generally Accepted Accounting Principles ("GAAP").[6] Organizations soliciting over $100,000 in a year must submit audited filings.

The resulting data for fiscal 1992, 1993, and 1994 appeared relatively complete. Because of New York's three-year record retention policy and its generous filing deadlines, the 1991 and 1995 samples were much smaller, and are biased toward late filers in 1991 and early filers in 1995. Accordingly, the analysis is confined to the three complete years.

The sample selection criteria are outlined in Table 1. The universe is the 11,213 organizations that reported having nonzero revenues in either 1992, 1993, or 1994. Organizations are excluded from the sample if the registration dates appeared implausible (e.g., years after 1995 or before 1954, when the state began requiring registration) or if extreme variations in total assets between years suggested decimal point errors. I also exclude two categories of organization, schools and hospitals, because they were subject to the somewhat different accounting requirements prescribed in specialized audit guides (AICPA 1994), and

Table 2. 1993 and 1994 Descriptive Statistics for a Sample of Nonprofit Organizations Filing Financial Reports with New York State (The Sample Excludes Religious Organizations, Schools and Hospitals.)

	Prior Year Audit Not Required		Prior Year Audit Required		Full Sample	
	1993	1994	1993	1994	1993	1994
			Panel A—Revenues			
		(Means, Medians, and Standard Deviations)				
Direct Contributions	52	46	2,082	2,193	983	1,028
	30	29	430	425	84	84
	254	98	7,878	8,655	5,433	5,950
Indirect Contributions	198	176	161	145	181	162
	0	0	0	0	0	0
	5,402	4,612	1,877	1,665	4,172	3,579
Government Grants	491	535	931	988	693	742
	30	33	0	0	8	9
	4,268	4,355	8,806	9,874	6,743	7,411
Program Income	843	931	1,360	1,468	1,086	1,177
	7	9	7	8	7	9
	11,850	12,776	8706	9,105	10,527	11,249
Other Revenue	103	95	801	713	423	378
	5	5	51	48	14	13
	959	1,034	5,336	3,784	3,698	2,687
Total Revenues	1,696	1,784	5,334	5,507	3,365	3,487
	202	223	1,009	1,051	439	458
	14,600	15,085	18,322	19,044	16,511	17,110
N	3,502	3,559	2,968	3,000	6,470	6,559
Direct Contributions as % of revenues						
Mean	31%	29%	58%	59%	43%	43%
Median	11%	11%	63%	66%	35%	35%
			Panel B—Expenses			
		(Means, Medians, and Standard Deviations)				
Program Expenses	1,446	1,535	4,130	4,307	2,677	2,803
	148	167	680	693	309	330
	13.572	14,069	5,140	16,066	14,374	15,078
Administrative	206	227	528	533	354	369
	29	31	135	129	60	60
	1,844	2,175	1,530	1,521	1,714	1,910
Fund-Raising	26	16	305	309	154	150
	0	0	36	37	1	1
	759	408	1,428	1,459	1,125	1,042
Total Expenses	1,678	1,778	4,963	5,149	3,184	3,320
	190	213	921	956	414	428
	14,822	15,537	17,111	18,031	15,996	16,807
Administrative %	18.5%	18.1%	16.8%	16.3%	17.8%	17.3%
	13.5%	13.6%	13.2%	12.7%	13.3%	13.1%
	18.9%	18.1%	14.5%	14.7%	17.0%	16.7%
Fund-Raising %	4.7%	4.3%	8.1%	8.0%	6.2%	6.0%
	0.0%	0.0%	3.9%	3.9%	0.2%	0.2%
	14.0%	13.0%	12.2%	12.2%	13.3%	12.8%
Price—						
Mean	$2.30	$1.96	$1.60	$1.73	$1.98	$1.85
Median	$1.20	$1.19	$1.27	$1.26	$1.24	$1.23
Std. deviation	$13.83	$6.63	$3.43	$6.73	$10.43	$6.68
Maximum	$557.82	$213.30	$142.9	$315.00	$557.82	$315.00

(continued)

Table 2 (Continued)

	Prior Year Audit Not Required		Prior Year Audit Required		Full Sample	
	1993	1994	1993	1994	1993	1994
Panel C—Other Descriptive Statistics						
Age (Years registered)						
Mean	12.4	11.7	17.3	16.7	14.6	14.0
Median	9.0	9.0	13.0	12.0	11.0	10.0
Std. Deviation	9.8	9.8	12.5	12.8	11.4	11.6
% under 4 years old	16.8%	21.9%	12.2%	16.7%	14.7%	19.5%
Total Assets ($000's)						
Mean	1,475	1,422	7,978	8,277	4,466	4,562
Median	122	135	883	954	316	336
Std. Deviation	15,257	14,080	40,695	41,355	29,963	30,039
% reporting low direct contributions*	59.8	60.4	16.3	16.2	40.4	40.2
% reporting "implausible data"*	70.2	72.4	30.6	32.6	51.9	54.1
% Non-New York	4.7	4.0	25.7	25.9	14.3	14.0
% by Type						
Health	12.9	12.8	14.7	15.2	13.7	13.9
Social Welfare	35.6	36.9	19.2	19.1	28.1	28.8
Civic	10.4	10.2	7.3	7.4	9.0	8.9
Cultural/Educational	17.9	17.7	21.1	21.1	19.4	19.3
Animal/Environment	2.6	2.8	3.9	3.7	3.2	3.2
Social/Fraternal	4.8	4.7	3.2	3.0	4.0	3.9
Support	6.4	6.0	14.7	14.8	10.2	10.0
Public Policy	5.3	5.2	11.9	11.3	8.3	8.0
Foreign Relations	0.5	0.3	2.2	2.1	1.3	1.1
Other	3.5	3.5	1.9	2.1	2.8	2.8
N	3,502	3,559	2,968	3,000	6,470	6,559

Notes: The values shown for each revenue item are sample means, medians, and standard deviations for the samples described in the text. New York State requires an audited registration filing if an organization solicits over $100,000 in contributions in the state in a year. Revenue numbers are in thousands of dollars.

Expenses are in thousands of dollars. The "Administrative %" and "Fund-Raising %" captions express the administrative or fund-raising expenses as a percentage of total expenses. Price (total expenses/program expenses) is a measure of the pre-tax cost to the donor of obtaining a dollar of program cost output.

*Organizations are considered to have "low contributions" when prior year direct contributions were < 10% of total income, and are considered to have "implausible data" if in the prior year either administrative or fund-raising expenses were zero.

because New York had special filing rules for colleges. These criteria reduce the available sample to 9,625 organizations. Because the baseline regression model in Sections VI and VII requires data from two consecutive years, the sample is further reduced to 6,470 (6,559) organizations for the 1993 (1994) regressions. These samples are divided into two subsamples, based on whether the organization would have been required by New York State to file an audited report in the prior year.

Table 2 presents descriptive statistics for the full sample and both subsamples for 1993 and 1994 (1992 statistics, not presented, are similar to 1993 and 1994). In each year about 46 percent of the organizations were required to have audits. Since the audit requirement is based on receiving aggregate contributions exceeding $100,000 in the prior year, it is not surprising that the "audited subsample" organizations are larger, with median 1993 (1994) total revenues of $1,009,000 ($1,051,000), versus $202,000 ($223,000) for the "unaudited" organizations. They are also more reliant on direct contributions, which account for 63 percent (66%) of total revenue for the median audited organization in 1993 (1994), versus 11 percent for the unaudited organizations each year. The ratio of direct contributions to total revenues is significantly higher (p-value < 0.01) for the audited organizations, using a Wilcoxon test. The unaudited organizations tend to be relatively more dependent on program income and government grants.

Panel B of Table 2 indicates how the two subsamples differ in their use of funds. The median organization in the full sample spent between 19.4 and 18.6 percent of total expenses on supporting services (administration and fund-raising) in 1993 and 1994, leaving about 81 percent for programs. While median organizations in the two subsamples expended about the same fraction of their funds on programs each year, this conceals a difference in spending on administration and fund-raising. The audited organizations expended relatively more on fund-raising, causing a higher median price. In contrast, approximately 64 percent of the unaudited organizations reported zero fund-raising costs each year. Price and fund-raising percentage are both significantly different between samples, using a Wilcoxon test, while administrative cost differences were not significant.

The existence of extreme observations causes skewing of results and some large differences between the mean and median figures reported in Table 2, panels A and B. In particular, the mean statistics for price are clearly influenced by extreme observations, as organizations with zero program costs in the denominator would have prices approaching infinity. One organization's price in 1993 was $557.82, implying it spent less than 0.2 percent of total expenses on programs. Such high prices were exceptional. Over 95 percent of the organizations in each subsample had prices less than $3, and almost 99 percent had prices below $10. To reduce the impact of outlying observations, prices were arbitrarily truncated at $10. This affected 93 observations each year, 26 in the audited sample and 57 in the unaudited sample.[7]

The descriptive statistics in panel C of Table 2 indicate differences between the two subsamples in various factors posited to affect the decision-usefulness of price. These factors include age, size, dependence on direct contributions, data plausibility, geographic location, and organizational type.

Age assumes a value of 1 to 40, representing the number of years the organization has registered with the state, a practice which began in 1954. About 5 percent of the observations are truncated at 40. The audited charities are somewhat older, with a median age in 1994 of 12, versus nine for the unaudited organizations. Many organizations in the sample appear to be relatively young. Almost 20 percent of the full sample, and a significant fraction of each subsample, had been registered with the state for three years or less in 1994. Consistent with Grimes (1977), I find that these new organizations have significantly higher fund-raising percentages in 1993 and 1994 than the more established organizations, but the administrative cost percentages were not significantly lower. Price, which depends on both the administrative and fund-raising percentages, is not significantly different.

The audited organizations are larger in terms of total assets, with 1993 (1994) medians of $883,000 ($954,000), versus $122,000 ($135,000) for the unaudited sample. They are more likely to rely on direct contributions for a significant fraction of their revenues. While about 60 percent of the unaudited organizations reported receiving less than 10 percent of revenues from contributions each year, only about 16 percent of the audited group received such low levels of donations. Since the audit requirements are based on donations raised in New York State, the audited sample contains numerous out-of-state organizations.

I define organizations reporting either zero administrative or zero fund-raising expense as having "implausible data." Section III, above, discusses accounting and data issues which may result in organizations reporting zero administrative or fund-raising expenses.[8]

Panel C indicates that the services offered differ in the two subsamples. The largest groups in the full sample in 1994 are social welfare groups (28.8%), cultural/educational groups (19.3%), and health organizations (13.9%). The audited subsample contains relatively more health charities, support organizations (e.g., United Way), and public policy groups, and fewer social welfare and civic groups.

V. REGRESSION RESULTS FOLLOWING STEINBERG'S APPROACH

Steinberg's (1983, 1986b) model regresses the change in contributions on the changes in each of the three expense categories (fund-raising, administrative, and program) in both the current year and the prior year. The differenced form implicitly controls for omitted variables

Table 3. Regressions Using a Modification of Steinberg's Model, Regressing First Differences in 1994 Direct Contributions on First and Second Differences in Expenses and the Difference in Price

	Regression Coefficients (absolute values of t-statistics)		
	Prior Year Audit Not Required	Prior Year Audit Required	Full Sample
Intercept	13,561*	−121,977**	−46,041***
	(7.7)	(2.2)[b]	(1.7)
1994 Δ Fund-raising costs	−0.00	2.47*	0.94*
	(0.1)[a,b]	(10.1)	(10.7)
1993 Δ Fund-raising costs	−0.01	0.03	0.01
	(1.0)	(0.3)	(0.1)[a,b]
1994 Δ Administrative costs	0.00	0.27**	0.17*
	(0.5)[a]	(2.1)[a]	(2.6)[a,b]
1993 Δ Administrative costs	−0.01	0.07*	0.47*
	(0.8)[b]	(11.5)[a]	(11.3)
1994 Δ Program costs	0.00	0.42*	0.37*
	(1.6)[b]	(32.2)	(41.9)
1993 Δ Program costs	−0.00	0.44*	0.31*
	(0.1)[a]	(22.6)	(25.4)
1993 Δ Price	−802	16,731	1,181
	(0.4)[a]	(0.2)	(0.0)
F-test p-value	0.30[b]	0.00	0.00
Adjusted R^2	0.00	0.31	0.25
N	3,133	2,896	6,029

Notes: *, **, *** Significant at 1%, 5%, or 10% levels, on two-tailed tests.
To illustrate the sensitivity of the results to highly influential observations, the effects of excluding the observations with leverage values above 0.3 are indicated by notes a and b. Between four and seven observations in each sample met this criterion.
[a] Sign of coefficient changes if high-leverage observations are deleted.
[b] Significance level changes to/from the 5% level if high-leverage observations are deleted.

that are stable across time. Results using this approach, with the addition of the prior year change in price, are shown in Table 3. Because three years of data are required for this model, only 1994 donations could be tested.

The first important observation is that the price variable is not significant, consistent with Steinberg's results. If the regressions are repeated by industry, price remains generally insignificant.[9] A second observation is that the current-year change in fund-raising is significant while the lagged change in fund-raising is not, suggesting that fund-raising's effects are short-lived. However, the results should be treated with caution because they are sensitive to the effects of outliers. For example, if between four and seven high-leverage observations are deleted from the samples, eight of the 24 coefficients in Table 3 would change sign, and the significance level of six would change to/from the 5 percent level. The presence of extreme observations reduces the robustness of the model's results.[10]

The relationship between first differences in contributions and changes in expenses can be expected to be noisy. Contributions are subject to transitory shocks, such as large gifts in any one year, which can result in extreme changes in reported contributions in that year and the following year. The standard deviation of the 1994 first differences in contributions for the full sample was approximately 31 times the mean. Correlation analysis finds only a low positive correlation between 1993 and 1994 changes in contributions. The Pearson correlation coefficient was 0.09, significant at 1 percent on a sample of 5,901 organizations. Budgeting practices and accounting processes, such as depreciation, may dampen the response of expenses to transitory revenue shocks.

Further data analysis suggests that this model is not appropriately specified for studying price elasticity. Price appears to be precisely the kind of stable, organization-specific characteristic that a difference model is designed to screen out. For the full sample, with price truncated at 10, the correlation coefficient between price in 1992 and 1993 is 0.73, and the 1993/1994 correlation is 0.78, both significant at 1 percent. The correlation between the 1993 and 1994 price changes was −0.33, significant at 1 percent, so price exhibits mean-reverting behavior.

VI. REGRESSION ANALYSIS USING LOG-LINEAR MODELS

The baseline model is a log-linear equation similar to Posnett and Sandler (1989), which relates levels of donations to levels of price, fund-raising, age (as a proxy for quality), and other revenue sources. The coefficient of price in this functional form is the price elasticity of donations. As a control for organization size, I have added the log of the prior year total assets to Posnett and Sandler's (1989) model, resulting in the following:

$$LDON = \beta_0 + \beta_1 LFR + \beta_2 LPRICE + \beta_3 LAGE + \beta_4 LASSET + \beta_5 LGOV + \beta_6 LPROINC + \beta_7 LOTHREV$$

where:

LDON	= the log of current year direct contributions
LFR	= the log of prior year fund-raising expense
LPRICE	= the log of the prior year price
LASSET	= the log of beginning total assets
LAGE	= the log of the organization's age, as discussed above
LGOV	= the log of current year government contributions[11]
LPROINC	= the log of current year program income
LOTHREV	= the log of current year revenue from other sources

Baseline results are shown for each sample in Table 4. Because White's general test indicates heteroscedasticity, asymptotic t-statistics are used as discussed in White (1980). The explanatory power of the model is higher for the audited subsample.[12]

The findings are consistent with the idea that donors reward efficient organizations, and with prior research by Weisbrod and Dominguez (1986), Posnett and Sandler (1989), and Callen (1994). The regressions show a negative association between price and subsequent donations, significant in each case at the 1 percent level. The price coefficients (elasticity) of the full sample in 1993 and 1994 are –0.55 and –0.53. The subsample of unaudited organizations has lower price elasticities (–0.21 and –0.15 in 1993 and 1994) than the audited subsample.[13]

The results for the age variable in Table 4 are interesting because the sign differs in the two subsamples. If age proxies for quality, then the coefficient should be positive. In Table 4 the coefficients are signifi-

Table 4. Baseline 1993 and 1994 Log-Linear Regressions of Direct Contributions on Levels of Explanatory Variables

	Regression Coefficients (Absolute values of t-statistics)					
	Prior Year Audit Not Required		Prior Year Audit Required		Full Sample	
	1993	1994	1993	1994	1993	1994
Intercept	9.89*	10.17*	6.7*	6.88*	5.36*	5.44*
	(36.8)	(40.6)	(41.3)	(46.8)	(38.3)	(39.0)
Log of Price$_{t-1}$	−0.21*	−0.15*	−0.54*	−0.59*	−0.55*	−0.53*
	(3.3)	(2.6)	(8.2)	(9.1)	(10.3)	(10.5)
Log of Fund-Raising Costs$_{t-1}$	0.23*	0.22*	0.30*	0.31*	0.52*	0.53*
	(8.8)	(9.0)	(28.5)	(30.1)	(47.7)	(47.2)
Log of Beginning Total Assets	0.02	0.02	0.32*	0.29*	0.27*	0.26*
	(1.2)	(1.0)	(17.9)	(17.3)	(15.7)	(15.4)
Log of Other Revenues	0.04**	0.03***	0.02	0.03**	0.07*	0.07*
	(2.3)	(1.8)	(1.4)	(2.4)	(5.1)	(5.1)
Log of Government Grants	−0.26*	−0.27*	−0.01**	−0.01	−0.19*	−0.20*
	(23.3)	(25.3)	(2.0)	(1.5)	(22.8)	(23.4)
Log of Program Income	−0.03*	−0.03*	−0.06*	−0.06*	−0.08*	−0.08*
	(2.9)	(2.7)	(7.9)	(7.4)	(9.1)	(9.1)
Log of Age	0.19*	0.21*	−0.14*	−0.11*	0.07**	0.09*
	(5.0)	(6.6)	(5.1)	(4.6)	(2.3)	(3.3)
Adjusted R^2	0.21	0.23	0.51	0.51	0.51	0.51
N	3,502	3,559	2,968	3,000	6,470	6,559

Notes: Extreme observations of price are truncated at 10. The asymptotic *t*-statistics are shown, since White's general test was significant at 1% in each regression (White, 1980).
*, **, *** Significant at the 1%, 5% or 10% levels, respectively, on two-sided tests.

cantly positive for the unaudited sample, but significantly negative for audited organizations. It is not clear why the coefficient should be significantly negative for the audited sample. The two subsamples differ due to the existence of a prior year audit, which in turn is dependent on size. If the audit or the organization's size conveys an assurance of quality, age may be redundant as a quality signal, and other organizational characteristics associated with age may dominate. One possibility is that age is negatively related to the "trendiness" of the organization's mission, since different types of organizations arose in different periods.

The other regression results are in line with the predictions of the model. The prior year fund-raising expense is positively related to donations, and the coefficients are statistically significant at a 1 percent level in both years for all samples. Total assets, used as a control for size, is significantly positive for the audited and full samples. The control variables for government grants and program income have negative signs, consistent with the idea that they "crowd out" donations, but the magnitude of the coefficients is small (and not significant in 1994) for the audited organizations. The higher crowding out effect in the unaudited sample may reflect greater use of government money by these organizations. When separate regressions by industry are performed on the full sample, statistically significant crowding out effects of government funding were detected for the health, social welfare, civic, cultural/educational, animals/environmental, public policy, and "other" categories in both 1993 and 1994, with coefficients ranging from −0.12 to −0.24. This result is generally consistent with the moderate crowding out effects discussed by Steinberg (1993).

When the regressions for the full sample are repeated separately by service type (Table 5), price coefficients are consistently negative and generally significant. All 20 coefficients shown in Table 5 for the full sample are negative, with values ranging from −0.19 to −1.17, and 16 are significant at 10 percent or higher levels.[14]

Both the magnitude and the significance of the price elasticities in Table 5 are generally lower for the unaudited organizations.[15] For example, the price coefficients for *unaudited* health, civic, support, public policy, and "other" organizations are insignificant in both years and have an unexpected (positive) sign in one year, while the price coefficients for the *audited* organizations in these groups are consistently negative, significant at the 10 percent level. More generally, the coefficients for audited subsamples are larger than the coefficients for the unaudited organizations of the same type in 18 out of 20 cases. All 20 price coefficients for audited organizations are negative, and 18 are significant at the 10 percent or higher levels. For the unaudited sample, only 12 of the 18 coefficients are the expected negative sign, and only three of these are significantly negative.

Within the audited subsample, where price is generally significant, the price coefficients range from −0.18 to −2.42. The differences in price sensitivity may not be due to inherent industry characteristics, but rather to the relative prevalence of factors discussed in Section III. For example, in 1994 social welfare agencies, the least price-sensitive

Table 5. Selected 1993 and 1994 Regression Results from the Baseline Model, to Provide Comparisons by Organization Type (The Table reflects the coefficient of Price, (t-statistic), and adjusted R^2 from each regression)

	Prior Year Audit Not Required		Prior Year Audit Required		Full Sample	
	1993	1994	1993	1994	1993	1994
Health	−0.04	0.07	−0.40**	−0.42***	−0.27***	−0.20
	(0.2)	(0.4)	(1.8)	(1.5)	(1.5)	(1.1)
	0.20	0.24	0.56	0.51	0.56	0.55
Social Welfare	−0.19***	0.01	−0.18	−0.26**	−0.33*	−0.19**
	(1.6)	(0.1)	(1.1)	(2.2)	(2.6)	(1.7)
	0.19	0.19	0.51	0.46	0.47	0.45
Civic	0.15	−0.16	−0.50**	−0.65**	−0.19	−0.40*
	(0.8)	(1.2)	(2.2)	(2.3)	(1.1)	(2.8)
	0.19	0.22	0.50	0.40	0.44	0.43
Cultural/Educational	−0.14	−0.17	−0.36*	−0.66*	−0.34*	−0.55*
	(0.8)	(1.2)	(2.8)	(4.2)	(2.6)	(4.5)
	0.18	0.23	0.48	0.54	0.46	0.50
Animals/Environment	−0.15	−0.87	−0.44***	−0.59***	−0.37***	−1.00**
	(0.5)	(1.2)	(1.6)	(1.9)	(1.3)	(1.9)
	0.32	0.33	0.74	0.69	0.72	0.67
Social/Fraternal	−0.50*	−0.36*	−0.71*	−0.54*	−0.66*	−0.63*
	(2.5)	(2.2)	(2.8)	(3.4)	(4.6)	(4.9)
	0.13	0.20	0.37	0.61	0.41	0.55
Support Organizations	−0.03	0.08	−0.69*	−0.70*	−0.62*	−0.62*
	(0.1)	(0.4)	(5.2)	(5.3)	(5.1)	(4.6)
	0.00	0.09	0.49	0.52	0.45	0.47
Public Policy	−0.09	0.18	−0.84*	−0.66*	−0.60**	−0.45***
	(0.3)	(0.5)	(3.0)	(3.6)	(2.0)	(1.5)
	0.21	0.23	0.59	0.62	0.62	0.64
Foreign Relations	NA	NA	−1.12	−2.42*	−0.47	−1.17*
			(0.9)	(3.2)	(0.8)	(2.7)
			0.52	0.62	0.60	0.65
Other	−0.06	0.30	−0.52***	−0.44***	−0.39***	−0.28
	(0.1)	(0.9)	(1.6)	(1.3)	(1.4)	(1.0)
	0.08	0.10	0.17	0.34	0.32	0.31

Notes: This table presents selected regression results using the baseline model used in Table 4 on 10 different service category subsamples in each year. Industries with samples less than 50 were not considered. Asymptotic t-statistics are used due to indications of heteroscedasticity from White's general test (White, 1980).
 *, **, *** Significant at the 1%, 5% or 10% levels, respectively, on one-sided tests.

category in the full sample, were more likely to receive low levels of donations, to report implausibly low supporting service costs, and to be start-up organizations than foreign relations organizations, the most price sensitive category.

VII. DIFFERENTIAL PRICE SENSITIVITY IN REGRESSION RESULTS

This section employs regressions using dummy variables to test the effect on price elasticity of factors discussed in Section III. For each factor, a zero/one dummy variable is added to the baseline model. In addition, the price variable is divided into two variables—a variable that equals price when the dummy equals one, and is zero otherwise, and another that equals price when the dummy equals zero, and is otherwise zero. Adding these two variables tests both the dummy variable's effect on the intercept and its effect on the slope of price. F-tests are used to test the differences between the price coefficients for significance. Table 6 shows the results of these tests.

The first factor tested was organization size. Small organizations are predicted to exhibit lower price elasticity. Because of the interplay of size and New York's audit requirement, only the full sample was tested for this characteristic.

I arbitrarily set a "small size" dummy variable equal to one in the 1994 (1993) regressions if 1993 *total revenues* were less than $143,000, the approximate 30th percentile level for the full sample. The dummy has negative coefficients of −0.14 and −0.24, significant at 5 and 1 percent levels. This is expected, as low total prior year revenues are correlated with low current year donations. However, the price coefficients gave unexpected values. The price coefficients of the small organizations are −0.57 and −0.61, while the coefficients for the larger organizations were −0.39 and −0.40, all significant at 1 percent levels. F-tests indicate the coefficients are significantly different at a 10 percent level in 1994 and a 5 percent level in 1993. Thus, small size, in terms of total revenues, is associated with higher price sensitivity of donations.

However, this size effect may not be robust to changes in the definition of size. If the definition of very small organizations is changed to be total *assets* below the approximate 1993 twenty-fifth percentile level of $70,000, then the price coefficients for large and small organizations for 1994 are not significantly different. Thus, the evidence for higher price sensitivity of small organizations is interesting but not conclusive.

A second consideration is whether organizations are in a start-up phase. Start-up organizations are predicted to be less price sensitive. As shown in Table 6, the price coefficients for organizations less than four years old are smaller. The difference in coefficients is statistically significant for the full sample in both years, but only significant for the audited sample in 1993.

A third factor is the degree of reliance on direct contributions. For organizations with low dependence on donations, lower price sensitivity is predicted. First, the percentage of revenues from direct contributions is used to test this assertion. A dummy variable is set equal to one if 1992 direct contributions were lower than 20 percent of revenues. The price coefficients for organizations depending heavily on direct contributions for the subsamples tested range from −0.57 to −0.78, significant at the 1 percent level, while the price coefficients for the other organizations are much smaller and not significantly different from zero, at a 10 percent level, in three of the four regressions. The two price coefficients are significantly different at 10 percent or better levels in each case. Second, the dependence on direct contributions was tested using an absolute dollar cutoff of $100,000 in 1992 direct contributions. The 1994 and 1993 price coefficients for the organizations with high levels of 1992 direct contributions were −0.96 and −0.78, significant at 1 percent levels, and significantly higher, at a 1 percent level, than the −0.07 and −0.10 coefficients reported for the other subsample. Thus, the evidence supports lower price sensitivity of organizations with low historic dependence on donations.

The fourth factor tested is the degree of dependence on indirect contributions. Price is predicted to be less relevant when indirect donations are high. Tests using a dummy variable, based on whether indirect support exceeded one third of public support,[16] revealed weak evidence for this hypothesis. The price coefficients are lower and generally less significant for organizations depending heavily upon indirect contributions. However, F-tests for differences in coefficients are not significant in three of the four samples. The results are somewhat sensitive to high-leverage observations, as noted in Table 6.

Local organizations are predicted in Section III to have lower price sensitivity. A simple division of the sample between organizations with New York and out-of-state addresses finds significantly lower price sensitivity for the New York organizations in the full sample in each year, with out-of-state organizations reporting price elasticities of −0.98 and −0.97 in 1994 and 1993, versus elasticities of −0.45 and −0.42 for the New York organizations. However, when the sample is restricted to the generally larger organizations of the audited sample, the difference between the two coefficients is smaller in size and no longer significant,

Table 6. Differential Price Sensitivity Tests, Using Dummy Variables in 1994 Baseline Regressions Selected Regression Results from Extensions of the Baseline Model to Test the Effect of Various Organizational Characteristics on Price Elasticity for Organizations Filing Regulatory Reports with New York State in 1993 and 1994

Organizational Characteristic Dummy	% of sample dummy = 1	Dummy Variable Coefficient	Price Coefficient (dummy = 0)	Price Coefficient (dummy = 1)	F-test p-value
Small Size					
1994 Full Sample	28.9%	−0.14**	−0.39*	−0.57*	0.08
1993 Full sample	28.9%	−0.24*	−0.40*	−0.61*	0.03
Startup					
1994 Full Sample	19.5%	0.21**	−0.62*	−0.26*	0.00
1993 Full Sample	14.6%	0.30*	−0.62*	−0.29*	0.00
1994—P/Y audit	16.7%	−0.03	−0.62*	−0.50*	0.42
1993 -- P/Y audit	12.2%	−0.03	−0.66*	−0.20**	0.00[a]
Low % Direct Support					
1994 Full Sample	40.2%	−1.89*	−0.78*	0.07	0.00
1993 Full Sample	40.4%	−2.29*	−0.65*	−0.03	0.00
1994—P/Y audit	16.2%	−0.81*	−0.63*	−0.32**	0.02
1993—P/Y audit	16.3%	−0.90*	−0.57*	−0.19	0.10

Low $ Direct Support				
1994 Full Sample	64.1%	-2.20*	-0.96*	-0.07***	0.00
1993 Full sample	62.2%	-2.37*	-0.78*	-0.10**	0.00
Indirect Support					
1994 Full Sample	10.5%	-0.98*	-0.54*	-0.31**,b	0.19
1993 Full Sample	11.2%	-1.02*	-0.55*	-0.42*,b	0.42[c]
1994—P/Y audit	4.6%	-0.47*	-0.60*	-0.18	0.29
1993—P/Y audit	5.2%	-1.01*	-0.54*	0.16[a]	0.02
Local Organizations					
1994 Full Sample	86.0%	-0.98*	-0.97*	-0.42*	0.00
1993 Full Sample	85.7%	-0.87*	-0.98*	-0.45*	0.00
1994—P/Y audit	74.1%	-0.53*	-0.63*	-0.52*	0.47
1993—P/Y audit	74.3%	-0.52*	-0.64*	-0.46*	0.21

Notes: This table presents key 1993 and 1994 results from applying different regression models to the samples discussed in Table 1. Each model is an extension of the baseline log-linear model used in Table 4, except that a zero/one dummy term is inserted and the price variable is replaced by two variables. One price variable equals zero when the dummy is zero, and equals log of price otherwise. The second equals zero when the dummy is one, and equals log of price otherwise. The F-test p-values are from tests that the two price coefficients are the same.

The dummy variables used are:

Small Size = 1 if 1993 total revenues < $143,000, the (rounded) 30th percentile level.
Startup = 1 if the organization has been registered for three years or less
Low % direct support = 1 if 1992 direct contributions < 20% of revenues
Low $ direct support = 1 if 1992 direct contributions < $100,000
Indirect support = 1 if 1993 indirect contributions > 1/3 of public support
Local organizations = 1 if address is in New York
Implausible data = 1 if Fund-raising or administration = 0 in 1993 or 1994

*, **, *** Significant at 1%, 5%, or 10% levels, on one-tailed tests, using asymptotic t-statistics.
[a] Significant at a 10% level if several high-leverage observations are excluded.
[b] Not significant at a 10% level if high-leverage observations are excluded.
[c] Significant at a 5% level if high-leverage observations are excluded.

implying that size (or the audit's impact on plausibility), more than location, is driving these results.

Finally, the sample was divided between organizations with "implausible data" (zero fund-raising or administrative expenses in 1993 or 1994) and those with "plausible" data. The sensitivity of donations to price is predicted to be lower when price is implausible. As indicated in Table 6, the price coefficients for the organizations with implausible data are lower in each case, and the difference in price is highly significant in three of the four regressions. Interestingly, the differences in price were somewhat smaller in magnitude and less significant for the audited subsample. This would be consistent with enhanced plausibility in general of audited data.

The results in Table 6 suggest that donations are most price sensitive for charities with plausible data and are highly dependent on direct contributions in either absolute or percentage terms. Donations are least price sensitive for organizations reporting either zero administrative or zero fund-raising expense, that depend very little on contributions in a base year.

To see whether these predictions dominate industry effects, I repeat the baseline regressions on two new subsamples. The results are shown in Table 7, where sufficient observations exist. Generally, the predicted results are obtained. The subsample of donation-reliant organizations has high price elasticity in every case, significant at the 5 percent or better level. The price coefficients for each industry are higher than those shown in Table 5. The price coefficients for the other subsample are uniformly lower in magnitude, and in seven of the 14 cases they have an unexpected sign. In only two cases are the coefficients significantly negative at the 5 percent level.

It is not clear from examining Table 7 whether any statistically significant industry-specific differences in price sensitivity exist within the first subsample. Support organizations have the highest price coefficients each year, but the other industries show no clear pattern. To address this question, I test a modified model, which allows the price coefficient to vary among the seven industries in Table 7, for both the "predicted high price sensitivity" and "predicted low price sensitivity" subsamples in 1993 and 1994. Chow tests indicate that the industry-specific price coefficients are not significantly different, at a 5 percent level, in three of the four regressions, although they are significantly different for the high predicted price elasticity sample in

Table 7. Comparative Price Elasticities, Using the Baseline Regression Model from Table 4, of Subsamples with Different Expected Price Elasticity, by Type of Charity
Table Contains Price Elasticities, N, and Regression R^2 Statistics

	Predicted high price elasticity subsample[a]		Predicted low price elasticity subsample[a]	
Organization Type	1993	1994	1993	1994
Health	−1.16*	−0.96*	−0.20	0.39
	113	108	299	303
	0.74	0.74	0.15	0.18
Social Welfare	−0.88**	−2.00*	−0.42**	−0.43**
	93	81	855	900
	0.72	0.65	0.17	0.16
Civic	NA	NA	0.14	-0.05
	28	29	171	166
			0.28	0.27
Educational/Cultural	−1.23*	−1.49*	−0.27	−0.13
	105	99	219	211
	0.70	0.65	0.30	0.33
Support	−2.35*	−2.67*	−0.18	0.48
	100	98	48	46
	0.57	0.57	-0.05	-0.02
Public Policy	−1.32*	−0.79*	0.46	0.73
	125	118	117	112
	0.63	0.71	0.21	0.10
Other	NA	NA	0.62	0.73
	6	6	94	93
			0.14	0.01

Notes: [a]The price elasticities shown are the coefficients of price, using the baseline model employed in Table 4. The organizations predicted to have low price sensitivity received less than 10% of revenues from direct contributions, had 1992 direct contributions < $1 million, and reported either zero fundraising or zero administrative costs in the prior year. The organizations in the second subsample had 1992 direct contributions > $1 million and > 10% of prior year revenues, and reported nonzero administrative and fund-raising expenses in the prior year.
If there were less than 40 observations, regression results were not reported.
*, ** ,*** Significant at 1%, 5%, or 10% levels, on a one-tailed test and asymptotic t-statistics.

1993. This test provides evidence that industry-specific price elasticity differences are generally not significant after controlling for dependence on contributions and data plausibility.

VIII. DISCUSSION AND CONCLUSIONS

Standard-setters believe donors are concerned with evaluating service efforts of nonprofit organizations and have established requirements for classification of expenses and for disclosure of joint cost data. The assumption is that expense ratios are of particular concern to donors. However, there has been little empirical research on the relationship between accounting data and donations. I find a significant relation between donations and price (as reflected in expense ratios) in situations when the data could be expected to be relevant and reliable. This finding is generally supportive of the current regulatory structure, which relies on disclosure to influence donors away from inefficient organizations.

My findings are consistent with a contextual view of the importance of financial information. Price elasticity depends on data relevance and reliability. Organizational characteristics that are strongly related to higher price sensitivity are age of the organization, dependence on direct contributions, and plausibility of data. A high dependence on indirect source of donations does not appear to affect price elasticity. The evidence on the effect of size is not clear, and depends on the proxy used for size. Additionally, differences in the effect of age are observed between large and small organizations. Differences in elasticity between local and other organizations are not strong after controlling for size. Similarly, industry differences in elasticity are not strong after controlling for other organizational factors.

ACKNOWLEDGMENT

This paper is based on my dissertation at New York University's Stern School of Business. It reflects comments and suggestions by my dissertation committee (Jeffrey Callen, Stephen Ryan, and Lawrence White) as well as Joshua Livnat, David Gelb, Itzhak Krinsky, Gary Simon, two anonymous reviewers, and seminar participants at the 1997 AAA National Conference. I gratefully acknowledge data collection assistance from the New York State Department of State and financial assistance from the Deloitte & Touche Foundation and New York University.

NOTES

1. Weisbrod and Dominguez assume that age proxies for the "stock of goodwill or trust among potential donors—which affects their perception of output quality."
2. Weisbrod and Dominguez's definition used total donations rather than total expenses.
3. The denominator of price simplifies to the ratio of program expenses to total expenses.
4. See Forbes (1998) for a survey of studies of organizational effectiveness.
5. Although not tested in this study, differences in accounting practices may affect the reported ratios. For example, consolidation practices and methods of allocating joint costs among program, administrative, and fund-raising expenses vary. The issue of accounting for joint costs of fund-raising and public information is discussed in Tinkelman (1998).
6. One exception to GAAP is that regulatory reporting excludes donated services. Second, the regulatory reports are on a legal entity basis, while organizations following AICPA SOP 78-10 (AICPA 1978) or the National Health Council's standards (National Health Council 1988) were required to prepare combined financial statements if certain criteria were met.
7. The use of the log of price also reduces the impact of outliers. Regression results without the truncation are similar to those presented here for the baseline sample.
8. Steinberg (1986b) also considered zero reported fund-raising or administrative expenses for a period of time as implausible. He attempted to restrict his sample to organizations with more plausible data, but found that resulted in an inadequate sample.
9. Price remains insignificant if it is defined as the level of price, rather than the change in price from the prior year.
10. The sensitivity of this model is also evident in Steinberg's (1986b) computed marginal donative products. The significance level of five of the 15 marginal donative products shown changes either to or from the 5 percent level when the sample inclusion criteria are changed.
11. Current year, rather than prior year, values are used for government grants, program income, and other revenues on the assumption that major changes in government funding or types of programs would become quickly known to the organization's supporters.
12. The results shown are robust to deletion of data points with high leverage statistics. Robustness was also tested by using rank regression, which yielded similar results. See Lang and Lundholm (1993) for an example of the use of rank regression.
13. Price is not significant in the differenced form of this model, for the reasons discussed in Section V. When the first differences in 1994 contributions, deflated by total assets, are regressed on the change in price, the organization's age, and deflated changes in fund-raising costs, other revenues, government grants, and program income, price is not significant. The explanatory power of the differenced model is very low, with adjusted R^2 of only 0.01 for the full sample.
14. Weisbrod and Dominguez's (1986) price coefficients range somewhat higher, from -0.73 to -2.65. Part of the difference may be due to their omission of administrative costs, which reduces the price.

15. Since theory predicts price to be negative, one-tailed tests are used.
16. Public support is the total of direct and indirect contributions.

REFERENCES

American Institute of Certified Public Accountants. 1978. Statement of Position 78-10, *Accounting Principles and Reporting Practices for Certain Nonprofit Organizations.* New York: AICPA.

———. 1994. Audit and Accounting Guide, *Audits of Certain Nonprofit Organizations.* New York: AICPA.

Bennett, J. T., and T. J. DiLorenzo. 1994. *Unhealthy Charities—Hazardous to Your Health and Wealth.* New York: Basic Books.

Callen, J. L. 1994. Money donations, volunteering and organizational efficiency. *The Journal of Productivity Analysis* 67(3): 215-228.

Council of Better Business Bureaus. 1994. *Give But Give Wisely.* Holiday Edition.

Engstrom, J. H. 1988. Information needs of college and university financial decision makers. *Research Report.* Stamford, CT: GASB.

FASB. May, 1980a. Qualitative characteristics of accounting information. *Statement of Financial Accounting Concepts No. 2.* Stamford, CT: FASB.

———. December, 1980b. Objectives of financial reporting by nonbusiness organizations. *Statement of Financial Accounting Concepts No. 3.* Stamford, CT: FASB.

Forbes, D. P. 1998. Measuring the unmeasurable: empirical studies of nonprofit organization effectiveness from 1977 to 1997. *Nonprofit and Voluntary Sector Quarterly* 27(2): 183-202.

Froelich, K. A., and T. W. Knoepfle. 1996. Internal revenue service 990 data: Fact or fiction? *Nonprofit and Voluntary Sector Quarterly* 25(1) (March): 40-52.

Grimes, A. J. 1977. The fund-raising percentage as a quantitative standard for regulation of public charities, with particular emphasis on voluntary health and welfare organizations. In *Research Papers Sponsored by The Commission on Private Philanthropy and Public Needs.* Washington, DC: U. S. Dept. of the Treasury.

Guidestar Directory of American Charities, 1996 Index. 1996. Williamsburg, VA: Philanthropic Research Inc.

Lang, M., and R. Lundholm. 1993. Cross-sectional determinants of analyst ratings of corporate disclosure. *Journal of Accounting Research* 31 (2) (Autumn): 246-270.

National Health Council. 1988. *Standards of Accounting and Financial Reporting for Voluntary Health and Welfare Organizations. Revised 1998—Third Edition.* National Health Council.

Posnett, J., and T. Sandler. 1989. Demand for charity donations in private non-profit markets: The case of the U. K. *Journal of Public Economics* 40: 187-200.

Steinberg, R. 1983. Two essays on the nonprofit sector. Doctoral Dissertation, University of Pennsylvania.

———. 1986a. Should donors care about fundraising? In *The Economics of Nonprofit Organizations—Studies in Structure and Policy,* ed. S. Rose-Ackerman, 346-364. New York: Oxford University Press.

———. 1986b. The revealed objective functions of nonprofit firms. *Rand Journal of Economics* 17(4) (Winter): 508-526.

———. 1993. Does government spending crowd out donations: Interpreting the evidence. In *The Nonprofit Sector in the Mixed Economy*, eds. A. Ben Ner and B. Gui. Ann Arbor, MI: The University of Michigan Press.

Stout, W. D. 1997. Materiality and nonprofit organizations: An empirical investigation of materiality thresholds of financial statement users. Doctoral Dissertation, University of South Florida.

Tinkelman, D. 1998. Differences in sensitivity of financial statement users to joint cost allocations: The Case of nonprofit organizations. *Journal of Accounting, Auditing and Finance*. Fall.

Weisbrod, B. A., and N. D. Dominguez. 1986. Demand for collective goods in private markets: Can fundraising expenditures help overcome free-rider behavior?" *Journal of Public Economics* 30: 83-96.

White, H. 1980. A heteroscedasticity-consistent covariance matrix estimator and a direct test for heteroscedasticity. *Econometrica* 48: 817-838.

HEALTH CARE ACCOUNTING RESEARCH
A REVIEW OF THE PROFESSIONAL LITERATURE, MODELS, DATA, AND RESEARCH OPPORTUNITIES

Dana A. Forgione

ABSTRACT

The U.S. health care industry has experienced unprecedented, market-driven change for more than a decade. With change comes major realignment of the economic factors and incentives that influence the management of health care organizations. The far-reaching economic magnitude and social significance of the trillion-dollar health care industry, when examined from the perspective of accounting and related theories, provides opportunities for research that are highly relevant and widely varied in scope. I review the salient professional health care accounting literature, consider research models and approaches, discuss major sources of data, and identify some of the many opportunities for future research and publication that exist in the area of health care accounting. I offer an adaptation of the agency theory model for comparative study of health care organizations, and describe a variety of alternative research venues.

I. INTRODUCTION

The health care industry experienced unprecedented, market-driven change for more than a decade. With change comes major realignment of the economic factors and incentives that influence the management of health care organizations. The ways in which health care organizations are financed, the array of assets in which they invest, and the spectrum of operations they pursue raise new and problematic issues for financial accounting and reporting. Issues of defining the reporting entity, revenue recognition, accounting for investments, mergers, acquisitions, and joint ventures between for-profit and nonprofit organizations, recognition of community benefit obligations such as charity care, accounting for agency relationships, risk contracts, assessments similar to taxes on tax-exempt organizations, and changing demands for public financial and operating information disclosures are just a sampling of the issues faced by accountants in the health care arena.

In the discussion that follows, I review the salient professional accounting literature. I also consider some research models and approaches, discuss sources of data, and identify some of the many opportunities for future research and publication in health care accounting.

II. PROFESSIONAL LITERATURE

The predominant, authoritative financial accounting and reporting literature for health care organizations consists of pronouncements and publications by the Financial Accounting Standards Board (FASB), the Governmental Accounting Standards Board (GASB), the American Institute of Certified Public Accountants (AICPA), the U.S. General Accounting Office (GAO), the U.S. Office of Management and Budget (OMB), the Healthcare Financial Management Association (HFMA), and the American Hospital Association (AHA).

Accounting regulations are also prescribed by Medicare and Medicaid for cost reimbursement purposes, by the U.S. Internal Revenue Service (IRS), by individual states, and by other regulatory agencies for measuring attributes relevant to reimbursement, certificate of need, and other public health care policy matters. These matters are important for research endeavors which depend on data derived from regulatory disclosures, or for research designs that include tests or controls of regulatory effects relative to certain variables. I focus on financial accounting and reporting matters, and generally refer to such regulatory accounting prescriptions only when they relate directly to the immediate discussion.

The relevant FASB pronouncements include the Statements of Financial Accounting Concepts (SFAC), and Statements of Financial Accounting Standards (SFAS). The GASB pronouncements include primarily the Statements of Governmental Accounting Standards. The AICPA publications consist primarily of the Statements of Position (SOP), the AICPA *Audit and Accounting Guide: Health Care Organizations* (*Audit Guide*), and the AICPA *Audit Risk Alerts: Health Care Industry Developments*. These pronouncements constitute the primary authoritative literature for health care accounting in the private, or state and local government sector.

U.S. governmental publications include the GAO's *Government Auditing Standards*, known as "The Yellow Book," and the OMB Circular A-133: *Audits of Institutions of Higher Education and Other Nonprofit Institutions*.[1] These pronouncements apply to federal government hospitals and to recipients of federal funds, including state and local government-controlled and private health care organizations.

The HFMA pronouncements include eight currently outstanding Principles and Practices Board (P&PB) Statements of Position. The HFMA also now produces the former AHA document, *Chart of Accounts for Hospitals* (Seawell 1995). The primary AHA publication related to accounting is the document, *Estimated Useful Lives of Depreciable Hospital Assets*. These pronouncements constitute the primary industry guidance for health care accounting.

The financial professionals who help manage the U.S. health care industry are privately organized in the HFMA. The HFMA was founded in 1946, and now consists of more than 30,000 members in 70 chapters. In 1974 the HFMA membership established a task force to examine health care accounting and the HFMA's role in formulating positions on issues. The result in 1975 was formation of the P&PB. The P&PB consists of 12 members, and develops position statements through a deliberative process. Similar to the FASB, the P&PB first develops a background paper, then prepares a discussion memorandum. Next it considers feedback from the professional community and prepares an exposure draft. Then, after incorporating additional feedback, the P&PB issues its final Statement of Position.

To date, the P&PB has issued 20 original Statements of Position that have increased rapidly in substance and complexity. Level E of Generally Accepted Accounting Principles (GAAP) is the source of authority that includes industry guidance under AICPA Statement of Auditing Standards (SAS) No. 69. As early as 1990 the HFMA's P&PB statements were explicitly recognized by the AICPA as Level 4 GAAP—the equivalent predecessor to today's Level E GAAP,[2] as identified under the then current SAS No. 52. The 1990 AICPA *Audit Risk Alert* for the health care industry states, "There is some confusion regarding the hierarchy of generally accepted accounting principles (GAAP) of health care entities....HFMA Principles and Practices Board Statements are considered level 4 GAAP under SAS No. 52."

Until recently, the jurisdictional boundaries in accounting standards for hospitals were not clearly defined. Considerable overlap seemed to exist between the GASB and FASB. The FASB has authority to prescribe accounting standards that apply to for-profit and private nonprofit hospitals. The GASB has authority to prescribe accounting standards for state and local government hospitals. However, FASB rules also apply to state and local governmental hospitals under GASB jurisdiction to the extent that GASB specifically refers to the applicability of such FASB rules—such as in the case of state and local government-owned hospitals that use the enterprise fund accounting and reporting model (*Audit Guide*). In addition, the GAO and OMB prescribe accounting standards for federal government hospitals, such as military and Veterans Administration hospitals, as well as for organizations that receive federal funds, including private health care organizations.

In the private sector the HFMA is the only organization in the United States that provides detailed, substantive industry guidance on the technical peculiarities of accounting and reporting for institutional health care providers. The HFMA's P&PB may also be viewed as a substantive lobbying effort with regard to influencing the formation of authoritative health care accounting standards. A few years ago the AICPA resisted strenuous industry opposition led by the HFMA on issues relating to changes in charity care accounting and reporting (Kovener 1990). The above AICPA statement quoted from it's 1990 *Audit Risk Alert* may have been, in part, an assertion of the FASB's authority in the standard setting process at the time.

Over the years, some of the P&PB Statements of Position were superseded by later statements, and due to obsolescence and/or superseding authoritative literature, in 1997 the P&PB withdrew some of it's statements. Of the 20 original P&PB Statements of Position, statement Nos. 5, 11, and 15–20 are currently outstanding and effective. All others were superseded or withdrawn.

In Appendix A, I present a concise list of the major authoritative documents for health care accounting, including P&PB statements that are now superseded or withdrawn. In Appendix B, I present a brief, annotated review of each of the current, authoritative documents, with emphasis on the outstanding HFMA's P&PB statements, their publication history, and identification of those superseding any previous statements. In the following section I discuss related opportunities for research in the effects of accounting standards for the health care industry.

III. RESEARCH OPPORTUNITIES

In 1997 Americans spent $949 billion on health care (ProPAC 1996). That represents one of the single largest portions of gross domestic product in the entire U.S. economy. The far-reaching economic magnitude and social significance of the health care industry, when examined from the perspective of accounting and related theories, and using the plethora of high-quality available data, provides opportunities for research that are highly relevant and varied in scope. In this section I describe a number of research opportunities, beginning with application of an agency theory perspective. I also discuss research opportunities based on a variety of other perspectives, including the information content of sociometric data in performance evaluation, behavior and ethics, international comparisons, bankruptcy and illiquidity, technology effects on financial performance, and longitudinal analyses.

A. Agency Theory

Considerable evidence from the P&PB statements indicates that the health care industry's perceptions about constituent groups and user needs are highly analogous to constructs of the agency model. For example, Statement No. 3 (1980) identifies constituent groups as management, creditors, investors, donors, and regulators. Statement No. 6 (1984) identifies bond covenant and regulatory (political cost) effects of reported accounts receivable turnover measures. Fama and Jensen (1983) and Wallace (1987) both provide early discussions of the agency problem within nonprofit organizations in general, while Conrad (1984), Forgione (1987), and Foster (1987) develop and apply aspects of the model within the health care industry context.

The agency paradigm can be used to describe the relation between the economic incentives brought to bear on, for example, hospital management, by the constituent regulators, donors or investors, and creditors, and the associated choices made by hospital managers. Hospitals use accrual accounting, and the existence of both for-profit and nonprofit organizations operating, and often directly competing, in the same markets offers an excellent opportunity to observe the incentive effects of differing forms of organizational control on both the real-valued (financing, investing, and operating) choices, and the accounting choices of hospital managers. Figure 1 presents an adaptation of the agency model (Forgione 1987) that is useful for the design of research in health care accounting.

As depicted in Figure 1, the equity investor has two choices in the health care capital market. The first is to buy stock in a for-profit health care organization, such as a proprietary hospital system, in which case the investor receives a typical return on equity. The second is to make a donation to a nonprofit organization, such as a community hospital system, in which case the investor receives the present value of any tax effects, plus valued goodwill. The goodwill generated may result in enhanced publicity, public image, and consequent improved business opportunities and cash flows for the donor in other proprietary endeavors.

In the model depicted in Figure 1, the for-profit investor requires profit-based financial reporting in order to monitor management's production of the return on investment. The nonprofit donor requires separate-fund-based financial reporting in order to monitor manage-

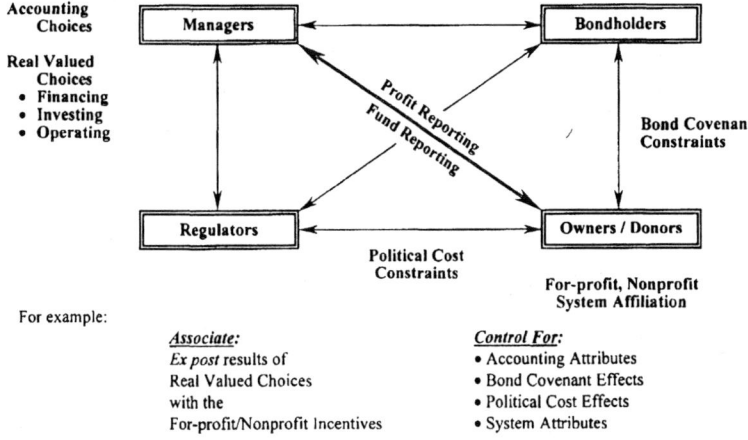

Figure 1. Economic Relationships

ment's production of the specific forms of valued goodwill identified under restricted-fund donations, for example, construction of a children's wing, or investment in a cancer research center bearing the donor's name as benefactor. The importance of this nonprofit, separate-fund stewardship factor is described and emphasized in P&PB Statement No. 8.

While substantial profit sharing incentive systems are used to help align the economic interests of for-profit managers with those of the stockholders, substantial profit sharing systems are not permitted by the IRS in the case of nonprofit organizations (*US IRC* Sec. 501(c)3). Nevertheless, in place of profit sharing systems, donor-held seats on the board of directors, public scrutiny, U.S. Securities and Exchange Commission (SEC) sanctions, and other forms of monitoring exist that provide nonprofit managers with strong incentives for behavior that is consistent with serving the objectives of equity donors.

In his analysis, Conrad (1984) uses an agency theory argument to demonstrate that in equilibrium, the two different types of returns produced by the for-profit and nonprofit organizational forms will provide equivalent value to the investor. He observes that, "The philanthropist will demand a demonstration that the value of the hospital's investment is equivalent to that of financial opportunities of comparable risk, even though the payoff to donated capital is in nonpecuniary terms (e.g. charity care)." Concerning the hospital's cost of equity versus debt capital, Conrad further observes that, "Whether payment is in the form of interest on debt or the search costs incurred by non-profits in seeking to attract philanthropy, these are real social costs which cannot be avoided." Thus, in Conrad's argument the historical failure of cost-based payors such as Medicare to pay nonprofit organizations rates that incorporated a return on equity, prevented the nonprofits from being able to reinvest those returns in the production of services which would yield the kind of net intangible returns on investment valued by the equity donors (philanthropists). For example, a donor may value the goodwill that comes from sponsoring a cancer research institute, the children's wing of a hospital, or a prenatal charity care clinic. Failure to pay the nonprofit organization a return on donated equity that could be put to work producing the forms of goodwill valued by the donor was considered tantamount to a 100 percent tax on the equity returns of the nonprofit organization, and thus produced a shift in the investment equilibrium.

In a related study, Foster (1987) uses agency theory and an access to capital argument to assess the hospital's choice of organizational form. He concludes that access to capital is associated with the choice of for-profit organizational form. That is, the costs of attracting donated equity for his observed organizations exceeded the costs of attracting for-profit stockholders. Two more recent studies (Martin and Kwon 1996; Kwon, Moldofsky, and Martin 1997) address the related issues of capital structure choice in nonprofit hospitals, and the economic theory of gift-giving. Their findings are consistent with those of Foster.

Probably the major factor influencing the choice of organizational form in health care is the availability of investors who perceive the organization as being able to produce a level of expected earnings that they value more highly than the level of expected tax benefits plus the goodwill it can produce. This is also related to the investors' individual income tax situations, such as whether they possess appreciated property that can be used for donated investment at the current fair market value, and whether they have sufficient ordinary income to absorb the tax deductions accruing from such a donation.

The model in Figure 1 adapts the agency framework to include the two forms of private equity capital investment and associated returns that exist in the health care industry, as well as the respective forms of financial reporting demanded by the investors. In one application of this model, Forgione (1987) finds a significant association between the for-profit/nonprofit economic incentives and real-valued financial and nonfinancial management performance measures observed during the first year of the Medicare Prospective Payment System, in both multihospital systems and independent hospitals.

The political cost constraints found in health care that are identified in Figure 1 are considerably more explicit than in the commercial business domain, and consist of explicit threats of revocation of tax-exempt status based on inadequate provision of measurable charity care and other community benefits or, in the case of Medicare, lack of payment for patient length of stay in excess of prescribed (based on industry average days) amounts. Recent cases include new assessments similar to taxes imposed on nonprofit health care organizations by state regulators. P&PB Statement No. 17 *Assessments and Arrangements Similar to Taxes on Tax-Exempt Institutional Healthcare Providers* was issued specifically to address the accounting implications of such political costs.

The U.S. Federal Bureau of Investigation recently received a government mandate to make the investigation and prosecution of health care fraud and abuse one of its highest priorities (Owens 1997). The U.S. Department of Health and Human Services, Office of Inspector General has also significantly increased it's investigations of health care fraud and abuse under the program "Operation Restore Trust" (Brown 1997; Dugan 1997). These are graphic examples of political costs incurred by health care organizations whose managers engage in abusive billing and other practices that are contrary to the law and the public interest. Nonprofit health care managers who consume excessive perquisites in breach of the public interest mission of such organizations also draw the attention of regulators. Boards of directors of nonprofit hospitals have been sued for breach of fiduciary responsibility in failing to provide factual and meaningful amounts of public community benefits, while their managers consume lavish compensation and nonpecuniary benefits from organizational resources (State of Texas 1990).

Management's self-interest maximization at the expense of equity capital providers, creditors, or the public interest is evident from lawsuits which allege consumption of excessive nonpecuniary benefits in the form of related-party transactions, risk-free real estate "sweetheart deals" established by management, hospital-owned hunting lodges for the benefit of management, and so on (Swasy 1990; State of Texas 1990; SoRelle 1991). Under it's Coordinated Examination Program, the Exempt Organizations Division of the IRS has aggressively pursued audits of most major hospitals throughout the United States. The IRS has specifically examined unrelated business income and private inurement issues, and an official of the IRS was quoted as warning that, "one or two truly adverse positions," would probably be taken based on these audits (Tax Analysts 1993). Researchers investigating factors associated with tax court decisions on exempt status will find P&PB Statement No. 15 especially useful, as charity care measures have been used as important criteria in these cases.

As the AICPA *Audit Guide* and the P&PB statements indicate, health care managers have considerable latitude in making both accounting and real-valued choices. In addition, regulators may aggressively pursue their own political agendas. However, doctors also represent a significant stakeholder group in health care organizations. They have traditionally been the primary customers of the hospital, who would schedule use of the hospital's facilities in order to market their own services to patients. The patients traditionally paid for the services and use of the hospital facilities either directly, or through some insurance arrangement.

However, doctors today are often contracted hospital employees, engaged like star baseball players, in order to present a "star lineup" that will attract the most (and best paying) patients to the hospital. Doctors may also be investors in the hospital (as well as in clinical laboratories, outpatient clinics, or other health care facilities), and may obtain significant managerial roles—thereby reducing the principal-agent gap. An example of political costs is the physician self-referral prohibitions (*US Code* 42 USC 1395nn), known as the Stark rules, that were enacted to protect the public from physicians maximizing their returns on investment by referring patients for improper or unnecessary medical treatments to facilities where the physician possesses a financial interest. Lee and Mahenthiran (1994) consider an activity-based management perspective which includes assessment of the role of doctors' independent contractor versus employee status in hospital cost management. They conclude that employee status for doctors will produce a substantial reduction in hospital costs by providing incentives that promote the reduction of non-value-added activities by physicians.

As depicted in Figure 1, bond covenant relationships also exist in health care organizations, as in commercial enterprises. The most frequent accounting-related constraint found in, for example, hospital bond covenants, is the debt service coverage ratio—which is basically the ratio of cash flow available for debt service to total debt service requirements. A typical standard for this ratio found in SEC Official Statement filings (analogous to 10-Ks for commercial enterprises) is a minimum of 1.0 to 1.5 times debt service coverage (e.g., Catholic Health Corporation 1990). Apart from this specialized measure, application of the bond covenant hypothesis of agency theory, as adapted in Figure 1, is essentially the same as for commercial businesses.

Thus, the agency model as applied to health care organizations is similar in many respects to the versions used in accounting research for commercial organizations. It is particularly useful for incorporating the effects of profit sharing factors, political cost factors, and bond covenant factors in assessments of managerial incentives and choice behavior in health care organizations.

Management's real-valued choices, and comparative analyses within the health care industry are also the subject of research studies (e.g., Cleverley 1990; Chilingerian and Sherman 1987; Herzlinger and Krasker 1986), but much of the early work used relatively simple statistical methods comparing costs and financial or operating ratios, and contained little, if any, linkage to a theoretical framework. Many areas can be developed further, and an agency theory approach can be useful in redesigning such research studies based on expected direction of findings relative to economic incentives, as modeled in Figure 1.

For example, nonprofit hospitals may have equity capital that is restricted by donors for use in the provision of prenatal charity care services, thus producing the specific form of goodwill valued by the donor. Lawsuits, assessments in lieu of taxes, and other political costs associated with the provision of inadequate amounts of charity care are greater for nonprofit hospitals than they are for-profit hospitals due to the federal public benefit requirement for nonprofits. Yet, provision of charity care is expensive, and reduces a hospital's ability to produce quarterly earnings for investors and/or meet debt-service coverage ratio requirements specified in bond covenants. Measuring charity care based on gross charges forgone rather than actual cost, or redefining charity care amounts to include reclassified bad debts, courtesy discounts provided to hospital employees or affiliates, or contractual adjustments on Medicaid payments received, all increase the amounts of charity care reported in the financial statements. Thus, agency theory leads to the expectation that the amount of reported charity care expenditure incurred by a hospital's management, and the selection of accounting methods that affect reported charity care amounts in the financial statements, will be associated with the degree to which the managers are constrained by the three economic factors—profit-sharing, political costs, and bond covenant constraints. Therefore, all prior research studies that have not sufficiently controlled for all three of the economic factors plus the accounting choices of management, can be redesigned and reexecuted to provide research results that are more reliable and less subject to omitted variable problems.

The study of management's accounting choices in itself is also of particular interest to financial accountants. For example, the discount rate used in accounting for pension plans has an analog in the discount rate used by Continuing Care Retirement Communities in computing the present value of their future service obligations (P&PB Statement No. 9). The income and cash flow management strategies, or other economic factors, associated with managerial choices in selecting or changing that discount rate to increase or decrease reported accounting measures could be studied within a Watts and Zimmerman (1986) type framework. Survey research on accounting choices is also a possibility. To date, I have not identified any health care studies that employ survey research in accounting choice behavior. Two field studies within the UK National Health Service, however, addressed the subject of hospital doctors' decision-making and management styles and accounting constraints in the changing hospital environment (Lapsley 1996, 1997). Lapsley found that doctors' decisions were associated with the accounting environments under which they operated.

The P&PB statements also offer an opportunity to observe an emerging deliberative process in formulating health care accounting standards (Forgione and Schiff 1994). In one study analyzing this process, Forgione and Giroux (1989) find evidence in comment letters submitted to the HFMA on P&PB Statement No. 8 that hospital managers lobbied either for or against the guidelines of Statement No. 8 (which advocated single-fund reporting several years before the FASBs adoption of its new fund accounting model in SFAS No. 117) in a manner consistent with their individual economic circumstances. They employ an agency theoretic approach and find that independent hospitals with relatively greater amounts of endowment income lobbied against single-fund reporting, while larger, more profitable health care organizations with smaller endowments lobbied for single-fund reporting. The P&PB Statement No. 19 (on resource transfers among affiliated entities), SFAS No. 116 (on contributions received and made), and P&PB Statement No. 15 (on charity care and bad debts) may also be amenable to studies of accounting methodology lobbying behavior by managers of institutional health care providers.

B. Information Content and Event Studies

Other studies that can be of value to investors include adaptations of event-type studies that associate, for example, bond market returns or duration with relevant financial and nonfinancial disclosure announcements. That is, disclosure announcements of income measures, regulatory payment system changes, abnormal Medicare mortality rate statistics, changes in debt service coverage ratios, discount rate changes, and/or patient volume and mix changes all may affect returns in the tax-exempt bond market for nonprofits, or the stock market for for-profits. Along a related line, Craycraft (1994) analyzes the incremental information content of sociometric data in evaluating hospital performance, and finds significant associations with hospital bond ratings. Studying the effects of the types of disclosures prescribed under P&PB Statement No. 18 *Public Disclosure of Financial and Operating Information by Healthcare Providers* on bond duration or other market phenomena may also be a fruitful avenue for future health care accounting research.

C. Behavior and Ethics

The effectiveness of corporate compliance plans is a very timely area for behavioral and ethics research, particularly in conjunction with the U.S. Internal Revenue Service, U.S. Federal Bureau of Investigation, and U.S. Department of Health and Human Services, Office of Inspector General anti-fraud and abuse initiatives, attendant political costs, and standards on accounting, for example, charity care in hospitals (Relman 1988; Mattox 1989; Forgione and Blankley 1996; Forgione 1998). As noted above, many hospitals are having their tax-exempt status challenged based on alleged failure to provide "adequate" levels of charity care (State of Texas 1990).

In a situation of limited monitoring, moral hazard issues in financial reporting for charity care, for example, are also timely. One research avenue might be a classification of the reasons for legal challenges to hospital exempt status, and the possible association of such reasons with the degree of donor and bondholder representation on the board of directors and/or independent auditor characteristics. Independent auditor characteristics might also be studied in relation to accounting choices within health care organizations. For example, when a health care organization's debt service coverage ratio declines to a level that is in close proximity to its threshold for technical default on bond covenants, to what degree is audit quality associated with the timing and magnitude of changes in the estimated discount rate, expected earnings rate, and/or salary-increase rate used by the organization in determining its pension expense and funding status disclosures? Or, alternatively to what degree is audit quality associated with the timing and magnitude of changes in the estimated mortality rates, morbidity rates, withdrawal rates, or other salient factors used by Continuing Care Retirement Communities in determining their patient survivorship rates, as well as the discount rate, selected amortization method, and consequent accounting liability for future patient care obligations?

Opportunities to integrate and apply theoretical perspectives from disciplines outside the accounting literature also exist. The health care environment may be viewed as "selecting" different kinds of health care organizations (Hannan and Freeman 1977; Aldrich 1979). Alternatively, health care organizations may be viewed as adapting to available resources in the environment (Pfeffer and Salancik 1978). Statements by the P&PB and similar bodies may function as environmental variables which facilitate, or hinder, selection or adaptation. The constructs of organizational power relationships (Pfeffer 1981; Morgan 1986) may be used to analyze the relationship between the HFMA, FASB, GASB, and the AICPA in setting health care accounting standards. Also, research on professional organizations (Hall 1968; Jackson 1970; Freidson 1983) can be used to understand, and perhaps facilitate, the advancement of the HFMA in the health care accounting standard-setting process.

At the group level, theories of group conflict and problem solving may be applied to certain issues, such as the charity care accounting conflict between the HFMA and the AICPA mentioned in a previous section. For example, Hoffman's (1979, 1982) hierarchical model of problem solving groups states that different groups view a joint function, such as standard-setting, from their own particular perspectives. Therefore, each group may have difficulty valuing the proposals offered by the other group. Various recommendations for minimizing this type of conflict are derived from Hoffman's model, such as composing task force subgroups from both sides of an issue, identifying criteria that both groups have in common, and so on. Other approaches to group conflict and problem solving which could be used as a basis for behavioral research in this area include social judgment theory (Hammond et al. 1977) and methods investigated by Rohrbaugh (1981), Hirokawa (1985), and Schweiger and colleagues (1986).

D. International Comparisons

Industrial countries throughout the world are facing similar cost containment dilemmas with their respective health care systems. In spite of the varied approaches which range from largely private, entrepreneurial health care in the United States, to nationalized systems in Germany, all developed countries are facing escalating costs and increasing consumer expectations, with limited financial resources. Many countries are experimenting with capitated payment systems and prospective payments similar to the Medicare hospital and physician payment systems in the United States (Forgione 1997). For example, Heald and Scott (1996) offer lessons to be learned from the UK experience in applying new capital cost payment systems in the National Health Service.

The area of international comparisons presents many other opportunities and challenges. Comparisons of incentives, performance, and measures of the quality of care under different pricing and market mechanisms in different countries under different social welfare systems are just a few examples. Differences in the economic factors and monitoring devices that constrain health care management in accordance with the demands of public and private constituencies can be investigated. The difficulties with such research include inconsistent definitions of data items, different cost collection approaches that make comparisons convoluted, and selecting the appropriate currency parity index from among competing alternatives, such as currency exchange rates, general purchasing power indexes, health care purchasing power indexes, or other inflation measures. Nevertheless, some excellent data sources exist.

The practical meaning of "charitable purpose" for tax-exempt status of nonprofits in the United States also needs to be explored relative to other countries. Many tax-exempt nonprofit organizations in the United States are converting to for-profit status to gain access to the stock markets and free top management from compensation limitations and the profit sharing and stock ownership prohibitions. According to U.S. law (*US IRC* 501(c)3) the disposition of nonprofit assets in a conversion to for-profit status must be made to another nonprofit organization that will continue to provide public benefits similar to the converting organizations original nonprofit mission. None of the assets or net earnings of the nonprofit may inure to the benefit of any private shareholder or individual. Thus, when proposed conversions involve top management of the nonprofit organization becoming the top management of the new for-profit organization, and receiving stock shares as compensation, yet maintaining their role in control of the nonprofit organization that receives majority stock in the for-profit as primary consideration in the nonprofit asset disposition, inurement will take place. What factors are associated with nonprofit conversions to for-profit status? How do such conversions take place in other countries? How do the factors affecting such conversions differ across differing economic systems and approaches to health care financing and delivery? What criteria are used to determine the stock value in such conversions?

Much ground can be broken in the area of international comparative analysis, particularly in understanding why some societies finance health care publicly, and why others like the United States do so both publicly and privately. Rakich (1991) provides a useful comparative analysis of the Canadian and American health care systems, with emphasis on the differences in social norms and perceptions. Application and integration of alternative theoretical models may contribute to the development of research designs in this area. Obtaining and analyzing comparable, international data, has become increasingly easier with the development of the extensive Organization for Economic Cooperation and Development database (OECD 1996). Differences in political and social environments, as well as in national health care financing approaches, costs, and accounting methods, present both challenges and opportunities for accounting researchers studying this area.

E. Bankruptcy and Illiquidity

In addition to research that is approached under a particular theoretical paradigm, opportunities exist to explore issues where no well-defined theoretic model has been articulated. A variety of methods have been used in this latter category for health care accounting research. For example, investigation exists in the area of hospital bankruptcy (Cannedy et al. 1973), but early studies use relatively simple research methods. Wedig and colleagues (1988) address hospital leverage and bankruptcy risk. Much of this early research can be developed further, particularly in light of the recent spread of capitation and other major changes in hospital payment methods that significantly affect cash flow patterns, and the resultant pervasive changes in economic relationships that have occurred in the industry since these studies were done.

Similar potential topics include discriminant or multinomial probit analyses of hospital illiquidity in association with selected financial ratios (such as receivables turnover, or the debt service coverage ratio), while controlling for differences in forms of ownership. Additionally, comprehensive sets of financial and nonfinancial performance measures could be factor analyzed and related to varying degrees of illiquidity, or subsequent recovery from financial distress (see Forgione, Schiff, and Crumbley 1996).

Accounts receivable and revenues in health care organizations are critical, complex, and difficult to audit. They incorporate thousands of medical procedure codes (which must be verified by qualified medical experts in an audit), and include issues of upcoding and bundling or unbundling of charges, assumptions about allowable and nonallowable reimbursement or payment claims for services, estimates of unexpected third-party adjustments and disallowances, dozens of different and conflicting payor rules and claims procedures, estimated accounts that will become uncollectible due to medical costs that escalate beyond the insurance and personal financial resources of otherwise solvent patients, and issues of separating bad debts from charity care, courtesy discounts, and contractual adjustments. Bankruptcy studies in particular will thus benefit from the analysis provided in P&PB Statement No. 16 on accounts receivable measures because it clarifies a number of definitional and classification issues that are important to understanding this complex accounting item in health care organizations.

The severity of bond covenant constraints and exposure to political costs are variables which may also have a systematic association with illiquidity measures. Consider the following excerpt from a comment letter written to the HFMA by a hospital manager in opposition to single fund reporting under P&PB Statement No. 8, "Many of our hospitals do not want to disclose investment income in their reports to the public. They do this today by either setting up foundations or simply encouraging the acceptance of restricted gifts" (Forgione and Giroux 1989). Consistent with the economic incentive to avoid political costs, this manager prefers to segregate and not disclose investment income in order to limit the hospital's exposure to public pressures for a reduction in payments. There may be a measurable association between the degree of exposure to such political costs, entity structure and reporting choices, and current or future financial distress.

F. Technology Effects on Financial Performance

In the area of relative technical efficiency, data envelopment analysis is used to explore the relative technical efficiency of hospitals and subcomponents thereof (Greenberg and Nunamaker 1987; Borden 1988; Nyman et al. 1990; Valdmanis 1990). Many more opportunities for this type of research exist, and there is a need for better operationalization of constructs, variables, and definitions of input and output for health care organizations.

In the existing data envelopment analysis research, issues such as the definition of hospital inputs and outputs, with adjustments for case-mix differences, are found to be significant factors that will no doubt need additional study before effective implementation of efficiency measures can be made. Different forms of ownership control might also be studied in association with differences in the relative technical efficiency of hospitals. For example, do for-profit hospital incentive structures induce managers to operate them more efficiently than managers of nonprofit hospitals? How do we define financial efficiency relative to quality of care? What does this imply for the contracting behavior of third-party payors such as Medicare, or health care purchasers?

G. Longitudinal Analyses

Longitudinal analyses of changes in economic relationships are also a potentially beneficial area of inquiry. Medicare now has the first 12 years of hospital data under the Prospective Payment System available, and has increased the already wide range of variables in its many public-use files. Opportunities for longitudinal policy assessment, such as studying the effects of Medicare payment policy initiatives and changing managerial incentives on the real-valued and accounting choices of hospital management over the duration of the Prospective Payment System initiative, will improve as the related data continue to accumulate.

IV. DATA SOURCES

Unlike many other areas of governmental and nonprofit accounting research there is an abundant supply of useful data in the health care area. The primary directory of databases is the *Inventory of U.S. Health Care Data Bases* published by the U.S. Department of Health and Human Services (DHHS 1988). This directory lists hundreds of data sources with specifics of the title, sponsor, purpose and scope, subject headings, input source, universe, sample, frequency, years available, cost if any, contact address and phone information, and other information for each database. It is an invaluable resource for researchers in the health care arena.

The primary governmental data source is the Medicare Bureau of Data Management and Strategy (BDMS). The BDMS produces data tapes of hospital cost reports for all Medicare hospitals, physician payment data, case-mix indexes, provider specific attributes, expected and actual mortality data—which is useful in establishing quality proxies and unexpected mortality measures for correlation with economic factors—and a wide range of other large databases. Medicare charges for the data, and I have found that the file record layouts are not always completely reliable. A broad spectrum of comparable international data, as mentioned above, is available from the OECD on CD-ROM. The CD-ROM also contains software for graphic and statistical summarization of the data on the disk. The spectrum of variables is comprehensive and includes case mix, lengths of stay, and several monetary conversion rates for each of the 27 OECD member countries.

Data on *Hospital Statistics* and the *National Hospital Panel Survey Report* are also available from the AHA. Health Care Investment Analysts, Inc. is a commercial data vendor and offers the *Comparative Performance of U.S. Hospitals: The Sourcebook*, and several other publications. The Center for Healthcare Industry Performance Studies offers the *Almanac of Hospital Financial & Operating Indicators*. The Group Health Association of America, Inc. offers the *HMO Industry Profile*, and most states in the United States maintain excellent public-use data bases for health care organizations operating within their jurisdictions. For-profit health care organizations publish corporate annual reports and often have 10-K filings with the SEC. Nonprofit organizations often have public bond issues and file Official Statements with the SEC, which are analogous to 10-K disclosures.

These data sources represent only a few of the hundreds of public use data files available to accounting researchers. The availability of such a wide array of significant data in the health care arena provides excellent opportunities for accounting research and cross-functional research designs.

V. SUMMARY

My first objective in this review is to summarize the professional health care accounting literature. My second purpose is to describe the related research opportunities in health care accounting and identify useful databases. I identify various approaches and topics, and observe that constituent groups and constructs consistent with an agency theory framework are described within the health care accounting literature. The existence of both for-profit and nonprofit health care organizations competing in the same markets provides an opportunity to study the effects of different forms of organizational control on both the real-valued and accounting choices of management—both domestically and across international boundaries.

I also describe a variety of other research venues, and cite a number of studies that only begin to tap the research opportunities available in the health care accounting area. The opportunities for future research are manifold, high-quality data is available, and the topic carries a timeliness, and economic and social relevance that is unparalleled by many other lines of inquiry.

APPENDIX A

Health Care-Related Professional Pronouncements

FASB Statements

Statement of Financial Accounting Standards No. 124: *Accounting for Certain Investments Held by Not-for-Profit Organizations* (1995).
Statement of Financial Accounting Standards No. 117: *Financial Statements of Not-for-Profit Organizations* (1993).
Statement of Financial Accounting Standards No. 116: *Accounting for Contributions Received and Contributions Made* (1993).
Statement of Financial Accounting Standards No. 93: *Recognition of Depreciation by Not-for-Profit Organizations* (1987).
Statement of Financial Accounting Standards No. 62: *Capitalization of Interest Cost in Situations Involving Certain Tax-Exempt Borrowings and Certain Gifts and Grants* (1982).
Statement of Financial Accounting Concepts No. 6: *Elements of Financial Statements* (1985).
Statement of Financial Accounting Concepts No. 4: *Objectives of Financial Reporting by Nonbusiness Organizations* (1980).

GASB Statements

Statement No. 29: *The Use of Not-for-Profit Accounting and Financial Reporting Principles by Governmental Entities* (1996).
Statement No. 20: *Accounting and Financial Reporting for Proprietary Funds and Other Governmental Entities That Use Proprietary Fund Accounting* (1993).

AICPA Pronouncements

Audit and Accounting Guide: *Health Care Organizations* (May 1, 1997).
Audit Risk Alerts: *Health Care Industry Developments—1996/97* (1996).
SOP 92-9: *Audits of Not-for-Profit Organizations Receiving Federal Awards* (1992).

U.S. Government Publications

GAO: *Government Auditing Standards* ("The Yellow Book") (1994).
OMB Circular A-133: *Audits of Institutions of Higher Education and Other Nonprofit Institutions* (1997).

HFMA P&PB Statements

Statement No. 20: *Health care Mergers, Acquisitions, and Collaborations* (Exposure Draft [ED]: July 17, 1996; Approval Date: August 11, 1997; *Healthcare Financial Management (HFM)* Publication Date: October 1997).
Statement No. 19: *Transactions Among Affiliated Entities Comprising an Integrated Delivery System* (ED: July 14, 1995, *HFM* Publication Date: June 1996, Updated August 1996, Supersedes *P&PB Statement Nos. 10* and *12*).
Statement No. 18: *Public Disclosure of Financial and Operating Information by Healthcare Providers* (ED: August 1, 1993).
Statement No. 17: *Assessments and Arrangements Similar to Taxes on Tax-Exempt Institutional Healthcare Providers* (ED: April 1, 1993, Approval Date. March 29, 1994).
Statement No. 16: *Classifying, Valuing, and Analyzing Accounts Receivable Related to Patient Services* (1993).
Statement No. 15: *Valuation and Financial Statement Presentation of Charity Service and Bad Debts by Institutional Healthcare Providers* (1993, Supersedes *P&PB Statement No. 2*).
Statement No. 14: *The Presentation of Patient Service Revenue and Related Issues* (Supersedes *P&PB Statement No. 7*, Withdrawn 1997).
Statement No. 13: *Timing Differences Pertaining to Third-Party Payment* (ED: 1990, Withdrawn 1997).
Statement No. 12: *Accounting for Resource Transfers among Affiliated Entities* (*HFM* Publication Date: October 1990, Superseded by *P&PB Statement No. 19*, Withdrawn 1997).
Statement No. 11: *Accounting and Reporting by Institutional Healthcare Providers for Risk Contracts* (*HFM* Publication Date: August 1989, See also *AICPA SOP 89-5*).
Statement No. 10: *Accounting and Reporting Issues Related to Corporate Reorganizations Involving Tax-Exempt Institutional*

Healthcare Providers (*HFM* Publication Date: February 1989, Superseded by *P&PB Statement No. 19*, Withdrawn 1997).

Statement No. 9: *Accounting and Reporting Issues Related to Continuing Care Retirement Communities* (*HFM* Publication Date: August 1986, See also *AICPA SOP 90-8*, Withdrawn 1997).

Statement No. 8: *The Use of Fund Accounting and the Need for Single Fund Reporting by Institutional Healthcare Providers* (*HFM* Publication Date: March 1986, Withdrawn 1997).

Statement No. 7: *The Presentation of Patient Service Revenue and Related Issues* (*HFM* Publication Date: April 1986, Superseded by *P&PB Statement No. 14*, Withdrawn 1997).

Statement No. 6: *How to Measure Working Capital: Classification and Definition Issues* (*HFM* Publication Date: September 1984, Withdrawn 1997).

Statement No. 5: *Accounting and Reporting Agency Relationships* (*HFM* Publication Date: December 1983).

Statement No. 4: *Reporting of Certain Transactions Arising in Connection with the Issuance of Debt* (*HFM* Publication Date: June 1982, Withdrawn 1997).

Statement No. 3: *Supplemental Reporting of Hospital Financial Requirements* (*HFM* Publication Date: December 1980, Withdrawn 1997).

Statement No. 2: *Defining Charity Service as Contrasted to Bad Debts* (*HFM* Publication Date: July 1978, Superseded by *P&PB Statement No. 15*, Withdrawn 1997).

Statement No. 1: *Uniform Accounting and Uniform Reporting in Hospitals* (*HFM* Publication Date: June 1977, Withdrawn 1997).

Other HFMA Publications

Chart of Accounts for Hospitals (1995).

AHA Publications

Estimated Useful Lives of Depreciable Hospital Assets (1997).

APPENDIX B

Annotated Review of Major Authoritative Pronouncements

FASB Pronouncements

SFAC No. 4: *Objectives of Financial Reporting by Nonbusiness Organizations* (1980)

This statement identifies distinguishing characteristics and provides a framework for accounting and reporting for nonprofit organizations.

SFAC No. 6: *Elements of Financial Statements* (1985)

This statement expands the definition of the elements of financial statements to encompass nonprofit organizations.

SFAS No. 62: *Capitalization of Interest Cost in Situations Involving Certain Tax-Exempt Borrowings and Certain Gifts and Grants* (1982)

This statement addresses important issues relating to tax-exempt interest, gifts, and grants relevant to nonprofit health care providers.

SFAS No. 93: *Recognition of Depreciation by Not-for-Profit Organizations* (1987)

This statement addresses the issue of depreciation for nonprofit organizations, including health care organizations. Private health care organizations generally employ the full accrual method of accounting and reporting.

SFAS No. 116: *Accounting for Contributions Received and Contributions Made* (1993)

This statement represents a major advancement in the accounting and reporting principles for contributions. It establishes criteria for accruing pledges receivable when the pledge is made, with an accompanying allowance for uncollectible pledges, and imposes accounting uniformity in this area of major economic significance for many health care organizations. This is a change from the former common practice of recording pledges when collected.

SFAS No. 117: *Financial Statements of Not-for Profit Organizations* (1993)

This statement introduced the first sweeping overhaul of accounting and reporting for nonprofit organizations in the history of modern accounting. It abandoned the former systems of separate fund accounting (such as used by health care organizations, i.e., general fund, endowment fund, specific purpose fund, and plant expansion and replacement fund), and adopted the concept that fund restrictions effectively apply only to the net assets (equity) section of the balance sheet. Net assets are now identified only as unrestricted, temporarily restricted, or permanently restricted in the equity section of the balance sheet. Assets whose use is limited are identified through captions or other notations and disclosures.

SFAS No. 124: *Accounting for Certain Investments Held by Not-for-Profit Organizations* (1995)

This statement applies the concepts of SFAS No. 115, on accounting for investments, to nonprofit organizations. Thus, nonprofit health care organizations must now also use the concepts of trading securities, available for sale securities, and held to maturity securities, with the accompanying guidance on when unrealized holding gains/losses are included in income, or bypass income and transfer directly to the equity accounts.

GASB Pronouncements

Statement No. 20: *Accounting and Financial Reporting for Proprietary Funds and Other Governmental Entities That Use Proprietary Fund Accounting* (1993)

This statement provides guidance for proprietary fund, including enterprise fund, accounting. This is highly significant because governmental proprietary activities should apply all applicable GASB pronouncements as well as any FASB Statements and Interpretations, Accounting Principles Board Opinions, and Accounting Research Bulletins issued on or before November 30, 1989, that do not conflict with or contradict GASB pronouncements. However, governmental proprietary activities are also allowed to apply all FASB statements and interpretations issued after November 30, 1989, that do not conflict with or contradict GASB pronouncements—on an all-or-none basis. Thus, the choice of enterprise fund accounting, as opposed to selecting a governmental fund accounting model, is the determining factor in whether the health care organization's financial reports are structured more extensively under FASB or GASB accounting guidelines. Governmental organization managers who choose enterprise fund accounting can be more extensively subject to FASB rules, than those choosing the governmental fund accounting model. Thus, for example, two substantially identical city hospitals could produce two substantially different sets of external financial reports, depending upon the choice of accounting model selected by the hospital's governing authorities.

Statement No. 29: *The Use of Not-for-Profit Accounting and Financial Reporting Principles by Governmental Entities* (1996)

This statement establishes guidance in nonprofit accounting and reporting used by governmental entities, including health care organizations such as state hospitals, state university hospitals and clinics, city hospitals and clinics, and county or hospital district institutional health care providers. This statement prohibits its applicable entities from following SFAS Nos. 116 and 117.

AICPA Pronouncements

SOP 92-9: *Audits of Not-for-Profit Organizations Receiving Federal Awards* (1992)

This statement provides accounting and auditing guidance for nonprofit health care organizations subject to OMB Circular A-133.

Audit Risk Alerts: Health Care Industry Developments—1996/97 (1996)

This publication is an annual supplement to the AICPA *Audit and Accounting Guide: Health Care Organizations*. It provides an excellent, concise summary of the latest economic, regulatory, and financial accounting issues that affect health care organizations.

Audit and Accounting Guide: Health Care Organizations (May 1, 1997)

This publication is the primary, authoritative document in accounting and reporting for health care organizations. It incorporates and applies the provisions of SFAS Nos. 116, 117, and 124 to health care entities. Its scope applies to virtually all types of health care organizations, including:

- clinics, medical group practices, individual practice associations, individual practitioners, emergency care facilities, laboratories, surgery centers, and other ambulatory care organizations
- Continuing Care Retirement Communities

- Health Maintenance Organizations and similar prepaid health care plans
- Home Health Agencies
- hospitals
- nursing homes that provide skilled, intermediate, and less intensive levels of health care
- drug and alcohol rehabilitation centers and other rehabilitation facilities
- integrated delivery systems that include one or more of the above types of organizations

U.S. Government Publications

GAO: *Government Auditing Standards* ("The Yellow Book") (1994)
   This publication is the standard, federal, authoritative guidance for audits of federal, state, and local governmental units, as well as for contractors, nonprofit organizations, and other nongovernmental organizations that receive federal funds.

OMB Circular A-133: *Audits of Institutions of Higher Education and Other Nonprofit Institutions* (1997)
   This publication prescribes policies, procedures, and guidelines for implementing the Single Audit Act. It's scope includes nonprofit and public hospitals that are part of an institution of higher education.

HFMA Pronouncements

Statement No. 5: *Accounting and Reporting Agency Relationships* (Discussion Memorandum [DM]: May 1982, ED: March 1983 *HFM* publication date: December 1983)
   Assets and liabilities that are held in agency for a related organization (such as a controlled foundation holding donated funds on behalf of a hospital) should be reported as unrestricted. However, the reporting entity should disclose any related limitations. Any related income or expense should be debited or credited to fund balance, not to income. Shifting income and assets to separate foundations has become a common practice in financial reporting. The FASB has on its current agenda a project relating to the definition of "entity" in accounting for health care organizations.

Statement No. 11: *Accounting and Reporting by Institutional Healthcare Providers for Risk Contracts* (*HFM* publication date: August 1989)

This statement identifies risk contracts as contracts with managed care health care plans where the provider is exposed to a risk of gain or loss on the contract. This relates only to Health Maintenance Organizations or other managed health care plans, or organizations that arrange these services as "brokers" such as Preferred Provider Organizations. Statement No. 11 essentially enlarges the previous scope of Statement No. 7 to include risk contracts. The issues covered include revenue and expense recognition, loss accruals, risk pools and stop-loss insurance. The statement also requires the estimation of revenues and valuation allowances, and includes a useful glossary. The AICPA SOP 89-5: *Financial Accounting and Reporting by Providers of Prepaid Health Care Services* was very similar to this P&PB statement, and was apparently strongly influenced by its analyses and conclusions.

Statement No. 15: *Valuation and Financial Statement Presentation of Charity Service and Bad Debts by Institutional Healthcare Providers* (1993, supersedes Statement No. 2)

This statement and Statement No. 14 brought the HFMA position on charity care and bad debt reporting into conformity with the AICPA *Audit Guide*. The now withdrawn Statement No. 14 gave a reorganized discussion of revenue issues, and illustrated implementation of the *Audit Guide's* provisions on revenue reporting. Statement No. 15 discusses charity care and bad debt issues, and provides guidance for the valuation and footnote disclosure of charity care under the requirements of the AICPA *Audit Guide*. The HFMA led strong industry opposition to the AICPA/FASB/GASB position of deleting charity care from revenues and receivables, but ultimately acceded to these standards.

Statement No. 16: *Classifying, Valuing, and Analyzing Accounts Receivable Related to Patient Services* (1993)

Accounts receivable are highly complex, and highly uncertain for health care organizations. They also constitute one of the single most important and difficult to audit balance sheet items. They measure the primary cash inflow source for the health care organization and may enter into ratio calculations that define conditions for technical default in bond covenant agreements. Accounts receivable turnover is thus identified in this statement as critical to the liquidity and going concern status of health care organizations. This statement focuses on the importance of properly measuring accounts receivable and receivable turnover under the AICPA/FASB rules for revenue/receivable recognition presented in the AICPA *Audit Guide*.

Statement No. 17: *Assessments and Arrangements Similar to Taxes on Tax-Exempt Institutional Healthcare Providers* (ED: April 1, 1993, approval date: March 29, 1994)

Many nonprofit health care organizations are becoming obligated to either pay tax assessments or enter into arrangements similar to, or in lieu of, taxes for their consumption of governmental services such as fire protection, security, and public works services. This statement prescribes accounting and reporting for payments for

1. governmental services
   - If a specific tax exists for all entities, report the tax as part of the item being taxed (e.g., include a telephone tax as part of telephone expense)
   - If only exempt organizations pay the tax, report it as general government support expense
   - If health services are exchanged in lieu of payment for governmental services, record both revenue and general governmental support expense at the fair value of the services exchanged
2. charity pools
   - If recovery of amounts paid is guaranteed, record recoverable amounts as a receivable
   - If recovery is not guaranteed, the net amount paid is recorded as general governmental support expense
   - When the provider has a legal entitlement to receive payment from the charity pool, record unrestricted amounts received in excess of payments made as patient service revenue; record restricted excess amounts in accordance with the restriction
3. general governmental support
   - Record as general governmental support expense.

Statement No. 18: *Public Disclosure of Financial and Operating Information by Healthcare Providers* (ED: August 1, 1993)

This statement recommends disclosures that include complete, comparative GAAP financial statements and footnotes, along with a management discussion and analysis that covers certain details regarding:

- general information
- trends in operating results and key financial ratios
- employees, medical staff and governing board
- regulatory environment
- risks and uncertainties
- statistical data
- major sources of revenues
- plans for the future

Statement No. 19: *Transactions Among Affiliated Entities Comprising an Integrated Delivery System* (ED: July 14, 1995, *HFM* publication date: June 1996, updated August 1996, supersedes *P&PB Statement Nos. 10 and 12*)

This statement updates, expands, and further develops the accounting concepts identified in P&PB Statement Nos. 10 and 12 with respect to applying principles of investment, affiliation, and consolidation accounting to nonprofit health care organizations.

1. Loan or advance (evidenced by intent and ability to repay)
    - If the recipient is wholly owned or controlled, reclassify any impairments in value as an equity transfer
    - If the recipient is not wholly owned or controlled, the facts and circumstances determine if any impairment is reclassified as an equity transfer, or is reported as specified by SFAS Nos. 15, 76, 114, or 118
2. Equity investment (evidenced by evidence of ownership, expectation of a return on investment, residual ownership rights, or participation in management or governance)
    (a) For investments in equity securities, apply Accounting Principles Board (APB) Opinion No. 18, SFAS No. 94, or superseding standards (Note: SFAS No. 124 was issued subsequent to P&PB Statement No. 19 and supersedes prior

accounting literature on investments by nonprofit organizations)
- (b) For investments evidenced by other means (such as in the membership of an nonprofit entity)
  - If there is no expectation of a return on investment, record as an equity transfer
  - If there is an intent and ability to provide a return on investment and other characteristics of an investment in equity securities, record as an investment in equity securities
3. Equity transfer (evidenced by no expectation of repayment or ownership interest)
   - If the recipient is wholly owned or controlled, report resource transfers as changes in net assets at book value, and exclude them from the determination of operating results
   - If the transfers are frequent, the facts and circumstances determine if the transfer is an ongoing subsidy of operating losses, and thus recorded as a loss or expense, and gain or income
   - Both the transfer or and transferee accounting method should be consistent, and any future commitment to continue funding losses should be disclosed
   - If the recipient is not wholly owned or controlled, the facts and circumstances determine the appropriate accounting
4. Contributions: report as specified in SFAS No. 116
5. Distribution of income from affiliated nonprofit entities
   - If there was a prior resource transfer, record the income distribution consistent with the prior transfer
   - If there was no prior resource transfer, record the income distribution as an equity transfer
6. Provision of goods or services: record according to the substance of the transaction, and disclose the terms of the transaction
7. Sale or dissolution of an affiliate: proceeds are recorded consistent with the prior resource transfer and any gain or loss is recognized in income.

Statement No. 20: *Health care Mergers, Acquisitions, and Collaborations* (ED: July 17, 1996, approval date: August 11, 1997, *HFM* publication date: October 1997)

This statement parallels the current FASB project on the subject of entity and mergers/acquisitions of nonprofit entities.

1. Health care business combinations should be accounted for as similar to a:
   - purchase (with a step-up in the basis of assets and liabilities), or a
   - pooling of interests (with no step-up in the basis of assets and liabilities)
2. Collaborations in which control is shared should be accounted for as joint ventures (usually with no step-up in the basis of assets and liabilities).

Other HFMA Publications

Chart of Accounts for Hospitals (1995)
This document offers a detailed, model chart of accounts for hospitals. Originating in 1922 by the American Hospital Association, it is one of the earliest modern documents to provide industry guidance on accounting for health care organizations.

AHA Publications

Estimated Useful Lives of Depreciable Hospital Assets (1997)
This document is a valuable source reference for establishing useful depreciable lives for health care assets. It is the accepted source for purposes of Medicare depreciation reimbursement calculations. It is of particular value to health care accounting research endeavors where the research design requires variables that reflect an estimation of the age of plant and equipment.

ACKNOWLEDGMENT

The author gratefully acknowledges the helpful comments of the Editor Paul Copley, and an anonymous referee.

NOTES

1. An earlier OMB Circular, A-128: *Audits of State and Local Governments*, applied to health care organizations for a number of years, but was rescinded by the 1997 revision of Circular A-133.

2. Level E GAAP (Other Accounting Literature) includes pronouncements issued by other professional associations such as the HFMA, or regulatory agencies and applies when there are no principles established on a particular issue by the FASB, GASB or AICPA.

REFERENCES

Aldrich, H. 1979. *Organizations and Environments*. Englewood Cliffs, NJ: Prentice-Hall.

American Hospital Association. 1998. *Estimated Useful Lives of Depreciable Hospital Assets*. Chicago, IL: American Hospital Association.

———. 1998. *Hospital Statistics*. Chicago, IL: American Hospital Association.

———. 1997. *National Hospital Panel Survey Report*. Chicago, IL: American Hospital Association.

American Institute of Certified Public Accountants. 1992. *Statement of Auditing Standards No. 69: The Meaning of* Present Fairly in Conformity with Generally Accepted Accounting Principles *in the Independent Auditor's Report*. New York: American Institute of Certified Public Accountants.

———. 1990. *Audit Risk Alerts: Health Care Industry*. New York: American Institute of Certified Public Accountants.

———. 1992. *Statement of Position 92-9: Audits of Not-for-Profit Organizations Receiving Federal Awards*. New York, NY: American Institute of Certified Public Accountants.

———. 1996. *Audit Risk Alerts: Health Care Industry Developments—1996/97*. New York: American Institute of Certified Public Accountants.

———. 1997. *Audit and Accounting Guide: Health Care Organizations* (May 1). New York: American Institute of Certified Public Accountants.

Borden, J. P. 1988. An assessment of the impact of diagnosis-related group (drg)-based reimbursement on the technical efficiency of new jersey hospitals using data envelopment analysis. *Journal of Accounting & Public Policy* 7(2): 77–96.

Brown, J. G. 1997. Testimony of June Gibbs Brown, Inspector General, Department of Health and Human Services, Hearing Before the House Ways and Means Subcommittee on Health. (July 17). Washington, DC.

Cannedy, L. L., D. D. Pointer, and H. S. Ruchlin. 1973. Viability and hospital failure: methodological considerations and empirical evidence. *Health Services Research* (Spring): 27–35.

Catholic Health Corporation. 1990. *Official Statement* (March 1).

Center for Health Care Industry Performance Studies. 1997–1998. *Almanac of Hospital Financial & Operating Indicators*. Columbus, OH: Center for Healthcare Industry Performance Studies.

Chilingerian, J. A., and H. D. Sherman. 1987. For-profit *vs.* nonprofit hospitals: the effect of the profit motive on the management of operations. *Financial Accountability & Management* (Autumn): 283–303.

Cleverley, W. O. 1990. Improving financial performance: A study of 50 hospitals. *Hospital & Health Services Administration* (Summer): 173–187.

Conrad, D. A. 1984. Returns on equity to nfp hospitals: theory and implementation. *Health Services Research* (April): 41–63.

Craycraft, C. 1994. The incremental information content of sociometric data in evaluating hospital performance. *Journal of Management Systems, Special Series Issue: Research in Healthcare Financial Management* 6(3): 39–52.

Dugan, J. K. 1997. Federal government expands compliance initiatives. *Healthcare Financial Management.* (September): 54–58.

Fama, E. F., and M. C. Jensen. 1983. Agency problems and residual claims. *Journal of Law and Economics* 26(2): 327–349.

Financial Accounting Standards Board. 1980, 1985. *Statements of Financial Accounting Concepts Nos. 4 and 6.* Norwalk, CT: Financial Accounting Standards Board.

———. 1982–1995. *Statements of Financial Accounting Standards Nos. 62, 93, 116, 117 and 124.* Norwalk, CT: Financial Accounting Standards Board.

Forgione, D. 1987. Incentives and performance in the health care industry: The case of for/non profit multihospital systems. Doctoral dissertation, University of Massachusetts, Amherst, MA.

———. 1997. Healthcare financial & quality measures: international call for a "balanced scorecard" approach. *Journal of Health Care Finance* 24(1): 55–58.

———. 1998. Corporate compliance plans in healthcare organizations: A top-down perspective. *Journal of Health Care Finance* 24(4): 87-92.

Forgione, D., and A. Blankley. 1996. Ethical issues facing private not-for-profit hospitals in the U.S.: The case of The Methodist Hospital System. *Public Budgeting & Financial Management* 8(3): 334–353.

Forgione, D., and G. Giroux. 1989. Fund accounting in nonprofit hospitals: a lobbying perspective. *Financial Accountability & Management* (Winter): 233–244.

Forgione, D., and A. D. Schiff. 1994. The contribution of the HFMA to healthcare accounting standards: opportunities for research. *Journal of Management Systems, Special Series Issue: Research in Healthcare Financial Management* 6(3): 1–21.

Forgione, D., A. D. Schiff, and D. L Crumbley. 1996. Assessing hospital performance: An inventory of financial and nonfinancial metrics. *International Association of Management Journal, Forum on Research in Healthcare Financial Management* 8(2): 65–83.

Foster, R. W. 1987. Hospitals and the choice of organizational form. *Financial Accountability & Management* (Winter): 343–365.

Freidson, E. 1983. The reorganization of the professions by regulation. *Law and Human Behavior* 279–288.

Government Accounting Standards Board. 1993, 1996. *Statements of Government Accounting Standards Nos. 20 and 29.* Norwalk, CT: Government Accounting Standards Board.

Greenberg, R., and T. Nunamaker. 1987. A generalized multiple criteria model for control and evaluation of nonprofit organizations. *Financial Accountability & Management* (Winter): 331–342.

Group Health Association of America, Inc. 1997. *HMO Industry Profile*. Washington, DC: Group Health Association of America, Inc.

Hall, R. 1968. Professionalization and bureaucratization. *American Sociological Review*: 92–104.

Hammond, K., J. Rohrbaugh, J. Mumpower, and L. Adelman. 1977. Social judgment theory: Applications in policy formation. In *Human Judgment and Decision Processes in Applied Settings*, eds. M. Kaplan, and S. Schwartz, 1–27. New York: Academic Press.

Hannan, M. T., and J. H. Freeman. 1977. The population ecology of organizations. *American Journal of Sociology* 929–964.

Heald, D., and D. A. Scott. 1996. Lessons from capital charging in the U.K. National Health Service. *International Association of Management Journal: Forum on Research in Health care Financial Management* 8(2): 29–45.

Health Care Investment Analysts, Inc. 1997. *Comparative Performance of U.S. Hospitals: The Sourcebook*. Baltimore, MD: Health Care Investment Analysts, Inc.

Healthcare Financial Management Association, Principles & Practices Board. 1977–1997. *Statements of Position Nos. 1–20*. Westchester, IL: Healthcare Financial Management Association.

Herzlinger, R. E., and W. S. Krasker. 1986. Measuring the economic performance of for-profit and nonprofit organizations. In *Research in Governmental and Non-Profit Accounting*, Vol. 2, ed. J. L. Chan, 151–172. Greenwich, CT: JAI Press.

Hirokawa, R. 1985. Discussion procedures and decision-making performance: A test of a functional perspective. *Human Communications Research* 203–224.

Hoffman, L. R. 1979. *The Group Problem-Solving Process: Studies of a Valence Model*. New York: Praeger.

———. 1982. Improving the problem-solving process in managerial groups. In *Improving Group Decision Making in Management*, ed. R. A. Guzzo, 95–126. New York: Academic Press.

Jackson, J. A. (ed.). 1970. *Professions and Professionalism*. New York: Cambridge University Press.

Kovener, R. R. 1990. New rules affect bad debt, charity care reporting. *Healthcare Financial Management* (October): 48–57.

Kwon, I. W., N. Moldofsky, and D. G. Martin. 1997. Economic theory of gift giving in the healthcare industry: A case of charity care. *International Association of Management Journal: Forum on Research in Healthcare Financial Management* 9(2): 15–26.

Lapsley, I. 1996. The puzzle of hospital doctors decision-making: An exploratory case study. *International Association of Management Journal: Forum on Research in Healthcare Financial Management* 8(2): 1–19.

———. 1997. The new public management diaspora: The healthcare experience. *International Association of Management Journal: Forum on Research in Healthcare Financial Management* 9(2): 1–14.

Lee, W., and S. Mahenthiran. 1994. Managing healthcare costs through structural rearrangement of hospitals: An activity based management perspective. *Journal of Management Systems, Special Issue: Research in Healthcare Financial Management* 6(3): 22–38.

Martin, D. G., and I. W. Kwon. 1996. Wealth shifting and capital structure choice in not-for-profit hospitals: An Agency approach. *International Association of Management Journal: Forum on Research in Healthcare Financial Management* 8(2): 20–28.

Mattox, J. 1989. *Special Task Force to Study Not-For-Profit Hospitals and Unsponsored Charity Care* (March 10). The Attorney General of Texas, Austin, TX.

Morgan, G. 1986. *Images of Organization*. Newbury Park, CA: Sage Publications.

Nyman, J. A., D. L. Bricker, and D. Link. 1990. Technical efficiency in nursing homes. *Medical Care* (June): 541–551.

Organization for Economic Cooperation and Development. 1996. *OECD Health Data on CD-ROM*. Paris, France: OECD Publications.

Owens, C.L. 1997. Health Care Fraud: Statements of Charles L. Owens, Chief, Financial Crimes Section, Federal Bureau of Investigation, Before the U.S. House of Representatives Committee on Ways and Means Subcommittee on Health (October 9). Washington, DC.

Pfeffer, J., and G. R. Salancik. 1978. *The External Control of Organizations: A Resource Dependence Perspective*. New York: Harper & Row.

Pfeffer, J. 1981. *Power in Organizations*. Marshfield, MA: Pitman.

Prospective Payment Assessment Commission. 1996. *Medicare and the American Health Care System: Report to Congress.* (June) Washington, DC: Prospective Payment Assessment Commission.

Rakich, J. S. 1991. The Canadian and U.S. health care systems: profiles and policies. *Hospital and Health Services Administration* (Spring): 25–42.

Relman, A. S. 1988. Are voluntary hospitals caring for the poor? *New England Journal of Medicine* (May 5): 1198–1200.

Rohrbaugh, J. 1981. Improving the quality of group judgment: Social judgment analysis and the nominal group technique. *Organizational Behavior and Human Performance*: 1–17.

Schweiger, D., W. Sandberg, and J. Ragan. 1986. Group approaches for improving strategic decision making: a comparative analysis of dialectical inquiry, devil's advocacy and consensus. *Academy of Management Journal*: 51–71.

Seawell, L. V. 1995. *Chart of Accounts for Hospitals*. Chicago, IL: McGraw-Hill.

SoRelle, R. 1991. Methodist Hospital, facing charity suit, sells duck lodge. *The Houston Chronicle* (Jan. 24): A17.

State of Texas vs. The Methodist Hospital; The Methodist Hospital System; and [Members of the Board of Directors] (1990). Petition No. 494,212 in the District Court, 126th Judicial District, (November) Travis County, TX.

Swasy, A. 1990. Challenge to Erie Hospital's tax status gains attention of cash-poor U.S. cities. *The Wall Street Journal* (Feb. 16): A7.

Tax Analysts, Tax Notes Today. 1993. (Feb. 3).

U.S. Code. 42 Section 1395nn. Limitation on certain physician referrals.

U.S. Department of Health and Human Services. 1988. *Inventory of U.S. Health Care Data Bases.* Washington, DC: U.S. Department of Health and Human Services.

U.S. General Accounting Office. 1997. *Government Auditing Standards.* Washington, DC: U.S. Government Printing Office.

U.S. Office of Management and Budget. 1997. *Circular A-133: Audits of Institutions of Higher Education and Other Nonprofit Institutions.* Washington, DC: U.S. Government Printing Office.

U.S. Internal Revenue Code. Section 501(c)3. Exempt organizations.

Valdmanis, V. G. 1990. Ownership and technical efficiency of hospitals. *Medical Care* (June): 552–561.

Wallace, W. A. 1987. Agency theory and governmental and nonprofit sector research. In *Research in Governmental and Non-Profit Accounting*, Vol. 3, ed. J. L. Chan, 51–70. Greenwich, CT: JAI Press.

Watts, R., and J. Zimmerman. 1986. *Positive Accounting Theory.* Englewood Cliffs, NJ: Prentice-Hall.

Wedig, G., F. A. Sloan, M. Hassan, and M. A. Morrisey. 1988. Capital structure, ownership, and capital payment policy: The case of hospitals. *Journal of Finance* (March): 21–40.

A COMPARATIVE ANALYSIS OF THE EVOLUTION OF LOCAL GOVERNMENTAL ACCOUNTING IN ALGERIA AND MOROCCO

Alan D. Godfrey, Cherif Merrouche, and Patrick J Devlin

ABSTRACT

The purpose of this analysis is to fill a gap in the literature by considering local governmental accounting in two North African countries: ex-French colonies, Algeria and Morocco. Using more recent generations of Luder's contingency model (Chan, Jones, and Ludev 1996) and elements of Rogers' diffusion of innovations theory (1995), we argue that in the two countries the evolution of local governmental accounting systems and subsequent innovations are the product of the colonial era, the chosen path to economic development, and the impact that natural resources had in shaping the outlook of each country. We identify possible reasons for the marked timing difference in the relative rate of adoption of governmental accounting innovations in the two countries.

I. INTRODUCTION

In their editorial article Chan, Jones, and Luder (1996) point out that, except for some more recent studies, only a dozen country studies have been written since the mid-1980s, and the focus has been on Western democracies. They argue further that most countries in Asia, Africa, and South and Central America are absent from comparative international governmental accounting research (CIGAR) studies. Our purpose is to fill part of this gap by considering the evolution of local governmental accounting in two North African countries: ex-French colonies, Algeria and Morocco.

The discussion that follows is divided into five sections. In Section II we argue that the differing postcolonial backgrounds of local government in the countries of North Africa have influenced the relative desire and ability to generate local governmental accounting innovations. We concentrate on Algeria and Morocco to analyze the development of their differing politico-economic systems. Section III outlines local governmental accounting in Algeria and Morocco both pre- and post-independence, highlighting the French influence of the former colonial power, and seeking to highlight some dilemmas which have made innovation problematic. Section IV hypothesizes that the rate of adoption of accounting innovation has varied among the countries of the region. This may be because of the differing perceptions of the attributes of such innovation through differences in stimuli, such as political determinism coupled with natural resource strength in Algeria, and international agencies and international standardization in Morocco. Section V summarizes the present position of local governmental accounting in Algeria, Morocco, and France, and suggests possible reasons for the continued difficulties experienced in finalizing a consistent model, despite the considerable accounting innovation which has already taken place throughout the region.

II. BACKGROUND OF LOCAL GOVERNMENT

Appendix A gives some indication of the present status of Algeria and Morocco in terms of world development. Panels 1, 2, and 3 indicate that there are similarities which place both countries within the lower-middle income category of economic development. However, there are important structural differences in the economies of the two countries. Algeria is richer than Morocco because of the increasing discoveries of large petroleum and gas reserves since 1956.[1] As a result, marked differences appeared, particularly in the 1960s and 1970s, in relation to government revenue and the financing of government operations in the two countries. Recourse to foreign resources in overall treasury financing was almost one-fourth in Morocco but was negligible in Algeria (IMF 1977). Another impact of this difference in natural resource strength was apparent in the relative size of the public sectors of both countries. In the 1970s the public sector in Algeria accounted for a predominantly large share of capital formation whereas in Morocco private investment, which had been stimulated by fiscal incentives, accounted for roughly half the total investment annually undertaken (IMF 1977).

In the two countries, development planning has been a recognized means of setting targets for economic growth and employment and providing guidelines for investment allocation and financing. The basic aims of development planning have been to raise standards of living, reduce disparities in the distribution of income, and strengthen the country's economic and social infrastructure. Local authorities in both countries play a significant role in attaining these objectives.

Algeria and Morocco share a common history over much of the nineteenth and twentieth centuries as both were colonized by France. Algeria was declared a part of metropolitan France in 1848, having been invaded in 1830. The occupation of Algeria led to French involvement in the neighboring monarchy of Morocco. Morocco became a French protectorate under the Treaty of Fez in 1912.

A. Pre-Independence

The French encouraged immigration to both countries with the result that there was a relatively large French population (in agriculture and business) in addition to the French administrators who ran the governments. As had been intended, French education nurtured an elite which prized French culture. However, an unforeseen development was the growth within this elite of modernizing nationalists who were attracted to the idea of independence—which, when combined with other (conservative and Muslim) groupings opposed to a French presence, represented a significant force for change.

The French found themselves in an impossible position—some government ministers wanted to meet nationalist movements more than half-way while others did not want to make life difficult for the French settlers. Thus, French governments were rendered ineffective (Calvocoressi 1991, 478). In Morocco, negotiations exposed the gap between the French position (a program of democratic gradualism) and that of the nationalists (who wanted immediate independence). Bilateral agreement proved to be a failure and France ceded independence to Morocco in 1956.

The situation in Algeria was very different. Here, independence was won in 1962 only after a prolonged armed struggle which began in 1954. As Calvocoressi (1991, 480) explains, circumstances in Algeria were without parallel in the rest of Africa—the European population had been a part of the country for much longer than any other settler community, was much nearer to the mother country, and in the main cities was as numerous (or almost as numerous) as the native population; the services provided by the settler community were conspicuous; constitutionally, Algeria was a part of metropolitan France. Thus, it may have been the case that there were very good economic reasons (e.g., the discovery of oil in the Sahara) for France to have viewed Algeria differently. But the unique relationship almost certainly also played a part.

B. Post-Independence

Algeria

Post-independence, the government of Algeria focused primarily on reviving the economy and reorganizing the institutional structure of the country by taking control of the major economic and financial sectors with the exception of petroleum. However, in common with many former colonial territories, the departure of the French left the country facing major difficulties, the most serious of which was the shortage of qualified manpower. The overwhelming majority of senior administrators and managerial and technical experts left the country. Management in most sectors of the economy vanished. Production fell, while unemployment and underemployment reached extreme levels. The mass exodus of French administrators left the new government with insurmountable problems at all levels. In terms of the Governmental Accounting Innovation Model 2B (Chan, Jones, and Luder 1996, 7)—hereafter referred to as the 2B model—this weak *administrative structural variable*, particularly in the years immediately following independence, represented a considerable barrier to administrative innovation, including accounting systems reform. Thus, the approach favored at the time was not to tamper with the inherited administrative-legal structure which was heavily dependent on a written and codified body of law. Meanwhile, to help overcome the administrative structural problem, Algeria prioritized education and training.

The emergence of the state as a major force in the economy resulted not only from the underlying socialist philosophy of the country, but also reflected this exceptional combination of circumstances that accompanied independence. The adoption and institutionalization of the socialist participative self-management system—Autogestion—in the modern agricultural sector (a "carbon copy" of the Yugoslav participation system) is probably the most typical example of increasing intervention.

The period 1962 to 1971 represented a period of stabilization, consolidation, and restructuring of the industrial sector. From 1966 onward, a series of nationalization programs was undertaken, the aim from the outset being to consolidate Algerian patrimony and lessen outside domination of the economy. All firms abandoned by their owners on the eve of independence were transferred into national corporations (nationalized enterprises), each responsible for a particular industry. The attempt to set a clear administrative structure for the country resulted in local elections (communes) in 1967, provincial elections (*wilayas*) in 1969, the adoption of *la charte nationale* (in essence, the constitution) in 1976 and, finally, elections for the National Assembly (Assemblee Nationale) in 1977.

Creating a new economic order, based on state ownership of most sectors of the economy, without the involvement of local authorities, was not perceived as a guarantee of success. It was important for the state to increase the role of local authorities, particularly their responsibilities for social and economic development in the new post-independence environment. Correspondingly, the present structure of local government evolved with 48 provincial administrations, each governed by a provincial governor (*wali*) who is appointed by central government, is responsible to the Minister of the Interior and is assisted by an elected assembly and executive council. These provinces are in turn divided into 227 administrative districts (*dairaats*) and more than 1,500 communes, each commune having its own elected assembly to run local affairs.

By the end of the 1970s Algeria was being transformed from a relatively poor agricultural country to one with a growing diversified and industrial economy. Oil and natural gas represented the country's greatest wealth and served as springboards for economic development. By 1978 the only parts of the economy that remained under private control were a fraction of the traditional agricultural sector, some small consumer manufacturers, and small-scale retail trade. Thus, initially the *political structural variable* (model 2B) in Algeria's case was strong and positive, probably as a direct result of the battle to achieve independence, coupled with the international political power derived from the nationalization of natural resources, especially oil and gas. However, during the 1990s Algeria has been troubled politically since the army cancelled the elections in 1991 and took control of the government of the country (*Financial Times* 1997).

Morocco

Morocco chose a different political path post-independence by establishing a monarchy when the Sultan became king in 1957. At around the same time the Spanish relinquished most of their interests in Morocco retaining only a small number of cities and territories. Although suffering from similar *administrative structural variable* problems as Algeria—the loss of expatriate skilled labor, particularly the impact of the departure of many French administrators, which left the new government with considerable problems at all levels—Morocco flirted with a democratic parliamentary political structure. However, this proved unworkable after the first Moroccan general elections were held in 1963.

Accordingly, the king acts as head of state and is empowered to appoint the country's prime minister and cabinet and can dissolve the country's legislature. Hagigi and Williams state that the government can be characterized as centralized, socialistic, paternalistic, and fairly stable (1993, 70). The same authors suggest that two characteristics of the monarchy, identified originally by Entelis (1989), have a possible impact on financial reporting practices: a highly developed system of "clientelism," where a paternalistic government distributes scarce resources to key persons in return for economic and political support; and, related to this, the level of corruption and bribery that is reputed to prevail in political and business activities (1993, 70).

However, after the last legislative elections in November 1997 a new prime minister was appointed to lead the coalition government. The new prime minister has entered into a partnership with the palace, whereby the king retains many powers under Morocco's new constitution while the prime minister will respect the monarchy but work to his own agenda. The prime minister is quoted as saying: "we want to institute fundamental reforms because it is unforgivable that at the end of the 20th century and after 40 years of independence, we should continue to have more than a 50 per cent rate of illiteracy, that our education system should be in crisis, that rural areas should be in a state of unimaginable neglect, some without water or electricity" (*Financial Times* 1998b). The new prime minister has set his sights on reforming the administration and the justice system which have long been seen as large obstacles to investment. The budget deficit is forecast to reach 4 percent in 1998, and about three-quarters of the budget is taken up by debt service and public salaries.

Moroccan local government consists of 65 provinces (including seven urban prefectures) and 1,544 communes. Provincial governors are appointed by the king and are answerable to central government. It could be argued that, in terms of the 2B model, the *political structural variable* in Morocco, at least initially, was more benign toward the former colonial master state which perhaps exerted a negative effect on the potential for governmental accounting innovation.

Thus, differences in the *political structural variable* of model 2B would appear to exist between the two countries of the region. Fresh from the rigors of hard-won independence, Algeria developed a strong sense of national determinism and a drive for economic development, assisted subsequently by the benefits derived from the acquisition of nationalized natural resources such as oil and gas. On the other hand, it would appear that Morocco, with its less contested path to independence and, at the time, its more limited natural resource strength, may initially have had less political desire to break away from adopted colonial systems.

III. LOCAL GOVERNMENTAL ACCOUNTING IN ALGERIA AND MOROCCO

The roots of governmental, and indeed commercial, accounting in North Africa are very firmly based upon the colonial model imposed by France during its period of occupation—a situation similar to that pertaining in the former British colonies of East Africa where colonial influence was found to be the major factor shaping governmental accounting (Godfrey, Devlin, and Merrouche 1996, 201). Thus, the development of the French Plan Comptable General (PCG 1957) (see Appendix B) over the early years of their independence provided the foundations for potential innovations in the accountancy systems of the nations of North Africa.

A. Pre-Independence

The local authority accounting system used in both Algeria and Morocco pre-independence was based on the French public accounting system of the time, where the central concern of public accounting was one of control (Montagnier 1981, 235). However, although these countries had different political status (Algeria being a part of France, whereas Morocco was a state in its own right under the protectorate of France) the financial system was much the same. It was drafted by French civil servants before being enacted in Algeria by French decree in 1862, and in Morocco by dahir in 1917. Within this common system the budget played a fundamental part. Not only did it constitute a provision for revenue and expenditure but equally it was the source of authorization for the generation of revenue and the incidence of all expenditure.

The commune (district) budget consisted of two elements, the basic budget and the supplementary budget. These were subdivided into three parts or titles: ordinary income and expenditure; exceptional income and expenditure; and, income and expenditure from "closed" operations. The budget was prepared by the president (chairman) of the commune and was required to be voted by the full council at its

July meeting (the financial year followed the calendar year). Under the French system of control any disagreement over the approved budget was required to be resolved by the "higher authority" (the prefect or governor). Indeed, the budget was overseen by the higher authority, even although it was put into operation by the municipal collector (or state accountant) and the authorizing officer (the president of the commune).

It is interesting to note the overarching powers of the higher authority where the commune budgets, supplementary funds, extraordinary contributions or loans, and local taxes were only enforceable after having been approved by the higher authority. In fact, the higher authority had powers to reject or reduce voted expenditure (but not to increase or introduce new expenditure), to vote finance where insufficient or no funds had been voted, and to remove specific items to stabilize a budget projecting a weak financial situation.

Also inspired by the French system, local authority accounting in both countries was, and still is, governed by a radical separation between the authorizing officer (the "ordonnateur" or person entitled to authorize the generation of revenue and the payment of expenditure, "the order giver") and the public accountant. This division of authority between "the signatory and the payer" is an age-old principle of French administrative and financial organization (Perreault 1996, 368). The authorizing officer decides upon what is to be generated or incurred, and it is then the public accountant's responsibility to make sure that receipts are cashed and payments are made on the basis of the documents issued by the authorizing officer. The public accountant is a professional civil servant of the Ministry of Finance (MOF) and, therefore, is independent of the local authorities.

It is important to understand that, under the French Public Accounting School, the public accountant has considerable powers and responsibilities, including personal liability for any omission or irregularity. They are not mere cashiers in charge of receipts and payments; they must check also that the orders from the authorizing officer conform with approved budgets and financial rules and regulations. If not, then they must deny execution of such orders, unless the authorizing officer requires their compliance, in writing. The main purpose of this separation is to allow the accountant to control, on a regular basis, the activities engaged in by the authorizing officer. Also, this dual responsibility is under the surveillance of the higher authority.

This process results in two parallel accountings being kept: that of the authorizing officer, and that of the public accountant. It is important to note that the authorizing officer's accounting starts and finishes with the issue of the order while that of the public accountant is based on proper bookkeeping procedures. The accounting system used in both countries, based on the French system of the time, was a single-entry model. (France changed to a double-entry format in the late 1950s/early 1960s, with the introduction of M11 and M12—see Appendix B.) Under the 1862 decree in Algeria and the 1917 dahir in Morocco, the public accountant was required not only to keep day-by-day accounts but also to produce monthly summaries and annual accounts. These annual accounts recorded under *receipts:* forecasts, actual collections, and any exemptions or interest to collect; and separately, under *payments*: opening finance, payments made, and the balances still to pay.

Under the same legislation, the president/chairman of the local authority was required to keep an accounting system showing all receipts and payments authorized. Annually he reported on the execution of the budget in the form of an administrative account. Both the administrative account and the public accountant's annual report were submitted for approval to the local authority's assembly. These reports were checked for mutual compliance and were approved by the assembly in the absence of the president. The approved reports were then sent to the Ministry of Finance, and to the Ministry of the Interior, to be used in preparation of the annual report of all local authorities. External audit of local government was, and still is, undertaken by agents of the respective national audit agencies.

B. Post-Independence

Algeria

Historically public service theory, inherited from colonial times, applied throughout the region and provided the "cornerstone" of administrative law which was born in the context of economic liberalism. Originally, the aim was to demarcate the scope of intervention of the public authorities. As a result, the distinction between public law and private law was firmly established. In colonial times public authorities were responsible for administrative matters, while private enterprises concentrated on all matters of an economic, industrial, and commercial nature. Local authorities adopted a system of public sector accounting whose purpose was to protect public goods and prevent fraud or misappropriation of public funds. That is, the emphasis was on the regularity of operations and the means of controlling them.

This inherited system has been a source of confusion for local accounting within the new political reality and economic development path of post-independence Algeria. Local authorities experienced a radical shift in emphasis and direction with their increasing involvement in economic activities. Yet they still retained the historical public management system, including local governmental accounting as it existed pre-independence.

By the end of the 1960s Algeria found the accounting systems inherited from the French colonial period increasingly inadequate as an instrument of economic planning. This resulted in the Ministry of Finance initiating the formation of the Higher Council of Accountancy (CSC: Conseil Superieur de la Comptabilite), whose task was to design and implement a new national accounting plan (PCN: Plan Comptable National). The design stage of the PCN drew on the experience of four French "Experts Comptables" from the French National Council of Accountancy, two of whom took part in the drafting of the Organization of African French-Speaking Countries' (OCAM) accountancy plan some two years earlier.[2]

The general recognition by the Algerian authorities of the defects and inadequacies of the PCG 1957 was the basic motive underlying the creation of the CSC. Hence, the emphasis was placed upon a total revision of, rather than on superficial changes to, the PCG in use at the time. To that end, it was of paramount importance to design and implement a new accountancy plan[3] based on the needs of the emerging new economic environment. Thus, the Algerian Plan Comptable National (PCN) was adopted in 1976. This accounting plan contains a chart of accounts,[4] which is divided into eight classes (five covering the balance sheet and three for the profit and loss account), and accounting principles and techniques.[5]

Algeria regarded the PCN as the general framework, or "common platform," for the practice of accounting by all sectors of the economy. Yet, because of differences in accounting needs between the various sectors of the economy, the PCN was to be adapted either in the form of sectoral plans (PCS) or in the form of particular plans for individual enterprises (PCP).

The role of the PCN as a "common accounting platform" for all sectors of the economy without adaptation to the specific needs of local government resulted in some local authorities continuing to use the inherited system, others using the PCN, and others using a mixture of the two. Conflicting definitions contained within local authority legislation have led to confusion and as a result there is considerable discretion given to local authorities in their choice of accounting treatment. The role of local authorities in Algeria is defined by order (No. 67/24 of 18 January 1967, the local authorities code), supplemented by issued decrees of application. The code distinguishes between "local authority services" and "local authority enterprises," the former being further subdivided into services of an administrative nature and those of an economic nature. For instance, some local authorities, taking advantage of the imprecision of the legal definition in relation to economic public services and local authority enterprises, created enterprises to manage their public services, particularly in the areas of urban transport and the distribution of water.

Such services, though best fitting the "public service" definition, have been run as "enterprises" because of the advantages this legal form offers. Local authorities run cinemas which can be viewed as a public service by one local authority but as an economic service by another. An individual local authority can provide the same service (hotels) in some cases as a public service, in others as an economic service depending upon the relative fiscal advantage.

The reason for this choice in the provision of service is the fact that the local authority enterprise is not subject to the requirements of public law. As a result a local authority can:

- manage its own treasury without requiring the approval of the district collector of taxes;
- recruit staff more easily from the labor market by offering higher salaries (though this would not be possible were the enterprise to provide the same service under a different legal set up, i.e., economic public service);
- pay its suppliers in advance and receive early delivery of goods (whereas the economic public service entity could not); and,
- depreciate its fixed assets, which would not be possible if the enterprise were to change its legal set up.

Article 208 of the local authority code stresses that the administrative organization, the financial system and the functioning of authorities are fixed by the regulation in place. In reality, local authorities tend to refer to colonial decrees of 1926, 1933, and 1955 for guidance. These decrees are nowadays officially repealed, leaving some questions regarding the nature of local authorities. For instance, should the entities providing public services be considered as enterprises, hence subjecting them to the same taxes as the state-owned enterprises and private firms, or should they comply with the commercial code? Are their employees to be considered as public servants or as having the same status as those of the national enterprises and the private firms? These questions and others have for a long time remained unanswered.

Local authority accounting in Algeria, therefore, faced a choice between use of the PCN and the inherited colonial system (or indeed some hybrid of both). Correspondingly, during the 1980s the idea of addressing some of the problems of public sector accounting became a necessity. After many attempts, law no. 90-21 appeared in August 1990. It defined the accounting requirements that apply to public sector organizations ranging from budgets and financial operations of the state to those for public bodies of an administrative nature.

Article 2 of law 90-21 (*Journal Officiel* 1990, 978), like its predecessor, underlines the importance of the principle of the separation between the authorizing officer and the public accountant. It refers to the budget as the sole source of authority for the collection of revenues and the incurring of expenditure. The budget is to be balanced and should distinguish between the activities of the revenue generation section and other subsections: capital programs and economic investment. The revenue generation section is concerned with current revenues, such as taxes, levies, and other income. Any surplus of revenue over expenditure can be transferred to either the capital program or the economic investment subsections.

The capital program subsection's revenues are derived from subsidies, borrowings, and/or appropriations from the revenue collection section. The economic investment subsection is concerned with the activities, including the provision of services, of the economic enterprises. Through a system of transfers, or virement, every section must have a balanced budget. The so-called "crude" budget each year is modified in response to the results of the previous year. If the previous year's activities show an excess of revenue over expenditure, the excess will be considered as new revenue for the supplementary budget. Conversely, if a deficit arose in the previous year, this is considered as new expenditure. The purpose behind this is to attempt to deter further deficits in future years.

Unfortunately, despite may years in preparation, law no. 90-21 was aborted before its inception. While it tried to include and deal with all parts of the public sector, it failed to recognize and address the many differences that clearly exist among these constituent areas. Correspondingly, local authority accounting in Algeria still faces many dilemmas. At present, some local authorities rely on an inter-ministerial circular (Circulaire Interministerielle C2 sur les operations des Communes), although from anecdotal evidence it would appear that it is not in widespread use. The C2 document was prepared jointly by the Ministries of Interior and Finance. It takes its inspiration from the PCN and attempts to provide some harmonization to present local authority accounting practices. However, during the writing of this paper, the authors were made aware of a major review of local governmental accounting currently taking place. This review has been prompted by the delay, since the adoption of the PCN in 1976, in finding a satisfactory solution to the inherent problems of local authority accounting, including the formulation, and acceptance, of a PCS relevant to local government needs in Algeria at the present time.

Morocco

Major reforms of the Moroccan accounting system postdated by some 10 years those taking place in Algeria. A process of normalization of the French colonial accounting model to the new realities of independence was undertaken during the late 1950s and 1960s. This was followed in the 1970s by review and amendment in light of experience and lessons learned. During this latter period several important pieces of legislation were enacted including the local authorities charter (1976) and the accounts commission law (1979). However, throughout this period accounting systems were based firmly upon French models:

> ...financial accounting in Morocco is based on the 1957 version of the French standardized accounting system publication, the Plan Comptable General. The Plan is used both in the preparation of financial statements and tax returns (Hagigi and Williams 1993, 70).

In other words, the Moroccan accounting system prior to 1986 rested on two distinct formations: one related to the private sector and firmly based on the PCG (1957), the other to the public sector largely based upon the pre-independence single-entry system from the 1917 dahir—the only common bond being the strong colonial French influence, with the two systems developing independently of each other over time without much interaction. As in Algeria, local authority accounting in Morocco rests on the distinctive, French-inspired "dual-responsibility accounting" system which is considered to be an extremely important control and accountability mechanism in drawing a dividing line between the person entitled to authorize the transactions and the public accountant.

It was not until 1986 that, like Algeria 10 years earlier, a "common platform" for the two sectors was developed by the Ministry of Finance through the National Committee of the Accountancy Plan (CNPC: Comite National du Plan Comptable) in the form of the PCM (Plan Comptable Marocain). The motives underlying these changes were similar to those experienced by Algeria at the beginning of the 1970s. It was suggested that the inherited accounting system (PCG) did not respond to the economic realities of the country. Furthermore, although the PCG was the subject of many amendments since independence, it was accepted widely that for a long time the amended PCG had not been suitable to either the requirements of national accounting or those of private sector accounting in Morocco.

Thus, the PCM national accounting plan, which covers all economic entities, blends together both French-Germanic and Anglo-Saxon influences while also taking account of particular economic aspects of Moroccan society. In similar fashion to its French counterpart, it incorporates a uniform chart of accounts and a highly detailed accounting guide. This accounting guide includes accounting definitions, model financial statements, and measurement rules.[6] Reform of the governmental accounting system and that of local authorities is presently taking place in Morocco using the PCM as the common accounting platform to generate a public accounting variant. As part of this process, three basic problems had to be addressed:

- the poor quality of information collected (the accounting entries and organizational structure do not provide all types of information required);

- the transmission of accounting information (which is not carried out in an integrated manner); and,
- the under-utilization of transmitted accounting information at the central level.

In order to lessen the consequences of such problems in all public sector organizations, new accounting plans for government and local authorities have been prepared by the General Treasury of the Kingdom and are presently in the process of being adopted with implementation set for 1998. While responding to the particularities and needs of the public sector, the new accounting plans of the government and the local authorities form an integral part of national accounting for all of the public administrative sector and have taken cognisance of UN recommendations for harmonization of the public sector accounting systems of its members, International Monetary Fund (IMF) proposals, the PCM, and the PCG.

The wide-ranging objectives of these governmental and local authorities accounting plans in Morocco seek to have in place a transparent accounting framework which gives a true picture of the activities of the government and the local authorities; improves performance in relation to the implementation and control of activities; integrates the activities of the government and the local authorities in national accounting; makes these accounting plans instruments of efficient management; develops a common language for the preparers and users of governmental and local authorities accounting information which better informs and, as a result, encourages participation in the further development of accounting standardization; improves the management of the treasury; assists economic and financial analysis; and meets the informational and accounting needs required by the government's partners, such as international financial institutions and other economic agents.

Current Situation

The position of local governmental accounting in both countries at the present time (in the case of Morocco, up to the introduction of their new system in 1998) is very similar. The historical communal accounting model adopted from the French in pre-independence times, with minor alterations and adjustments over the years, is still in widespread use throughout the region. This model is very firmly based on the budget as the backbone of the accounting and reporting system. Local authorities in the two countries are obliged to adopt a specific nomenclature and a budget-accounting plan, defined and decided upon by the Ministries of Finance and Interior in both Algeria and Morocco.

The main difference in approach is that the Algerian system combines all revenues and expenses related to the same area within the same account, and deducts one from the other to generate a surplus/deficit which is subsequently posted directly to the annual budget summary statement. In the case of Morocco, the revenues and expenses are accounted for separately, then two statements are presented, one summarizing each class of revenues to give the total revenues for the period and the other following the same process for expenses. These summary totals of the revenue and expense classes are posted to the local authority's General Budget Summary.

The result of these processes is that local authorities are provided with two separate sets of very long and technical budget accounts, one prepared by the president/chairman of the local authority and the other by the public accountant. Both of these sets of accounts follow exactly the budget structure outlined above. These accounts are not particularly user-friendly due to their technical complexity and sheer volume (some accounts run to over one hundred pages or more). In addition, the accounts do not provide any indication of the short-term solvency of the local authority, as the principal focus is one of control rather than the provision of management information. A final constraint upon the accountability aspects of these systems is that local governmental accounting in Algeria and Morocco suffers greatly from a culture of secrecy and confidentiality, where the information requirements of central ministries take primacy over the management needs of local authorities.

IV. REGIONAL DIFFUSION OF GOVERNMENTAL ACCOUNTING INNOVATIONS

In terms of consequences in the real world (Jaruga and Nowak 1996, 28) and Model 3A (Chan, Jones, and Luder 1996, 9), diffusion of at least part of Algeria's innovations to other countries of North Africa was no doubt assisted by the "homophilious" nature of the relationship existing between members of the region. *Homophily* is the degree to which a pair of individuals who communicate are similar (Rogers 1995,

286). Correspondingly, Morocco has followed Algeria's lead in modifying its inherited accounting system, albeit only recently.

This *regional culture variable* was also found to operate among the countries of East Africa, as identified in the 2B model, where the homophilious nature of interstate relationships must assist diffusion. With respect to North Africa, however, some questions arise regarding the time delay involved in this process of regional influence and diffusion. In other words, why did Morocco wait 10 years to follow, at least in part, Algeria's innovation in developing its own national accounting plan? What implementation barriers were in place and why? According to Rogers (1995, 204), diffusion research literature largely ignores the investigation of how the properties of innovations affect their rate of adoption. He adds (p. 206) that 49 to 87 percent of the variance in the rate of adoption is explained by five attributes: relative advantage, compatibility, complexity, trialability, and observability. Applying these attributes to the slower rate of adoption in Morocco, it would appear that in the case of *relative advantage* (the degree to which an innovation is perceived as better than the idea it supersedes) and *compatibility* (the degree to which an innovation is perceived as consistent with the existing values, past experiences, and needs of potential adopters) perhaps there were fewer stimuli for movement away from the inherited colonial accounting model during the first 30 years of independence. Thus, although the *observability* (the degree to which the results of an innovation are visible to others) of earlier governmental accounting innovations in Algeria should not have been a problem because of the close *regional culture variable*, Morocco may not have perceived these innovations as better or consistent with existing values at that time. In the case of Algeria, strong stimuli, such as the fight for independence, an associated stronger national determinism, the desire for change away from the enforced colonial model, together with the country's natural resource strength and the wish to play a significant and strategic role in the region, perhaps encouraged earlier innovation.

Complexity (the degree to which an innovation is perceived as relatively difficult to understand and use) probably has more effect in the early stages of a country's independent development. The impact of the negative *administrative structural variable* in the period immediately following independence from colonial power may mean that the potential for governmental accounting innovations is severely constrained during this period because of the perceived complexity of the process.

Subsequently, as countries develop their administrative potential the impact of complexity on the innovation process should diminish. It may be the case that Algeria responded more quickly in remedying its administrative culture, through increased education and training, thereby removing the complexity impediment from the innovation process earlier than its neighbors.

Trialability (the degree to which an innovation may be experimented with on a limited basis) may also have an impact when linked with the complexity/weak administrative culture scenario described above. However, as an improved administrative culture develops the ability to trial governmental accounting innovations may be possible—for example, in selected ministries or local authorities or, indeed, within neighboring countries. (See Appendix B where Mariel [1996] ascribes at least part of the success of M14 to the piloting of the new system in 6,500 communes over three years prior to its general release.)

Table 1 considers the impact of Rogers's (1995) five attributes of innovation on the potential for developing governmental accounting change in the countries concerned over differing time periods.

1960s

There was a commonality between Algeria and Morocco during the 1960s, the period immediately following independence, in the negative impact of all attributes of potential innovation. In other words, the

Table 1. Impact of Rogers's Five Attributes of Innovation and Stimuli for Change Over Time

Homophily	Algeria +		Morocco +		
	1960s	1976	1960s	1970s	1986
Relative advantage	−	+	−	−	+
Compatability	−	+	−	−	+
Complexity	−	+	−	−	+
Trialability	−	+	−	+	+
Observability	−	+	−	+	+
Stimuli for change over time:	+National determinism		+International agencies		
	+Algerianization of accounting		+International standardization		
	+Natural resource strength		+Moroccanization of accounting		

Notes: The − and + signs signify negative or positive attitudes, respectively, to the attributes over time in the two countries.

ability to innovate was lacking even though desire for such action may, or may not, have existed.

1970s

The transition from a negative to a positive impact of the key attributes of potential innovation took place in Algeria during the 1970s with the development of the PCN during the early years of the decade. It could be assumed that these developments in one part of North Africa meant that the observability and trialability attributes moved from negative to positive in neighboring countries, through the positive regional culture variable. The stimuli for change in Algeria at this time were possibly the combination of politico-socioeconomic factors, such as national determinism, including the desire to Algerianize national accounting systems, demand for economic development of the country, and its natural resource strength, especially oil and gas. While in Morocco, perhaps, diffusion of the Algerian innovation did not occur at this time because the remaining three attributes remained negative. This situation may have arisen because Morocco was only just beginning to review its accounting systems in light of experience and lessons learned since independence.

1980s

With observability and trialability positive, the transition of the three remaining attributes from negative to positive allowed accounting innovation in Morocco to take place in the 1980s with the development of the PCM. The stimuli for this transition may have included the impact of international agencies such as the United Nations (UN) and the International Monetary Fund (IMF), the movement toward international accounting standardization—including European Community (EC) harmonization of accounting—and the desire to Moroccanize national accounting systems.

Reciprocal Diffusion of Innovations

From the standpoint of the study of accounting innovations in the underdeveloped world, an interesting feature of the Algerian experience is the reciprocal nature of diffusion of some of these innovations back to the former colonial master state.[7] The introduction of the Algerian national accounting plan in 1976 preceded the French revision of the PCG (1957) in 1982. French assistance was provided, along with

OCAM expertise, in developing the PCN which included a number of innovations from the French PCG 1957. However, as the following quotes confirm, some of these OCAM-inspired innovations found their way back into French accounting practice via the revised PCG 1982:

> It is important to note that the OCAM plan has been an important phase in the evolution of standardization "a la francaise," positively, thanks to its contribution which has been recognised, but may be negatively as well as a result of the reactions which its (the PCG 1957) inadequacies have created. For the 1982 Plan appears to be the inheritor...which would listen to the ultimate recommendations of its testator, inviting it to draw the lesson of its own discomfiture (Gouadain 1995, 241).

> It (the OCAM Plan) contains a certain number of innovations which have been the fruit of the experience with the 1957 Plan (p. 240).

> The 1982 Plan whose structure of course is essentially based on that of its major predecessors, inherits from the OCAM Plan in at least two major areas: le tableau de financement and le tableau des soldes (p. 241).

> Needless to say...the OCAM Plan has contributed to establishing a fertile dialogue...in relation to the vitality of the "French Accounting School" (p. 242).

This reciprocal diffusion occurred in spite of the more "hetrophilious" nature of the relationship between OCAM countries (particularly Algeria) and France, where *hetrophily* is defined as the degree to which pairs of individuals who interact are different in certain attributes (Rogers 1995, 287). This feature of reciprocal colonial influence can perhaps be associated with the middle-income status and related natural resource wealth of Algeria which allows for greater confidence and independence from former colonial influence. This in turn promotes the search for more innovative accounting solutions, which may produce consequences relevant and useful to more developed countries, where the common base assists this phenomenon. Certainly, this reciprocal diffusion of accounting innovations is not apparent in the low-income status economies of East Africa.

In summary, it would appear that the *regional culture variable* combined with the *homophily* existing between the countries of North Africa allowed the regional diffusion of governmental accounting innovations to take place. However, such diffusion occurred after a considerable time lag and it is hypothesized that the ability and/or desire of the two states to innovate was affected by the impact of Rogers's five attributes. As Table 1 indicates, these attributes changed from a negative to positive impact at different time periods in each country. The possible stimuli for such changes over time are identified.

As well as the existence of regional diffusion it appears that some elements of what we have termed *reciprocal diffusion* of accounting innovations, from the former French colonies back to France, also have taken place. This would appear to have occurred in spite of the more *hetrophilious* nature of the relationship existing between these states.

V. SUMMARY AND CONCLUSIONS

The public sector accounting literature has devoted little attention to accounting in North Africa. In addition, the question of whether Western governmental accounting is relevant to a particular developing country, or group of countries, has received little attention in the literature. The accounting literature in virtually its entirety supports the suggestion that no two countries are exactly similar. The supporting rationale is that nations differ in many respects—for example, environment, culture, religion, and even customs. As a result, it has long been accepted that for accounting to reflect the particular circumstances of a society, accounting must be strongly influenced, and ultimately shaped, by the particular factors that are specific to a given country. It follows then that no two nations' accounting systems would be exactly the same.

However, it has been shown in this analysis and elsewhere (Godfrey, Devlin, and Merrouche 1996) that African countries, in both East and North Africa (and elsewhere, perhaps), adopted governmental accounting systems that had been established in the first instance to reflect the particular circumstances of western European countries. Realizing, in the post-independence era, the inadequacies of the inherited accounting systems as a source of information for economic development and planning, new systems developed in North Africa. This situation, where considerable innovation from the former colonial model has taken place, is in marked contrast to the position in the countries of East Africa where little innovation has taken place over the years since independence. Part of the explanation for this regional difference within Africa may be related to the relative national income status of the groups of countries involved, with the low-income countries of East Africa less able to innovate successfully, compared to the middle-income status countries of North Africa. However, the geographical proximity of France to its two former colonies may provide an additional explanation for this regional disparity. Geography, as an independent variable, has largely been ignored in the literature concerning the export of accounting technology. We consider it a factor worthy of further study in attempting to understand, more fully, the transfer of accounting innovations from developed to developing countries.

In Algeria and Morocco it is clear that the new accounting systems have been shaped, to a large extent, by the former colonial system. Indeed, a reciprocal diffusion of accounting innovations appears to have taken place with the revised French national accounting plan being influenced by African experience. An interesting difference between Algeria and Morocco, however, is the length of time taken before each rejected the former imposed model and developed its own national accounting system. The earlier innovation which took place in Algeria would appear to reflect the strong sense of national determinism at that time, the desire to Algerianize accounting, and the natural resource strength existing within the country. Meanwhile, in the case of Morocco, perhaps, initially at least, a more laissez-faire attitude toward the inherited system prevailed, until pressure to reform and Moroccanize the governmental accounting system was felt from within the country and externally from international agencies and standard-setting bodies.

Table 2 highlights a further interesting observation, that, at the present time, both Algeria and Morocco have advanced by developing their own national accounting plans which are designed to act as general accounting platforms covering both commercial and governmental sectors. But in terms of local governmental accounting innovations, Algeria's attempt to introduce its sectoral accounting plan in the 1990s has failed, perhaps partly because of the internal political problems existing at the present time, and this has resulted in the continuation of the considerable dilemmas faced by local authorities over the choice of using either the former colonial model or the PCN. Morocco, on the other hand, albeit some years behind Algeria's attempted innovations, is just about to introduce its governmental sectoral accounting plan. Only time will tell if this will be a successful venture. Finally, as Appendix B indicates, France has developed further its local governmental accounting system—adopting a single budget and accounting model which utilizes wherever possible (under the guise of "new public management") a commercial accrual-based approach that takes full account of the specific features of French local authorities—and has committed itself to further developing this model.

Table 2. Summary of Governmental Accounting in Algeria, Morocco, and France

	Algeria	Morocco	France
Historic local governmental accounting system	1862-present (with minor modification)	1917-1998 (with minor modification)	1862-1954 (with minor modification)
General accounting plan/common accounting platform	PCG 1957-75 PCN 1976	PCG 1957-85 PCM 1986	PCG 1957 Revised 1982
Local governmental accounting based upon common accounting platform	PCS (90-21) 1990 (unsuccessful) "C2" 1994	to be introduced 1998	M11 1954 (revised 1974) M12 1964 M14 1997
Institution driving governmental accounting change (change agent)	MOF	MOF	MOF

Summary Position at 1998:	PCN or	Historic "C2"	Historic (New PCS planned for 1998)	M14
Main Features:				
*Accruals based	Yes	No	No	Yes
*Respects specific local authority features	No	Yes	Yes	Yes
*Single budget and accounting system	No	Yes	Yes	Yes
*Chart of accounts	Yes	No	No	Yes
*Chart - No. of account Classes	8	n/a	n/a	8
*Chart - includes cost analysis	No	n/a	n/a	No
*Chart based on European functional framework	No	No	No	Yes
*Single-entry (S/E) or double-entry (D/E) system	D/E	S/E	S/E	D/E
*Dual-responsibility (accountant/authorizing officer) system	Yes	Yes	Yes	Yes
*Elected authorization for all transactions	No	Yes	Yes	Yes

APPENDIX A

Background Data on Algeria and Morocco

Appendix A. Descriptive Data on Algeria and Morocco

	North Africa [Algeria Morocco]		East Africa Kenya	France	USA	UK
Panel 1. Background Data						
Area (thousands of sq. Km.)*	2,382	447	580	552	9,364	245
Population (millions) in 1994*	27.4	26.4	26	57.9	260.6	58.4
Population annual growth rate % 1990-94*	2.9	2.3	2.7	0.5	1	0.4
Life expectancy at birth (years) 1994*	69	56	59	78	77	76
Infant Mortality Rate (per 1,000 live births 1994)*	35	56	59	6	8	6
Adult illiteracy (%) in 1995*	38	56	22	<5	<5	<5
National income classification*	lower-middle	lower-middle	low	high	high	high
Former colonial power (20th century)	France	France/Spain	UK			
Date of independence	1962	1956	1963			
Government	republic	monarchy	republic			
Political democracy	multi-party	multi-party	multi-party			
Local government regional units	48	35				

Panel 2. Economic Structure

Total labor force (millions) in 1994*	8	10	13	26	131	29
-% Agriculture (1990)*	26	45	80	5	3	2
-% Industry (1990)*	31	25	7	29	28	29
GDP (million $) 1994*	41,941	30,803	6,860	1,330,381	6,648,013	1,017,306
-% Agriculture (1994)*	12	21	29	2	n/a	2
-% Industry (1994)*	44	30	17	28	n/a	32
-% Services (1994)*	44	49	54	70	n/a	66
Average annual growth rates % 1990-94*						
-GDP*	-0.6	1.7	0.9	0.8	2.5	0.8
-Agriculture*	-0.2	-1.5	-1.5	0.4	n/a	n/a
-Industry*	3.3	0.3	0.9	-1	n/a	n/a
-Services*	4.1	3.4	2	1.1	n/a	n/a
-Exports of goods & nonfactor services*	-0.4	2.1	0.4	3.8	6.7	1.9
-Gross domestic investment*	-6.8	-2.7	-2.2	-6.3	4.1	-2

(continued)

Appendix A (Continued)

	North Africa Algeria	Morocco	East Africa Kenya	France	USA	UK
Panel 3. Development Indicators						
GNP per capita ($) 1994*	1,650	1,140	250	23,420	25,880	18,340
GNP per capita ranking (out of 133 countries in 1996)*	71	58	17	124	115	128
Average annual GNP growth % 1985-94*	−2.9	1.2	0	1.6	1.3	1.3
Official development assistance (% of GNP) 1994*	1	2.1	10.2	n/a	n/a	n/a
External debt as % of GNP 1994*	74.3	76.3	112.4	n/a	n/a	n/a
External debt as % of exports of goods & services 1994*	312.1	257.1	275	n/a	n/a	n/a
Central government budget - total tax revenue (% GNP) 1994*	n/a	26.7	22.4	38	18.5	31.9
Average annual inflation % (GDP deflator) 1984-94*	22	5	11.7	2.9	3.3	5.4

Source: *From Plan to Market, World Development Report 1996-The International Bank for Reconstruction and Development/World Bank, 1996 New York.

APPENDIX B

Local Governmental Accounting in France

The Plan Comptable General (PCG)

After the Second World War France standardized its accounting system through the general accounting plan of 1957 (originally ratified by ministerial article of 18 December 1947) (Montagnier 1981, 231). The origins of this plan lie firmly rooted within the unique features of the French system where the government was in a very powerful position to plan and control all sectors of the economy (Samuels, Groves, and Goddard 1975, 14). These planning arrangements arose as a response to the realities of the post-Second World War situation, where a series of five-year economic plans was developed to create an *economie concerte,* with public and private investment working together to rebuild the economy.

However, there is general misunderstanding that the long tradition of centralization in France means that French accounting is controlled by the state. This misunderstanding is exacerbated by the notion that all sectoral accounting provides inputs for a national accounting system through which the government controls the economy. The reality is that enterprise accounting predates the national accounting arrangements and attempts to reconcile the two have largely failed (Alexander and Archer 1995, 171). However, as Jones and Luder (1996, 75) show, this failure is not unique to France.

The PCG (revised in 1982) was adopted as the basis for tax returns in 1965 (Alexander and Archer 1995, 173). It is essentially a chart of accounts with a system of ledger codes; recommendations on the valuation of assets and determination of costs, expenses, and results; model financial statements and statistical reports; and a discussion of the cost accounting procedures relevant to Class 9 of the plan.

This accounting plan and its sectoral variants, although fitting in a precise way into the structure of French law, are more in the character of accounting manuals than pieces of legislation. The PCG's general organization has been set out according to principles that have not evolved since its inception in 1947. These principles, identified by Cotte, Milot, and Nante (1996, 354), include:

The accounting standards constitute a system which should be consistent and be collected in one document. This sole document is the reference book for the development of general standards as well as their adaptation to specific cases when necessary. This document is the General Accounting Plan (PCG: Plan Comptable General).

Local Authority Accounting

Thus, France is a centralized state in the constitutional sense where local authorities (collectivites locales) are not autonomous, in that their organization is determined by law. France was also a centralized state administratively where central government, through the process of administrative supervision by its local representatives (prefects), could supervise the operations of local authorities and their elected members and officials (Magnet 1997, 1). This supervision was gradually relaxed with the introduction in 1982 of the decentralization acts.

Correspondingly, the financial management of local government followed a similar but lesser development where previously close supervision was exercised by the prefects or by officials of the Ministry of Finance (MOF). Now the newly established regional chambers of accounts (*chambres regionales des comptes*) carry out an external and independent ex post audit, while the prefects check on the legality of local acts and the Ministry of Finance monitors the ongoing transactions.

Local government in France is based on a three-tier system with 24 regions, 100 departments, and 36,500 communes (p. 2). The regions are relatively new and their budgets presently cover education and training, regional development, and transport. However, these areas of responsibility are not set in stone and some regional politicians would like to see more power being transferred, including roads, heritage, health and social planning, and tourism policy (*Financial Times* 1998a). The first departments were established in the late eighteenth century at the time of the French Revolution when 83 were set up and divided into districts. Communes range from the city of Paris, which is both a commune and a department, through every town and village to the "historic communes" of the First World War with no inhabitants (Mariel 1997, 2). Over 22,000 have fewer than 500 inhabitants while only 2,500 (the large communes) have populations in excess of 3,500 citizens.

In response to the extension of local government powers, the liberalization of their funding sources and the fact that communes had become major economic players in the 1980s, the Ministry of Finance (through its Public Accounting Directorate) issued a new accounting directive, M14. This replaced the previous directives M11 (introduced in 1954, revised 1974), which applied to communes with less than 10,000 inhabitants, and M12 (introduced 1964) which applied to those communes with more than 10,000 inhabitants. These directives marked the change from single-entry to a double-entry local governmental accounting systems. Whereas the revised M11 and M12 relied upon the PCG 1957 and its chart of accounts as their general accounting platform, M14 was derived from the revised PCG 1982. Since January 1, 1997, French communes and their dependent local agencies have been applying M14, the new budgetary and accounting system (p. 1).

The objectives of M14 are (i) to apply wherever possible corporate accounting principles and rules from the general accounting plan (PCG) and (ii) to respect the reality of French communes. The former meant the application of general accounting principles, such as prudence, consistency and fairness, to give an accruals-based view of activities. Whereas, respecting the reality of communes implied observance of three basic features: institutional features, budgetary organization, and public management rules.

The first of these realities recognized the problems of size, the not-for-profit public motive, and the tax-based funding with minimum fees charged for services. The budgetary organisation recognized the public financial law where every receipt and payment requires budgetary authorization from the elected body. It also recognized the 1982 decentralization acts which contained precise budget rules requiring two budgets (current operating budget and an investment budget) which must balance by law. The public management rules covered the public procurement code (which includes the separation of duties of the budget holder on the one hand and the controlling supervision of the public accountant on the other), the territorial civil service functions and the financial functions—like the requirement to deposit all local authority funds in the single State Treasury Account.

Thus, M14 operates within a single budgetary and accounting framework. This implies that every receipt or payment transaction must be recorded simultaneously and identically by the public accountant (local tax receiving officer, under the Ministry of Finance) in his accounts, and by the president or mayor in his commune budget accounts. As Mariel (p. 3) points out, this has two major consequences:

- the basic rules are laid down by law, as commune budgets are produced legally under the constitution; and,
- accounting rules automatically affect the budget.

Any accounting practice, for example, a depreciation charge, corresponds to a budgetary operating expense which must be "funded" by budget revenue to balance the operating budget.

The main features of M14 include a compromise whereby all communes with less than 3,500 inhabitants simply have to apply a new accounting chart and a new method of allocating income based on internal financing. For the "large communes," numbering some 2,500, a more complete accrual accounting system and a simplified functional code are introduced. The simplified code has 10 main, and 50 sub-functions and is based on the European functional classifications of the administrations (p. 4). Communes with more than 10,000 inhabitants can use this code to vote their budgets.

The preceding directives M11 and M12 were found to be too complex for both local decision makers and citizens as they lacked a genuine accruals-based overview and did not provide precise information on the main budget lines. They lacked, also, clear separation of calendar years and certain charges were not fully accounted for. M14 introduced the requirements for all charges and income to be accounted for within each calendar year, for mandatory depreciation of replaceable property, and the possibility of setting up provisions outwith the general accounting plan. It included, also, an overhaul of all budget documents.

Mariel (1997, 6) points out that all communes, except Paris (as both a commune and a department it is not required to implement the commune-based reforms immediately), have implemented M14 successfully. This success is based upon several factors including wide consultation, training, and the piloting of M14 in 6,500 communes over the period 1993-1996. It would appear that Rogers's five attributes of innovation were positive in France to allow successful change in governmental accounting practice to take place.

ACKNOWLEDGMENT

The authors would like to thank Mr. Salah Hamzaoui, President du Conseil Regional, Morocco, Mr. Jacques Magnet, President de chambre at the Cours des Comptes, France, and Professor Gabriel Montagnier, University Lyon III,

France, for their invaluable assistance in providing details of accounting innovations in France and North Africa. Thanks are due also to Mr. James C. Wright and Mr. Marc Fermin for assistance with translation. Finally, we would like to thank the two anonymous reviewers for their constructive contributions. However, the views expressed and any inaccuracies in this paper are exclusively the responsibility of the authors.

NOTES

1. Algeria has about 2 percent of the world's reserves of petroleum and about 3 percent of reserves of natural gas. In comparison, Morocco has phosphate rock as the only important mineral resource but it is now the world's biggest exporter of phosphates possessing approximately 75 percent of the estimated world's reserves (Hagigi and Williams 1993, 71).

2. OCAM (Organization Commune Africaine, Malagache et Mauricienne) was formed in 1965 as a regional organization representing the former French African states including Madagascar and Mauritius. Its objective was to promote economic, social, and technical cooperation and its formation was strongly supported by France. The most important legacy of OCAM is its Accounting Plan (Elad 1995, 71) which was first released in 1973 and is now in its third edition (Hagigi and Williams 1993, 74).

3. In his address to the CSC's members the Minister of Finance stated that:

> You are to elaborate a new general accountancy plan that will become a tool particularly adapted to the management necessities of the Algerian planning, as well as to the needs of the socialist enterprises. In other words this is to endow ourselves with an instrument that will ease both forecasting and decision making.... we must ensure that the national accounting has at its disposal, for its statistical and forecasting aims, information that is easy to aggregate, clear and significant ..." (Ministry of Finance 1972).

4. Jaruga and Szychta distinguish between a chart of accounts and a plan of accounts. The former is defined as a schedule of general ledger accounts while the latter is an accounting chart plus guidance on principles and techniques (1997, 523).

5. The classes of accounts in the PCN are Class 1 Own capital, Class 2 Investments, Class 3 Stocks, Class 4 Debtors, Class 5 Debts, Class 6 Expenses, Class 7 Revenues, and Class 8 Results (Societe Nationale de Comptability 1975, 5)

6. The PCM chart of accounts is divided into 10 classes using a decimal numbering system. The classes are Class 1 Permanent finance, Class 2 Fixed assets, Class 3 Current assets (excluding cash and bank), Class 4 Current liabilities (excluding cash and bank), Class 5 Cash and bank (liquid assets), Class 6 Expenses, Class 7 Revenues, Class 8 Results (profit/loss), Class 9 Cost analysis, Class 0 Special accounts (Perochon and Talbi 1993, 92).

The first five classes (1-5) represent the balance sheet accounts, the next three (classes 6-8) are grouped together as management (profit and loss) accounts while Class 9 covers cost analysis and Class 0 special accounts (e.g., opening and closing balance sheets). The 10 classes utilise the decimal system to provide a detailed framework of sub accounts. For example, in Class 2, account 22 is intangible fixed assets, while account 23 represents tangible fixed assets with account 231 being used for land, 232 for buildings, and so on. Under Class 3, account 31 covers inventories with account 34 recording debtors (accounts receivable).

7. For example, the tableaux of debtors and creditors and the value-added statement.

REFERENCES

Alexander, D., and S. Archer. 1995. *European Accounting Guide*. New York: Harcourt Brace Professional Publishing.

Calvocoressi, P. 1991. *World Politics Since 1945*. New York: Longman.

Chan, J. L., R. Jones., and K. Luder. 1996. Modelling governmental accounting innovations: An assessment and future research directions. In *Research in Governmental and Non-profit Accounting*, Vol. 9, ed. J. L. Chan, 1-19. Greenwich, CT: JAI Press.

Cotte, Y., J. P. Milot, and P. Nante. 1996. The French standard accounting system and accountancy of public institutions. In *Research in Governmental and Non-profit Accounting*, Vol. 9, ed. J. L. Chan, 354. Greenwich, CT: JAI Press.

Elad, C. M. 1995. The value added accounting principles of the OCAM plan: A theoretical appraisal. In *Research in Accounting in Emerging Economies*, Vol. 3, ed. R. S. O. Wallace, 53-82. Greenwich, CT: JAI Press.

Entelis, J. P. 1989. *Culture and Counterculture in Moroccan Politics*. Boulder, CO: Westview Press.

Financial Times. 1997. Observer doubts hit Algeria poll image. June 10.

———. 1998a. New regions, new network. March 3.

———. 1998b. Kiss that tells so much about Morocco's new prime minister. May 13.

Godfrey, A. D., P. J. Devlin, and C. Merrouche. 1996. Governmental accounting in Kenya, Tanzania, and Uganda. In *Research in Governmental and Non-profit Accounting*, Vol. 9, ed. J. L. Chan, 193-208. Greenwich, CT: JAI Press.

Gouadain, D. 1995. *L'Ecole Francaise de comptabilite, melanges en l'honneur du Professeur Claude Perochon* (The French School of Accounting, Miscellany in Honour of Professor Claude Perochon). Paris: Foucher.

Hagigi, M., and P. A. Williams. 1993. Accounting, economic and environmental influences on financial reporting practices in third world countries. The case of Morocco. In *Research in Third World Accounting*, Vol. 2, ed. O. Wallace, 67-84. Greenwich, CT: JAI Press.

International Monetary Fund. 1977. *Survey of African Countries* 7, Washington, DC: IMF.

Jaruga, A., and W. A. Nowak. 1996. Toward a general model of public sector accounting innovations. In *Research in Governmental and Non-profit Accounting*, Vol. 9, ed. J. L. Chan, 21-31. Greenwich, CT: JAI Press.

Jaruga, A., and A. Szychta. 1997. The origin and evolution of charts of accounts in Poland. In *The European Accounting Review,* Vol. 6, eds. A. Loft and P. Walton, 509-526. London, Chapman & Hall.

Jones, R. H., and K. G. Luder. 1996. The relationship between national accounting and governmental accounting: State of the art and comparative perspectives. In *Research in Governmental and Non-profit Accounting,* Vol. 9, ed. J. L. Chan, 59-78. Greenwhich, CT: JAI Press.

Jounal officiel de la republique algerienne No. 35 (Official Journal of the Algerian Republic), 1990. Algiers: Algerian government printers, 15 August.

Magnet, J. 1997. The external audit of local public corporations in France. Paper from *Comparative International Governmental Accounting Research Conference (CIGAR),* Milan.

Mariel, P-L. 1996. Presentation of the new accounting system for Communes. In *Research in Governmental and Non-profit Accounting,* Vol. 9, ed. J. L. Chan, 364. Greenwich, CT: JAI Press.

———. 1997. Modernization of the budgetary and accounting system of French Communes. Paper from *Comparative International Governmental Accounting Research Conference (CIGAR),* Milan.

Montagnier, G. 1981. *Principes de comptabilite publique (Principles of Public Accounting).* Paris: Dalloz.

Perochon, C., and A. Talbi. 1993. *Pour comprendre et utiliser le plan comptable marocain (For understanding and using the Moroccan accounting plan).* Paris: Foucher.

Perreault, J. 1996. The French public accounting system. In *Research in Governmental and Non-profit Accounting,* Vol. 9, ed. J. L. Chan, 368. Greenwich, CT: JAI Press.

Rogers, E. M. 1995. *Diffusion of Innovations.* New York: The Free Press.

Samuels, J. M., R. E. V. Groves, and C. S. Goddard. 1975. *Company Finance in Europe.* London: The Institute of Chartered Accountants of England and Wales.

Societe nationale de comptability (National association of accountants) 1975. *Plan comptable national (National Accounting Plan).* Algiers: SNC.

Printed in the United States
118855LV00003B/147/A